Last in the Tin Bath

Last in the Tin Bath

THE AUTOBIOGRAPHY

David Lloyd

with Richard Gibson

**SIMON &
SCHUSTER**

London · New York · Sydney · Toronto · New Delhi

A CBS COMPANY

First published in Great Britain by Simon & Schuster UK Ltd, 2015
A CBS COMPANY

1 3 5 7 9 10 8 6 4 2

Simon & Schuster UK Ltd
1st Floor
222 Gray's Inn Road
London WC1X 8HB

www.simonandschuster.co.uk

Simon & Schuster Australia, Sydney
Simon & Schuster India, New Delhi

A CIP catalogue record for this book
is available from the British Library.

Hardback: 978-1-4711-5044-9
Ebook ISBN: 978-1-4711-5046-3

Typeset in Bembo by M Rules
Printed and bound by CPI Group (UK) Ltd, Croydon, CR0 4YY

MIX
Paper from
responsible sources
FSC® C020471

Simon & Schuster UK Ltd are committed to sourcing paper
that is made from wood grown in sustainable forests and supports the Forest
Stewardship Council, the leading international forest certification organisation.
Our books displaying the FSC logo are printed on FSC certified paper.

To all my family

Contents

Introduction

I have probably qualified for the gold watch when it comes to cricket. Aside from the briefest of diversions in the early 1980s, it has provided me with my livelihood since being signed on at Old Trafford as an inky-fingered fifth former back in 1963. This year represents the fiftieth anniversary since my first full season as a professional with Lancashire. Not that I am after any kind of long-service award.

You see, the pleasure has been all mine. Yes, it has been some journey, and like all of substantial length it has contained its highs and its lows, catching the praise and dodging the brickbats, although I am pleased to report it has never become as disconcerting as the one experienced by mate Craig 'Donkey' Daniels in the 2015 Wilmslow half-marathon when, having bet against half our local pub that he would finish in semi-professional time, he was overtaken by a man pushing a wheelbarrow, a full-sized Paddington Bear and a pantomime horse in quick succession. By that stage, a few miles in, dripping with sweat, he anticipated being a good few pounds lighter by the finish line. Around £500, as I recall.

It was hellishly tough breaking into that Lancashire dressing room as a meek sixteen-year-old, but as I reflect on it from my privileged seat in the commentary box for Sky Sports, there is a recognition that it was the making of me. The testosterone-fuelled mickey-taking, the hard graft for little reward, the harsh lessons of failure coupled with the joy of victory and personal achievement held me in good stead. Life as a county cricketer was the garden of my life, but it was not always sunshine and roses, even though I yearned for the funny side of all events.

Thankfully, where there were tears, laughter was never far behind. Most notably, when Bob 'Knocker' White, who went on to become a bloody good umpire, was batting for Nottinghamshire at Old Trafford in the late 1960s, when, with a half-century to his name, he suffered a twinge in his back. Visiting teams did not have physios travel with them in those days and so our man Bill Ridding ran on. Knocker, bent double, had some Fiery Jack ointment rubbed into the area to relieve the pain and reduce the stiffness. It worked a treat, although Fiery Jack was a product that really lived up to the name on the tin. After resuming batting, Knocker began moving more freely and even got a sweat on, which was the cause of his retiring hurt soon afterwards, as the stuff began running down his arse cheeks. After numerous gulps and groans, his face turning redder and redder, eyes watering, he departed to place his derriere in the bath, leaving several other men on the opposition crying for a different reason.

Cricket is a sport that acts as a magnet for characters and I am grateful to have met many across all the roles I have held in the game – from young shaver at Lancashire, to England player, coach from grassroots to international arena, first-class umpire and latterly commentator. They have all helped fill the game's progress with fun. And how different it was back in the sixties when Bert Flack, the groundsman at Old Trafford, declared Pakistan's innings against Lancashire in a touring match by entering the field with the roller and telling the batsmen: 'It's our turn now.' Can you imagine that these days? There would be an ICC inquiry.

It is with a heavy heart that a cricketer gives up the comradeship of the dressing room and it might explain why I refused to pack in altogether when I came out of the county game in 1983, and even went back for another spell with my beloved Accrington Cricket Club not long before I turned pensionable age. Every April I long for the whiff of Ralgex in the nostrils and recall the hundreds of blokes I am proud to have called team-mates. There is even a thought or two for those I am not. Cricket, mirroring life, occasionally pitches you together with work colleagues you might not otherwise pass the time of day with.

While I have always cared deeply about the fortunes of the England team, and still do – never more so than when I had the privilege of coaching it for three years – neither have I forgotten where it all began, or where I passed through to get there. It is why, in recent years, I have put my name to the Lancashire League and Professional Cricketers' Association, serving as president of both organisations. The sport has given me plenty and this has represented a chance to give something back.

To be frank, if you put me in a darkened room and shone a bright light in my eyes under questioning, I would tell you that my natural devotion lies elsewhere. It's always been like that for me, really. Football has been my first love. My business has been cricket. It means I have come to like both of them equally. One of them is a real passion, something to keep me occupied on a social level, and yet it is the other one that has allowed me to make a living through expertise.

Sport in general makes me happy. I don't really know either of the rugby codes, never found the time to get into them, but as the years tick by and I speak to pals who do, I find myself wishing I had. Other lads that I played with and coached at Lancashire were into rugby league, but I wasn't born in that same M62 corridor heartland. And the red-trouser brigade who follow rugby union certainly never stopped off at Accrington. That's far too posh and anyone that knows anything of the area knows we don't do posh. But the bottom line is that competitive action tends to get me hooked. I can get lost watching the darts; I love watching snooker; the Do Not Disturb signs go up on our lounge door if I decide to sit down and watch a televised racing meeting. You probably know lots of folk like me. Just call me Mr Bloke.

Through the toughest times – the back end of my playing days with Lancashire, a personal crusade against entrenched English habits while coach of the national team – I hope that bloke was still recognisable. If he went missing temporarily, I always tried to get him back. Those whose careers took me in as both coach and co-commentator – such as Michael Atherton and Nasser Hussain – have been best placed to judge, I guess, but I retain confidence that all the friendships and loyalties developed during the late 1990s still remain intact as I sit back and put my lifetime in the sport to paper.

As a youth, I took a while to come out of the shell. My innocence and modest upbringing, combined with having a disciplinarian of a mother, slowed my transition from childhood into adolescence. But once I began to gain confidence, the simple advice of my father, a man with a strict devotion to his Methodist beliefs, has never been far away from my thoughts. 'Be yourself,' he used to tell me.

By nature, I am a positive person who likes the light-hearted side of life, and I hope that has come across in my commentary. This is not to say I refuse to be critical, merely that I try to paint players in the best possible light whenever given the chance. Of course, sometimes your judgements turn out to be severely skewed, and a player surprises you. One of the best things about sport, and forming opinions, as you have to do in my position, is being proved right. But I confess that it nearly always feels better to be proved wrong.

Take Steve Smith. As I write, he is the world's number one-ranked Test batsman. Yet when Australia first picked him in the 2010-11 Ashes it looked to me like they could have easily thrown in any member of the Alan Price Set, the group that sang about Simon Smith and His Amazing Dancing Bear, and been as well served. Fast forward four years and he looks a totally different player, captaining Australia successfully in Michael Clarke's absence in a Test series against India and churning out runs across all formats. Seldom has he failed since establishing himself in the Baggy Green at the end of our 2013 summer. Opponents have struggled to stop him, although I may have missed a trick in this regard. During the 2015 World Cup, I bumped into him and his partner in a restaurant. Would you believe it? He only had his bat with him! And he would have left it behind but for my intervention. It would have been better service to queen and country to have confiscated it.

He is not the only batsman to have made it to the top who has done me like a kipper. If I am watching a match at home it tends to be through a TV production eye rather than that of a cricket aficionado, considering things that have worked well and those that have not. But when I am at a match, doing my job, I become more interested in the skill, and similarly to Smith, the progress made by Hashim Amla since English viewers first got a sight of him back in 2004-05 has been fascinating. When he turned up on the world scene he was a walking wicket and the way he has transformed his game has been phenomenal. The best players do not always start on the international scene like world-beaters.

The progress of some speaks volumes for their determination to succeed. The way Mitchell Johnson went from bowling from the left, bowling to the right, to bowling straight at the batsman at the speed of light was a wonder to behold. To witness Mahendra Singh Dhoni suddenly come to life in an innings is intoxicating, even though he has done it to you several times before. Players like him truly get you lost in the moment behind the microphone. Then, there are the wondrous bowlers the unpredictable Pakistan continue to churn out. Long after I vacate the commentary box for a final time, they will be unearthing them, you can be certain of that.

The game advances in some ways and stays the same in others. There are a few of us now who watch what modern players do on a morning of a match to prepare and every single one of us would be of the opinion that the warm-ups they get through these days represent a lot of work before they get into the six or seven hours on the field. Jimmy Anderson – and clearly it is what he wants to do – will bowl something like thirty deliveries before the start of play. That's five flippin' overs. In the past, someone like Ken Higgs, a strapping bloke, would just get through the rhythm, nice and loose by stretching. Peter Lever was exactly the same. Then there is that anomaly that when all the prep has been done, they wander off, the captains have the toss and all the players are then sat around for half an hour back in the dressing room. I am sure a physiologist would tear me to pieces, but I feel that they have been doing too much. We had a cup of tea, did the crossword, then hit a few catches, had a hit and then had a bowl. It would all be over and done with and the only extra would be a stretch for the fast bowlers in the dressing room. I wouldn't call that unprofessional.

For 250 days of the year, I am assessing cricketers and watching the development of teams. In Joe Root I believe England have a player who will be spoken of as one of the best batsmen on the planet in future years and I place a quiet confidence in the new management team of Andrew Strauss, Trevor Bayliss and Paul Farbrace to deliver something special. It is early days, but the raw materials are there and the environment to progress is in place.

Even in my downtime I can be spotted at league cricket grounds, watching my grandchildren up at Accrington, or nipping along to see Saturday matches at Bramhall, in Cheshire, or Easingwold in North Yorkshire, clubs near to the bases I have set up in my life with Diana. There are other pursuits to be enjoyed, such as long walks with Tags our fox terrier – me on my second knee, Diana on a new hip – or a day out on my BMW F800ST motorbike. These activities, like some of the items on my bucket list, such as riding a horse or travelling about on a canal boat, provide a break from the old routine. Our great British pubs offer me further respite, and a refuge for conversation to meander onto other topics over a decent pint of ale, but it has never been a hardship to talk cricket and I will gladly natter about it at the bar if someone wishes. After all, it is, I am told, what I do best.

CHAPTER 1

Last in the Tin Bath

One of the trendy buzz phrases used in English cricket circles over recent times has been 'appointment to view'. According to the market research people, fans of the game wanted an allotted time slot in the week for their Twenty20 fix; a regular blast off, if you will. For some Friday night is music night and nothing else. For others, however, Friday night is NatWest night, that being the most popular time for our eighteen counties to conduct their family-oriented fun.

It was a family night for us too back in the 1950s. If you had made an 'appointment to view' visit on a Friday to 134 Water Street, Accrington, a short while after the town had digested its fish suppers, you would have had the displeasure of seeing yours truly, a twig of a lad with slightly sticky-out ears, covered in seven days' worth of grime being dunked and returned to my original milk-bottle-white complexion.

Think of one of those corner-set luxury whirlpool baths with multiple speed settings, an array of gentle bath soaks, shampoos and Egyptian cotton towels ... then erase it from your thoughts as you are getting completely the wrong idea.

It was more like sheep dipping, if truth be told.

Seldom did luxury come to town in Accrington. If it had it would have been run out by the mob, I reckon. A place like that offered a pretty rough-and-ready upbringing, but like most kids of my generation I made the most of the outdoors. Covered in dirt by Friday evenings, scrapes on my knees, bruises littered indiscriminately around my body, my habitual 'treat' was to scrub off the badges of honour during this weekly ritual. You see, Friday night was wash night.

The appearance of the tin bath full of suds in our back parlour was a regimented affair and like all regiments had an established pecking order. This was not just *my* night to scrub up, it belonged to the whole family, so I had to wait my turn. The cost of producing hot water restricted us to one soak a week and naturally it was adults first. And when I say family I don't just mean me and my parents. Oh, no. There were only three of us living on a permanent basis at 134 Water Street, but my Uncle Harry and Auntie Annie lived five blocks up with my cousins Brian and Jean. Now Auntie Annie must have been a bit of a tyrant because at various stages of my childhood, Uncle Harry, Brian and Jean came to live with us, and that meant I got knocked down a rung or two.

My dad, David senior, and Harry, his brother-in-law, worked up at the foundry, which no two ways about it was a really shitty, dirty job. They would come home utterly filthy and make do with taking a soap and flannel to themselves throughout the week before their big plunge on a Friday night to get properly clean.

I was an only child so you might have anticipated my lot not being so bad. But Uncle Harry would also have his turn to jump in before muggins here dipped a toe. Not that I could see my toe once it was in. You can no doubt imagine the colour of the water when it came to my turn and the reduction in its temperature since it had been filled. You will have heard the phrase 'as happy as a pig in shit'? Well, I conformed to the stereotype, without the contentment.

This once-a-week ceremony took place downstairs for the first few years of my life. Later, Dad created a DIY bathroom upstairs by partitioning part of my bedroom off with plasterboard and erecting a new floor out of pallets from the local glass factory that one of our family members used to collect for him. Establishing an upstairs bathroom was our doffing of our flat caps to modern life.

We stuck to using the outside lavatory, though, to avoid any accusations of opulence. Sure, the cleaning of teeth could take place inside, but going to the loo was always an outdoors expedition whatever the weather. You would have to make your way outside, as icicles formed on your imponderables, to sit on the throne, and there was no toilet roll to speak of – being an exorbitant item, it never made it onto our shopping list. Instead, there were bits of old newspaper that Mum and Dad would pin to the back of the toilet door. Who said recycling was a twenty-first-century fad?

Once read these rags would be put to a secondary use. Some people say they're full of shit anyway, but I've always been an advocate of a good newspaper, and not for the kind of use we got out of the *Daily Herald* and the *Daily Sketch*.

Kids of 2015 don't know they're born. We take so much for granted these days. Wake up in a morning during winter and your bedroom more often than not is like the Bahamas in holiday season. Central heating? Back then, there would be genuine frost on the windows – and I'm talking about the insides. The only chance of heat entering the house between October and March meant an Antarctic trek into the backyard to get a shovel full of coal. Even then, you would be shivering for a quarter of an hour before the fire took its full effect.

We used to collect the bottles of Sarsaparilla sold to us by the pop man on his weekly rounds and turn them into hot water bottles to take to bed with us at night. Electric blankets? Bunkum.

You would keep filling these things with hot water until they cracked, and only when you were well stocked for bottles did you consider selling your over-supply back to the pop man on his next visit.

Friday night wasn't only bath night; it was washing night as well. Mum would wash all our clothes by hand and lay them out to be pulled through the mangle. In later years, as I reached my teens, I became the mangle operator and the prolonged turning of the handle took place in front of the fire while watching our newly acquired television. Seeing Michael Miles present the ITV game show *Take Your Pick!* dismissed the sense of it being a laborious chore. Contestants could win monetary prizes for answering relatively simple questions, but it was those failing to get through the preliminary round – the 'Yes–No interlude' – that got me guffawing.

A fellow called Bob Danvers-Walker, the voice of Pathé News for four decades, was the show's announcer, while Alec Dane was effectively the gong of doom for those taking part. Michael Miles would interview the contestants for sixty seconds, with the name of the game being for them to avoid saying yes or no. I would be chortling away to myself as Michael Miles would say such things as, 'Hello, Richard, is it?' 'Yes.' *DONG!* Dane would come into his own in a nanosecond, at the slip of the tongue. It was brilliant stuff.

Last in the tin bath. Stood at the mangle. I knew my place all right. Home life was a strict regime that left me behind my peers in terms of growing up and seeing the real world.

Ours was a strict household dominated not by my father but my mother. To say I was well disciplined by her would be a bit like saying that Genghis Khan liked a spot of fisticuffs. She had old Genghis's aggression too. For example, she would think nothing of giving me a whack with the frying pan. In contrast, my dad would never raise a finger against me. I could get a hiding for next to nothing, really. All it took was for her to be that way inclined and woe betide me. On reflection, she must have suffered a few women's problems, I think, because I always seemed to be going to the corner shop to fetch some pills or other for her. When she wasn't in the striking mood I could be stood in the corner of the room for hours on end; told to face the wall and not turn around until instructed. People talk of their childhoods being happy. Was mine? Was it hell. I was frightened to death of my mother. She worked at a weaving mill from 7.30 a.m. to 5 p.m. five days a week, and my sense of dread only eased when she was sat at a loom rather than at our kitchen table. It was not until I was about eighteen that the fear that she might *actually* skin me alive passed.

Unconditionally, I knew my place – move from it and I would be dispatched those few hundred yards to Uncle Harry's gaff, one of a clutch of family members on the Aspin side to populate Water Street and its environs, to fetch his dreaded sailor's belt. It seemed to spend as much time on my backside as it did around his waist, and it was always Mum who thrust it there with a flick of the wrist reminiscent of Glenn McGrath propelling a seam-proud delivery down an off-stump line. She administered these lashes with the dedication of an Olympian too. Then, when she had finished this ceremonial beating, I suffered the ignominy of having to shuffle back to Harry's to return his leather weapon of justice with folk inevitably gawking at me, having heard the commotion from inside number 134. Talk about a bum deal.

When it came to Fridays, my stock was the equivalent of Albania in the Eurovision Song Contest. I would be bringing up the rear. We were also pretty far down the pecking order when it came to our social status. But like lots of families who grew up in the type of back-to-back cottage we called home, we got on with life. Sure, we had no money to speak of, but neither did the folk around us either. It was a harsh environment to be a part of – getting by was a darned hard slog for most – and that much was evident in the intimidating experience of waiting at the mill for my mother to finish work. The noise emanating from its walls was otherworldly in its volume. It reverberated around your body, and that was when you were stood outside. I couldn't have imagined having to spend nine and a half hours a day suffering it on the inside. But this was part of life in the Lancashire enclave in which I grew up.

This was us. Our lot. It never occurred to me that our family was from anywhere else, as we seemed to be and acted like Lancastrians through and through. The clue was in the surname, I guess. It should have given things away – and not been such a surprise to learn – that my grandfather Arthur Lloyd came from Cardiff. He had migrated north to find work in Shropshire, then latterly settled in Accrington.

He only had one eye, did Arthur. An affliction that didn't cause any hindrance generally but would prove a bit of a handicap when it came to earning a bob or two. You see, he used to work on the door at the Sydney Street Working Men's Club, and a prerequisite of the job was to collect payment from patrons on entry. On any given evening things would be fine, but some among the revellers would make it their business to try to sneak in on his blind spot. Cheeky bleeders! There are very few memories for me of one-eyed Arthur because he passed away when I was four, but I retain cartoon-like imaginary visions of him being duped by a stream of likely lads saving on their admission money so they could afford another pint at the bar.

Dad was a devout Methodist whose beliefs meant he was also a strict teetotaller. He never thrust that upon me, but I did not drink around him in later life as a mark of respect, and wouldn't have seen the inside of many establishments by the time it was legal for me to be ordering my own pint. At Christmas my mother would make a big sherry trifle, and a second booze-free one for Dad.

On one side of our family there was Dad, a fairly quiet and

reserved army of one. On the other, there was a shedful of Aspins. There were umpteen of them as Mum had thirteen brothers and sisters. A number of my aunties and uncles I never knew, but the Aspins of Accrington hailed from Plantation Street, a rather apt address, the crop they were cultivating clearly being children. Everybody lived within half a mile of each other, with the majority of us in adjacent streets. It was typical, I guess, of many families in northern towns. You could just walk into each other's houses at any time. In fact, there were so many of the Aspins you could have gone in blindfolded to any given house in Accrington and had a decent chance that it would belong to a relation.

My maternal grandfather was notorious in the area, and commonly known as Bill o'Moleside, named in recognition of the large hill next to the coppice where they lived. Moleside was so called because it was punctuated with lots of little caverns, as if giant moles had been working overtime on it. At weekends these caverns – referred to by locals as Gamblers' Caves – would be populated by blokes playing cards and dominoes for money.

He was a bit of a mover and shaker was Bill and he used to be at the forefront of this amateur casino, playing for ha'pennies and pennies. There were very few television sets around in those days, of course, particularly in areas like ours where money was tight, so Bill clearly got his entertainment from fraternising with fellow card sharps. When he wasn't out, the evidence presented suggests he was hard at work producing more heirs. No wonder he needed to win a few extra bob come Saturday. There were a lot of mouths to feed.

Dad started work in that hellish foundry – the unforgiving physicality of which was not something he enjoyed one iota – but ended up with a much more comfortable life for himself as a theatre technician at Accrington Victoria Hospital. For many years, I thought he was the bloke who operated some kind of cinema for convalescents. You know, the fellow that put newly released pictures on. It came as something of a disappointment to learn that he actually worked in the operating theatre, sterilising and disinfecting everything in sight so that surgery could take place.

He worked at the hospital for thirty-odd years, which added up to a fair amount of experience. As time went by, every now and again he would do an operation himself. Not top-end stuff like brain surgery or owt like that, mind. No, just the simpler stuff. For example, the full-time surgeons would think nothing of allowing him to whip out an appendix. He would then bring home these worm-shaped trophies, pickle them and place them in jars for display. You could see all the evidence of his handiwork hanging up in his shed.

From the centre of Accrington, Water Street ran all the way out to the countryside. It was the primary thoroughfare and the route people took to get to Peel Park, then home of the great Accrington Stanley. On Saturday afternoons, I would sit on the front step of our terraced house and watch all the players, followed by supporters an hour or so later, walk past. Living where we did meant I got to know these players, conversing with them as they went by, boots tucked under their arms.

What bound us all together in those days was that we were literally all bound together. Travelling out of town was not common; the world was a much bigger place. Your community was yours to be proud of, and folk were proud of it. People would stick to their own communities, displaying a sense of loyalty to the characteristics it possessed and its subsequent influence on their lives. Of course, it wasn't glamorous, but this old mill town represented our world. Its massive cinder area located adjacent to Peel Park at the end of Water Street – or Rec as it was more commonly known – was where the Stanley players would train. Out of hours, in early evening, at weekends and in school holidays, it would be transformed into an imaginary Old Trafford, for football in the winter, cricket in the summer. Kids would come from all over town to congregate for a game. It's where we learned our skills, honing them for hours as our parents went about their own daily chores. This waste ground was a sporting mecca of hopes and dreams. From dawn to dusk – or so it seemed – you could spot Accrington's youth transforming themselves into young Denis Comptons or taking off Duncan Edwards. Sure, if you were any good you learned the technical aspects of given sports elsewhere, but here was the stage to parade what you could do among your peers.

That scene on Accrington Rec would have been replicated the length and breadth of the United Kingdom. Playing outdoors with a ball with your mates was a rite of passage for any child of the 1950s and several subsequent generations too. Nowadays, the parks of our towns and cities look bleak and are sparsely populated. No jumpers for goalposts, no more Ron Manager; some FIFA-branded video game being played in the front room on an abnormally large TV screen, yes, but no magic taking place in the fresh air.

Equally empty are the inner-city streets we used to populate for a knockabout. When was the last time you saw a set of cricket stumps chalked on a wall? They were ten-a-penny in 1947, the year in which I was born. But times have changed. We are all more aware of the perils of allowing our children to unearth their own mischief, fearful that mischief or something worse will find them. The kids of this country are poorer for it. Of that I am sure.

The Rec was also the site of three air raid shelters, reminders of the Second World War. These shelters – no longer standing as the whole area has been bulldozed and tarmacked since – represented our dens, a refuge where we could hang out when we took a break from our sporting endeavours. We would dive into them, have a chinwag over our glasses of lemonade or cream soda – never beer, as under-age drinking didn't seem to appeal in those days – or tuck into our little penny loaves and crisps. A penny loaf was as you imagine from the description – bread baked in a tin about three inches long and an inch wide that would cost you a penny.

Dad had been a worthy and enthusiastic sportsman himself, turning out as a right-back for several amateur football clubs over a quarter of a century. He was proud of my progress as I came up through the ranks of the local teams, meticulously scouring the newspapers in search of mentions of my achievements. Several landmarks of my boyhood participation made it into his beloved scrapbook.

Despite our austere existence, I never wanted for kit. Poor we might have been, but Mum and Dad were typical of northern parents, I guess. I never knew how, but they always managed to find a way of purchasing the right clobber when it was required, whether that was flannels, bats, pads, cricket shoes or football boots.

Mum also took it upon herself to kit me out in what I can only say was distinctly the wrong gear from an early age. Now let's be clear – I don't have anything against cross dressing per se. I just don't feel it has ever been a pursuit for me. Mum obviously had different ideas, though. Disappointed not to get the daughter she had always craved (my parents had me relatively late in life by mid-twentieth century standards), Mum refused to let the facts get in the way of her fairytale story. So for the first five years of my life, I was her little girl.

If things had turned out exactly as she had planned, I would have been called Gwyneth. As it was she had to make do with putting waves through the long curly hair she let drop towards my shoulders, dressing me in a frock and adding accessories. Forget toy cars. The only thing I possessed with wheels on as a toddler was a pram.

Being an only child, I had to suffer in silence. Later in life I asked my mum why I had no brothers and sisters. 'We only did it once,' was her cheeky reply. My guess is that joking about it masked the truth. They'd had trouble conceiving. After all, when I was born they were both thirty-seven.

Putting my mother's disappointment about my gender aside, she did develop one other strange fixation when it came to me: she was convinced I had a hole in my head that used to let the cold in and was the chief cause of my asthma. She seemed to think that I would catch a chill, as the young heroes of Charles Dickens's novels always used to, so took to sending me to school with a flying hat on. It was for my own good, she used to tell me, and to make matters slightly worse she put me in a pair of clogs with metal soles, and baggy trousers with braces to boot. Let me tell you, it's no fun being dispatched to school looking like Roy Chubby Brown after he's been on a hot wash. When we went swimming, the teachers were told that making me wear a swimming cap was compulsory, so concerned was Mum about water getting in around my brain.

When it came to my health, she was always of the belief that there was something wrong with me, although for my part, other than the complex developed from dressing like a Bavarian circus extra with my lederhosen and European footwear, I generally felt fine outside the house. It was only inside that I would start coughing and wheezing. But I put that down to the multitude of birds my father brought home. The tally of canaries and budgerigars he kept throughout my childhood must have hit fifty, and I reckon it must have been a bit of budgie-fancier's lung that I developed.

My dad used to breed these feathered fiends and one of his early favourites was a budgie called Joey. It used to sit on his head, which meant it was covered in bird shit most of the time. In terms of his pate, imagine an albino version of Mikhail Gorbachev and you will have a pretty accurate image. Unlike me, these birds could get away with a bit of lip and Joey was the only being alive who would ever dare tell my mum what to do. 'Put kettle on, Mary!' it would chirp.

My parents met through my dad playing football with my mum's brothers. They did not see eye to eye on everything, mind you. For a start, Dad was deeply religious and my mother wasn't. He could be found at Cambridge Street Methodist Church three times every Sunday and throughout his whole life it was his second home. In later years, he finished up as its caretaker and became a lay preacher. It was not only his refuge but the hub of the community.

Accrington was littered with regular hangouts for me – the cricket club just on the outskirts, Peel Park where my beloved Stanley played, the Rec and the technical school where I was a pupil – yet the focal point was the church. As well as the multiple trips on a Sunday along with Dad, I would return most nights to attend the Institute's youth club and engage in sporting pursuits. I would be one of twenty or thirty lads playing snooker, table tennis and darts, or be stood around chatting with a bottle of Sarsaparilla or lemonade in hand. We ran four snooker teams in the church league and I was a member of the D team.

It was a brilliant existence, a great grounding in life. We had our own football team, a flippin' good outfit too. We were all mates together and there was no question of any of us going to the pub. In addition to the sports teams, there was a fantastic pop group – one of those skiffle bands with a washboard and a tea chest. They were truly terrific, and as well as playing at the church they would be booked to play other gigs around the local area. The Institute was a vibrant place every night. Handed six pence on the way out the front door by my mother, this pretty sum had to get me through an evening's entertainment. You would have to pay a contribution for the lights for the snooker, once your name was the topmost one left on the chalkboard. Table tennis, which came at no cost, was played in another room, so the rest of the money tended to go on fizzy pop.

The bloke that ran it all was called Norman Gresham. He played in the B team when it came to snooker, with a style of play a bit like Chris Gayle's batting. What he lacked in subtlety, he made up for in power. He just used to hammer the ball. Line it up with the cue and give it an almighty crack. He was a lovely old fella, who would give up his time every single night, Monday to Friday, taking the money for the various activities and handing out the change meticulously. But he was also part of what was a pretty special microcosm of Accrington life.

There was a real camaraderie down there and I would make that pilgrimage happily every night as a teenager, ensuring I was back home for between nine and ten o'clock. It was a real happy hangout for me, and held me in good stead for the dressing-room environments I would experience later in life as a professional cricketer with Lancashire and England.

Closer to home in Water Street you would normally find me with my best mate Alan Deakin. Alan – or Fatty, as I affectionately knew him – lived right at the top of our road. He was an unbelievably clever lad who had piano lessons and breezed through all his tests when it came to anything educational. Our families were very close, so much so that I called Alan's mum Auntie Elsie. Of course, she wasn't a conventional auntie, just an adopted one. We've all had one of those, haven't we? Not a blood relative but someone familiar enough to earn the title by default. We spent lots of time together, both us lads and our mums and dads, and we were all part of Cambridge Street's extended family.

He might have been Alan to Auntie Elsie but he was Fatty to me. Not that she was particularly fond of me using his nickname. 'He's called Alan,' she told me sternly, during one memorable ticking off when I knocked for him one morning and asked: 'Is your Fatty coming out?' It didn't matter to me what he was called. He was my best mate. It doesn't take a genius to deduce that he had a bit of weight on.

Those familiar cobbles in that particular residential area, which meandered down towards the town centre, have been razed now.

But they were the stepping stones to magic and mischief when I was young. We got up to some right shenanigans on and around them. If we weren't kicking around some ball or another or hitting one with a bat or a stick, then we would be playing marbles. Walk down a street like ours and you would see boys like me on those cobbles, shooting marbles towards the targets we marked in front of garage doors. It was a big game in the 1950s and 60s but has not stood the test of time for some reason. The same can be said of another one of my old favourites which was top and whip. You would chalk the top – a wooden block with a pointed end – in all different colours and then pick up the whip – a leather shoelace – to flick it round, trying to make it stand up on end and spin to create a rainbow of moving colours.

This was innocent enough, but like all boys we went a bit off piste at times. For example, one of our tricks was to tie the ends of a rope to two door handles from opposite sides of the street, and then bang on them alternately. Of course, try as one might, they wouldn't open, much to the frustration of those inside. Reserved, I might have been, but when pitched together with Fatty we became a dastardly duo.

Actually, I am not particularly proud of one of the other larks we got up to – in fact, on reflection it's shocking, absolutely awful, but as a reformed character I feel compelled to share it with you.

A lot of doors at that time had what we called snecks – a type of latch or catch to fasten them. You had to push the top bit down with your thumb and pull at the same time to open the door, and our prank was to force a drawing pin into the wood near the sneck and then attach a bit of dog shit to its head. When people put their thumb on the sneck they would inevitably feel the unusual substance on their fingers and thumb, causing them either to sniff it, or worse still lick it, to the considerable mirth of the two giggling onlookers stowed behind a wall or leaning on a lamp-post yards away.

I wish I could tell you that my adolescent years were all good, clean fun. But I was brought up not to tell lies. If I did, it meant a wallop from Mum.

Dad always liked to develop the 'family' theme when he played sport. Football was his love – it was through natural ability rather than an inherited interest that I fell into cricket – throughout his life. Once his playing days were over, he ran local football sides with a fair amount of success. Every now and again he would attempt to foster the team spirit with social nights round at our house. My school teams would get similar treatment. Mum would cook up a dozen or so servings of pie and peas, and everyone would natter about the game over supper.

When Dad hung up his boots, he took on the kind of challenge he relished. One of the amateur teams in Accrington, Cedar Swifts, were hopeless when he started. They were a lost cause, if truth be told – but that very fact gave him something to work with. Winning with the best did not appeal to my dad as it might to others. Turning around perennial losers did and, with the usual Lloyd template of togetherness applied, that is what he set about doing with great success.

Not that I took to cricket instantly, and certainly not at the age of ten. Like Dad, football has been the natural number one passion for me; cricket the slow burner that still flickers half a century later. My adolescence featured lots of links to the town's football club rather than its cricket equivalent. In those days Stanley had a nucleus of Scottish players, scouted north of the border and sent down to ply their trade in the English lower leagues. My Auntie Edith was the housekeeper at their collective digs, providing me with another link to the place and its squad. She would cook their meals, wash their clothes and generally see to it that they were comfortable in their new environment.

All this gave me my initial interaction with professional sport, and throughout my childhood I wanted to follow in their footsteps and become a footballer. I was pretty good at it and always encouraged at school. However, I was doing all right at cricket as well, and into my teens I was captain of the town teams in both sports.

It would not be economical with the truth to suggest I might have had a different sporting career but for my awkward social skills as a boy. Football League clubs from around the region had their eye on me and I signed for Burnley as a schoolboy. After a spell of training with them, it was the first-team manager Harry Potts who came to our house and got me to commit to a contract. These days there are about four levels of coaches and management between the first-team boss and those in charge of age-group teams, and so it is unlikely that you'd hear of Arsène Wenger popping along the road to Camden to meet the family of a fifteen-year-old with potential. But it was common practice at that time and was still so in cricket when, as Lancashire head coach in the 1990s, I paid a similar visit to the Flintoff household in Preston. More of that later.

Gawthorpe Hall, where Burnley trained, was a state-of-the-art facility back then, much better than anything else on the Division One scene, and I was coached by Jimmy McIlroy, another Clarets legend, so you would have thought all this was manna from heaven for a football-loving nut like me. Unfortunately, though, my heart simply wasn't in it, and I used to skip training. When it came to it I could play all right, make no mistake about that, but dressing room banter exploited my inherent shyness and alienated me. I certainly didn't feel as though I fitted in either there or at Blackburn, who also called me for training ground matches, and would tuck myself away in a quiet corner. Then, I sought excuses not to go; missed the bus, looked for other invites or purposely delayed my departure. Bungling an opportunity like that told its own story.

As a sheltered youth, I had always been comfortable playing in my immediate environment, alongside like-minded pals, starting with the Peel Park junior school teams. No wonder, perhaps, given that in one memorable season we racked up 63 goals in 11 straight wins without conceding once. Yep, played 11, won 11, goal difference 63.

Yet it wasn't as if the football clubs moved heaven and earth to secure me, either. For example, I might have got a personal call from Harry Potts to offer me a Burnley B team match, but after I declined to attend a Lancashire trial in Bolton due to a clash, no one came banging on my door to persuade me that I was making a mistake. With the benefit of hindsight a life in sport has given me, I know what it's like when you are recruiting for youth teams. There are a lot of talented young kids out there and as an organisation you don't want to be wasting your time on one, regardless of the talent in question, if his heart is not in it. You concentrate on the hearts that are.

Short in stature for my age and slight with it, I wanted to be someone like Johnny Haynes, one of the great inside-lefts, or Duncan Edwards, who caused me to cry my eyes out for a day as a ten-year-old when he died in the Munich air disaster. Edwards was my sporting hero and indisputably would have been one of England's best footballers if he'd survived. I wanted to be that Manchester United No. 6. But I was never one to be thrusting myself forward for extra recognition outside my own post code.

In Accrington, things felt completely different because even from a young age I felt I had a presence, as though people knew me and of my achievements on the sports field. The fact that folk might sing my praises was enough to relax me. Even in my dad's teams, when I was by far the youngest player, I was completely chilled out about being junior in elder company. Quite simply, I was one of these kids that needed familiarity to perform well. It was not a necessity later in life, but fast forward into my thirties and I still loved being transported back into that Accrington bubble playing local sport.

As well as running Cedar Swifts, Dad started up the church football team, and the Cambridge Street Methodists were a crack outfit, I can tell you. David Hughes, with whom I went on to share a cricket dressing room at Old Trafford, hailed from Newton-le-Willows but was talked into playing centre-forward for us at weekends because he was dating a girl from Blackburn. I was fourteen when I started playing and it felt like a genuine sense of achievement when this team evolved over subsequent years, culminating in the winning of the All-England Methodist Church Cup.

While David was a fine leader of the line – winning a healthy proportion of his aerial challenges – I was more a provider than scorer. That meant playing as the second striker – a Peter Beardsley with the looks, if you like – or on the left flank, as I did on occasion during a spell in the local non-league with Great Harwood, for whom Jack Simmons ploughed the forward furrow. Big Jack used his physicality to his advantage and would think nothing of bundling opposition goalkeepers over the goal-line in his quest to score. He did so with some success, contributing to his breaking of several league records, and unfortunately his leg on three occasions too. The final one ended his football fun for good.

Commitments with teams across a couple of sports throughout my teens meant trekking to and fro on public transport. At that time nobody had a car; there were literally none anywhere. So I would get the bus to do a couple of hours' training with Burnley after school – or not as the case may be – or to Old Trafford on Saturday mornings for net practice, returning from Manchester to play in a league match for the Swifts after lunch.

As a consequence my schoolwork got neglected and my education took a back seat. Being a technical college, our school offered the chance for lads like me to pick up the skills to learn a trade – an oldstyle apprenticeship on leaving. I was never going to have an obvious path to follow as there was nothing I particularly excelled in. My three O-level passes came in English, Woodwork and Technical Drawing, much to my surprise and even more to the surprise of our master, whose assessment of my ability proved more stinging than any other I received in subsequent cricket reports across the national press.

I was scheduled, rather bizarrely given my qualifications, to become a plumber's hand upon leaving school. I know, I couldn't see how that gig with the local council had been lined up, either. It mattered little, though, as instead, I took my first tentative steps as a professional cricketer that summer of 1963.

However, even while on the Lancashire staff I liked playing local amateur football and would do so under code names to avoid drawing attention from the Old Trafford hierarchy. My contracts prohibited this of course, and goodness knows what I would have done had someone put me in A&E with one of the horror tackles that proliferated on playing fields around the county. I reduced the chances of this occurring by pulling out of 50-50 challenges and even reassessing some 60-40s if the defender I was up against looked like a prize cage fighter. Despite this, I so loved the whole event of playing with my mates – having a laugh before kick-off in the dressing room, before giving it your all on the pitch for ninety minutes and then reliving it down the pub – that it all felt worth it. That 'When Saturday Comes' existence was great for me. I was simply itching for the arrival of every weekend.

As with all things, the Cambridge Street team eventually ran its course and was consigned to history, and its folding meant it was time for me to move on too. Even into my twenties I was clearly a sought-after property on the local scene, as evidenced by a couple of blokes who would have passed for nightclub bouncers, Tony Noonan and John Starkey, turning up at my house not long after word had got out about the demise.

These two hulks, captain and player-manager respectively, liter-ally filled the front room of my marital home in Ascot Way. It was only local league football but having a couple of heavies like that turn up made it feel like you were being recruited into a mafia family. Here they were asking me to sign up for their clan. It was a bit like being taken into the local militia. They wanted me to fight alongside them, all ten stone of me; a lightweight left-winger to add a different kind of punch. Their opening gambit was: 'Come and join us, we need some credibility.'

During the first eight matches of the season they had been at their consistent best: they'd had a man sent off every week and owed that much in fines they felt they needed some reforming. Signing up a Goody Two-Shoes like me was the answer. I was pretty proud of being the Gary Lineker of my day, not once having had my name taken by the referee.

The fact they wanted to sign a wet-paper-bagger to dilute their reputation should have told me what they were all about, although to be fair I had a good idea because a few mates were already playing for Willow Mount, the club in question. Not that the name of the club meant anything at all, really. You see, we had to keep changing what we were called on an annual basis because of our notoriety. Willow Mount we might have been, but we also went by Baxenden Football Club and Park Inn in other seasons. At one stage it felt like we were called something different every month. There were some terrific players – the goalkeeper Rubber Thompson, a postman whose parents hadn't delivered him a proper Christian name as far as I could tell, saved everything; then there were the two Daves, Pitt and Kay, Alec Mackereth and Phil Howarth, a terrific lad who later in life became the partner of my first wife Susan.

Suffice to say that whatever name we sported, we could handle ourselves in the rough and tumble of the Accrington leagues. Of course, as a good church-going lad I wasn't one of the main pro-tagonists when it came to problems, but as a collective I have to admit we were bloody reprobates. In that day and age it was anything goes on a football field and our tackling left nothing to the imagination. But could we play football? Boy, could we ever. We were a fantastic team, but the bottom line was that we would win by whatever means necessary. These were brilliant times for me, playing alongside blokes who promoted a real sense of 'us and them'. At times it could get really tasty on the field, but this was strictly social for me. For by now the seriously competitive stuff was already happening over in Manchester with Lancashire.

CHAPTER 2

Accy Thump

During his time on the international stage, ably grinding out innings over several hours, Paul Collingwood earned the name Brigadier Block. It was my old mate and long-term Sky Sports colleague Bob Willis who wonderfully dubbed him Double B. But I have news for Bob and you lot out there: when it came to defensive batting I was the original. Been there, yawn the T-shirt.

There are some other similarities between myself and Colly, whose redoubtable qualities have made him stick out in the modern era. Like me, he has no body piercings or tattoos. Not on public display, at least. And the way in which he put up the barricades against the odds to save Tests for England against the might of South Africa and Australia in the space of eight months in 2009-10 showed admirable depth of resolve. There was a real thou-shalt-not-pass attitude about him during the last rites of matches in Cardiff, Centurion and Cape Town. He proved himself master of the dead-bat.

Of course, you were made to wait until the end of matches for Colly's quality to out. But with me you could see it from the start of an innings. Because in my youth, I barely played a shot in anger; not that it bothered those who were developing me up at

Accrington. I was never discouraged from placing a high price on my wicket and staying in as long as possible, repelling whatever the opposition bowlers threw at me.

Playing Lancashire League cricket was a bit of a baptism of fire for a teenage wannabe, especially with a few international bowlers littered around the other clubs, not to mention the wily old pros alongside them who had graced the league for several years. Between these two groups they gave you little to hit and tested your technique and concentration.

During summer months, the church institute where I hung out with like-minded pals closed down temporarily, and so I found my entertainment elsewhere. Naturally enough, that meant virtually every evening in the school holidays involving a trek up to Accrington Cricket Club. My dad allowed my mum to run the house and he was content with his lot, his escapism coming when he played or managed football matches at weekends, while my escape route was proving to be up the stoney thoroughfare that was Thorneyholme Road.

Cricket was certainly not Dad's thing, but he was very supportive in all of my activities and so backed me in whatever I chose to take up. It was actually one of the blokes from his football team that started me off at Accrington Cricket Club by paying my initial annual membership fee. Peter Westwell was the goalkeeper from Cedar Swifts and it was probably as much of a thank you to my dad for his devoted duties as any thought of doing a good turn for a young lad.

Hours were spent grooving my bowling action or tinkering with my batting technique in the nets with other young players, either at official club practice or the Under-18s equivalent. If a midweek match took place I would be up there watching, taking the opportunity to have a knock-up in between innings on the outfield, as kids have tended to up and down the country through the generations; on some occasions the club groundsman Frank

Nash would even let us use a pitch on the edge of the square for an impromptu practice match during quieter periods of the six weeks' school holidays and at weekends.

My bowling, at least, was reaping the rewards of it all. At thirteen, I was already scalping third XI batsmen, and the thrill of taking wickets maintained my enthusiasm and persuaded me there was an alternative to football. Probably due to my lack of physicality when pitched against grown men, my batting didn't develop at the same pace. But by 1961, I was in the second XI on merit and being successful at that level too, taking five-wicket hauls versus Bacup and Todmorden. Dad, whose keeping of scrapbooks I was thankful for later in life, recorded all the details for posterity.

For a young lad of fourteen, this was an intoxicating world. Imagine being one step away from mixing with some stars of the global game. It was the equivalent of being in the team below one of the best players at the Indian Premier League playing at a club like Accrington. At that time, the Lancashire League produced its own yearbook with pen-portraits and photographs of the professionals recruited from overseas, a publication that actively encouraged the inner autograph hunter in every child. Of course, I was no different in wanting their signatures, but ambition meant I wanted to compete alongside them too and thankfully the wait for this to come to fruition was not a long one.

I made my Accrington first XI debut as a fifteen-year-old in July 1962 against Rishton, in a side that contained West Indies great Wes Hall. Wes's popularity – he even made it round to our house to sample my mum's pie on occasion – came from his willingness to be a part of our community. Forget his wonderful ability as a cricketer, he was also as generous with his support of others, myself included. He showed an interest in the club's younger players, and when you played alongside him he made you feel an equally important member of the team.

So there I was in my very first match, my only first XI

appearance of that particular season. What a thrill to be shoulder-to-shoulder with this supreme international athlete. Wes was in his mid-twenties, the prime of his career, and was a fearsome prospect for the best batsmen in the world, let alone the best players from our county. It must have felt like he was pushing off the sightscreen to opposition batsmen when he had that new ball in hand. The ferocity of his bowling was summed up by the fact that our wicketkeeper Jack Collier used to shove steaks down his gloves in a bid to reduce some of the impact. By the end of an innings those mitts would have been closer to well done than medium rare.

On this single occasion that I played alongside him, a drawn match up at Rishton's Blackburn Road ground, Wes opened both the batting and bowling. Although a renowned fast bowler, he was a capable enough batsman to have scored two Test fifties by the age of twenty-five, and showed some of his ability with 64 in a century opening stand. Such a start to our innings meant we were going to post a competitive total even though Rishton fought back. In fact, batting at No. 8, I arrived at the crease on a hat-trick, and considered averting such a result a major triumph. However, although I avoided the ignominy of being dismissed first ball, I didn't last long, making just one in my maiden knock.

No matter. By eight o'clock that Saturday evening I was able to reflect on a triple of my very own, the first three wickets of my first XI career. I had been picked to bat in the lower-middle order and bowl the combination of chinamen and googlies that had flummoxed kids of my own age and indeed second XI batsmen around the league. Accrington's captain, Lindon Dewhurst, provided me with a good window of opportunity too – all too often young lads are picked with promises of this and that, only to end up as glorified scarecrows in the field. I could have no such complaints though, being brought on first change after Wes had nipped out the top three. My debut figures of 6-0-24-3 were numbers to be proud of.

People like Wes, Bobby Simpson and Eddie Barlow, who all played in the league, were of another world in my eyes, gods mixing among the mortals, and I would hang off any word of encouragement they might offer. They all recognised I had talent and so would invest time in me and give tips on how I could improve further. All advice was good advice as far as I was concerned and I lapped it up freely enough, although because of the nature of their engagement by the club it wasn't always available on a freebie basis. Simpson, as was his prerogative as the professional over from Australia, charged a couple of shillings for private coaching sessions and our family simply could not afford to pay. But the one piece of recurring advice from these great cricketers actually echoed what the other senior players of the club would tell me. Simply, to never give your wicket away. The way you hurt the opposition when batting, they taught me, was to stay in. It therefore became your primary objective.

However, it was actually a less-heralded name from a foreign land who had most to do with my progression from a shorts-wearing schoolboy cricketer to a first-team regular. Before Wes Hall came to the club, the professional was not another pace bowler from the Caribbean but an off-spinning all-rounder from India, as luck would have it. Surjuram Girdhari – more familiarly known as SK, his initials – was not a gun player of Lancashire League cricket but he stuck around in the area after his 1958 season with the club, working as a male nurse, and kept his association going by coaching the up-and-coming youngsters. A player with a Ranji Trophy double hundred and a ratio of four wickets per first-class appearance at 20 runs apiece was someone worth listening to. His knowledge was a great help, coming at a time when my parents had acknowledged that my commitment merited kitting me out and venturing to Gibson Sports in the town centre to purchase my first bat: a coil-sprung Stuart Surridge 'Ken Barrington'.

Statistically speaking, I was unable to make the same kind of contributions initially with that bat as I was the ball. There were no problems with my technique, that was sound enough, but I possessed little power so I was unable to emulate my successes in schoolboy matches in senior cricket.

Against players of my own age, I was chaining together some decent scores and my highest to date came two days after that first XI debut, when I struck an unbeaten 71 for our Under-18s against Church. Matches were coming thick and fast for me at this point, and people in high places were taking note of my performances.

It was perhaps because of the disparity in numbers between my work as a batsman and bowler that most experts seemed to think that it would be as a left-arm spinner that I would make my mark, recognising my maturity with the ball while at the same time voicing some concern at a lack of attacking options at the top of the order.

However, there remained no pressure on me to score quickly when playing for Accrington, and they showed faith in me when as a sixteen-year-old, I started the 1963 season as first-choice opening batsman in the first team. There were no spectacular results in my initial outings; in fact, in the very first game of the season I made Geoff Boycott look like an absolute dasher, remaining steadfast at the crease for more than an hour for just 13. Rumour had it that I even sent glass eyes to sleep in the crowd. Of course, there were grumbles from folk who came to watch us – in those days you would think nothing of having 1000 or so 'on' – yet the people who mattered most stuck with me.

Jack Collier, our salt-of-the-earth keeper who never had a bad word for anyone, offered me words of comfort as I sat down in the dressing room, rubbing my shoulders like an amateur masseur and telling me: 'Ee, you were going grand … just gettin' yer eye in … I thowt you'd get fifty …' Every club needs a player like Jack, a real larger than life character. When Eddie Robinson – a leg-spinner only denied Lancashire honours due to the presence of Tommy Greenhough, Bob Barber, Brian Booth and later Sonny Ramadhin – sent down his googly, Jack would rarely pick it, and as he flagged another through for byes would shout: 'Ee, Eddie … they're comin' down like snakes … I'd given it up … thowt it had bowled him!'

I rarely reached the boundary with my strokes, and seldom got it off the square for that matter, but I was learning my trade in good company against good weekend cricketers, and there were no moves from any of the club hierarchy to reform me because they knew the reward of developing a young player. The role of a Lancashire League club was to produce cricketers to represent the county and their dedication to doing so was something I greatly appreciated.

Investing their time and trust in me was a mutually beneficial process, I guess. For me, being monitored by Lancashire offered the opportunity of a professional career. For the club, there was kudos in producing such players. It was not long before I began to produce more serious scores – which in those days were a bit like a particularly costly over at the Big Bash League.

At first, if I managed to get into the twenties against a testing attack I saw it as a real triumph. My baker's dozen away at Colne was followed the next week by a single-figure contribution in a home defeat to a Ramsbottom side featuring a nineteen-year-old Ian Chappell as their pro. In the draw with Rawtenstall the following day, I struck 33 – the highest score in the match. Later that month, I repeated the feat with 46 in a victorious cause versus Burnley at Turf Moor. The 137-run total that Burnley posted was comfortably the highest of any innings in my first five matches of that 1963 season – the average being just 101 – but we cantered home by eight wickets, and when I was dismissed there was plenty of time remaining to have gone on and celebrated a half-century.

Nevertheless, innings like this naturally swelled my confidence and provided the conviction that I was good enough to prosper in this esteemed company. Within half a dozen appearances I began to think and feel like a first XI cricketer. Any young player needs support to become established, and I could not thank those that I played with in those days highly enough for their patience and understanding.

The cricket was played in a tough environment, with opponents not giving an inch. Such an attitude heightened the competitive nature, but it also led to a negativity when it came to style of play. In those days, there was a general tendency for teams to bat on too long, probably because they encouraged lads like me to hone their batting skills on the job in the middle, which effectively killed off chances of positive results before everyone began munching on their teas. Delayed declarations and a proliferation of draws hurried on an era of limited-overs cricket at club level. The pitches could be treacherous too, particularly when damp in early season, nibbling about for the bowlers and demanding a watchful approach from batters. It required you to dig in, to get into game mode by not getting out cheaply, and promoted precise footwork and tight defence.

Away from the competitive stuff, where the heavy ball bowled into the pitch by your prototype league seamer proved as hard to get hold of as Harry Potter's snitch, I had developed a more expansive array of strokes. These were chiefly unleashed in the huge, open-age friendly games we used to have up at the Rec. The most memorable one I can recall got me in quite some bother. The occasion in question was a couple of years before getting my run in the first XI, when I clipped one off my legs beautifully and watched with pride as the ball sailed over square leg … and straight through Mrs Bidulph's front window.

Now I might have got away with this on any other day, but unfortunately for me one of the other players in this particular cricketing extravaganza was Keith, also of the name Bidulph, and a loyal son as it turned out. There was no way he would be turning a blind eye to my indiscretion, and my horror at the consequences of my actions completely overwhelmed me. Not that I was scared about what the Bidulphs would say or do; I was just scared to death about how my own mother would react. 'She'll go apeshit,' I thought, or some such phrase more befitting 1961, as I ran home in tears.

I was explaining what had happened to Mum – you've probably nicknamed her Scary Mary by now, right? – when there was a knock at the door. 'It was him that did it,' said Keith, pointing his finger towards me as my mother opened our front door. It had been a cracking shot – I picked it up beautifully and it just jetted towards the houses with a seemingly unstoppable momentum – but it cost me two shillings.

Whenever I was sent to age-group cricket trials I felt comfortable. Undoubtedly, in contrast to how I felt about football, it was because I knew I was better than my peers. Physicality didn't come into it as much and I was quite comfortable that I was more skilled than those I was up against. Playing for Lancashire schoolboys was a real thrill, because we used to play our games at Old Trafford and it was a real incentive to stay in the squad just to play more games at such a magnificent venue.

It was in no small part down to the enthusiasm of Bob Cunliffe, the physical education teacher at Accrington Secondary Technical School, that I was at so many of these trials. Although we didn't actually have a play area as such, making do with the school yard, Mr Cunliffe was dead keen on us participating at the highest level we possibly could. With no facilities, there was not even an official school team or fixture list – certainly not to compare with the kind that Lancastrian grammar school lads would have been familiar with. They would participate in weekly fixtures against other similar establishments.

Shame, then, that I was as proficient at my 11-plus at school as

South Africa were at reading a Duckworth–Lewis sheet at the 2003 World Cup. Not that my educational route (towards becoming a highly skilled tradesman) held me back one bit. Because what we lacked was more than made up for by Mr Cunliffe's enthusiasm. By hook or by crook we played four matches or so a summer, somewhere or other, and although I don't know for certain, I suspect it was all down to him. Certainly, Bob, fully aware of what I was doing at the weekends with Accrington, was not backwards in coming forwards when it came to promoting my cause. In conjunction with the cricket club, he would be recommending me to all of the representative teams in the wider area, and his dedication meant I got as many opportunities to impress as any clever clogs up the road. For a school with no cricket heritage we produced some good cricketers – Jack Simmons left the summer before I started.

So with both school and club supporting my case and pushing my credentials for higher honours, I had a pretty strong support network. My sheltered upbringing meant I had no other distractions. I was devoted to my weekly routines of church and cricket, and my parents were as dedicated to encouraging my interests as they were enforcing strong discipline. From the age of thirteen, I had been allowed to turn out for Accrington's third XI, and a year later I was being dispatched to my first schools trial.

National recognition also came my way for the first time while at Accrington Secondary Technical when I was selected for the annual English schools matches. I played pretty well in those North versus South matches, as I tended to do in the few games I appeared in at Old Trafford, under the noses of several committee members more often than not. All of which was useful, I'm sure, at getting me that first contract with Lancashire.

It was a great feeling when my name was called out in assembly by the headmaster. This happened whenever I was selected to play for representative XIs, and it meant making my way out to the front to accept the accolade on stage. Not that the entire teaching staff were supportive, mind you, even one who clearly liked cricket. Mrs Archer, the geography teacher, was totally dismissive of any notion that I would earn a living doing something I was beginning to love.

She never said so, but I suspect it was an incident involving me and her new motor – a Morris Oxford Shooting Brake – during what should have been lesson time that influenced her thoughts. Mr Cunliffe had taken me out of the classroom to work on my batting, and had taken another couple of lads too who acted as fielders. We were having this knock-up in the school yard, with Mr Cunliffe bowling, when I smacked this ball. It came straight out of the middle and proceeded straight through the window of Mrs Archer's gleaming new pride and joy. She'd only had this car a day, as I found out from her personally after Mr Cunliffe made me go and explain what had happened.

'I don't know why you bother with this cricket business,' she used to say to me. 'You should concentrate on being a bit more academic.' I was already intent on making my dream a reality, so whenever she offered her two penn'orth on the subject all I ever heard was 'blah, blah, blah'.

It was years later when her words came back to me in the strangest of places. I was walking down the steps at Dean Park, Bournemouth, with my Lancashire opening partner Barry Wood, halfway through what turned out to be a Gillette Cup quarter-final victory over Hampshire in 1972 when a distinctive shrill caught my ear. 'I hope you've improved, Lloyd,' a female voice warned. Blow me down, sat among this full house was the very same Mrs Archer. It turned out she had moved down to the south coast in retirement. Barry Richards had scored a wonderful 129 to put us under pressure, but from the moment Peter Lee got him out we never looked like losing, so I think I had the last laugh on that one.

Academically I was all right – no better than all right – although I could never shake the feeling of injustice that I was at the wrong school. I might not have been the brightest button at Peel Park, but I always felt I would have been better off at a different educational establishment. The technical college was designed to help trades people prepare for later life. For those that wanted to become electricians, draughtsmen and plumbers, skilled manual workers, it was ideal, but it just wasn't me. I would have much rather studied Geography and History and learned French. But these three were all subjects that you had to drop in year two to concentrate on more practical areas. Unfortunately, the compulsory subjects were Woodwork, Metalwork and Technical Drawing.

I was conscious that my hands were going to be useful to me, and so I didn't want to jeopardise that by blowing them up or chopping a finger off. By the age of fourteen, I began to spend plenty of time away from school, playing sport, mainly cricket, and having the school's blessing to do so. I didn't really bother with homework, and to be honest I didn't really have time. After-school cricket practice became more and more regular, and when I say practice I don't just mean for an hour. I'd be there for three hours, and there was the travelling to and fro to consider as well.

Even when I wasn't at a designated training session, I would be creating my own little practice routines, such as attaching a ball to a washing line and hitting it repeatedly, or going to the cricket club with just one cricket ball and bowling it hour after hour at a set of stumps. There was no need for an outside edge or a wicket-keeper's gloves at the other end. I would go down there with not a soul around and literally bowl and fetch until my arm felt like dropping off. The only respite during marathon spells was the fifty-yard round trip in between deliveries to fetch the ball from the back of the net.

For a young spin bowler, doing the same thing over and over again, repeating it hundreds and hundreds of times, helped groove my action. There are no short cuts when you are trying to make it as a professional in any sport, and very few get there by luck or natural talent alone. It doesn't happen by accident, aspiring cricketers have to put a lot of work in, and this was my homework during my formative years. I really enjoyed practising because I didn't know anything else. I just knew that I loved playing sport. Even in my early teens, I had huge ambition to play professionally.

It might be said that my successes in cricket brought me out of my shell a little bit, although I would never claim to have been an outgoing sort of character. I remained relatively shy in public and ultra quiet in the house, mainly because of the hold that my mum had over me, although as the years went by I became less scared of her.

Funnily enough, in terms of my personality I have discovered that I am much more my mum than my dad. For a start, I possess her fiery temper. I've always had that short fuse and can go off if someone riles me, but I'm miles better now than I used to be, because in young adulthood I would be a bit like Vesuvius. It would take the slightest thing for me to go off. Now, on the rare occasions that I do flip my lid, more often than not I smile to myself: 'That's my bloody mother.'

All of my mum's family was extremely supportive as I set out on my cricketing career. There were relatively few on my dad's side, but there was still my Uncle Alf, my Uncle Harry and my Auntie Mary. I have goodness knows how many cousins scattered around Accrington but I've not seen most of them for years, because whereas they have stayed around the area they grew up in, my job has taken me all over the world. When we were all confined in this tight-knit community, things were different. We were all as much Accrington as the chimneys and cobbles.

One of my bugbears was being denied the opportunity of playing for Accrington at cricket once I had been signed on at Old Trafford. Like my colleagues, I fell foul of a rather silly league rule that did not allow players who made a living at Lancashire, even inexperienced kids like myself, to continue relationships at the clubs that had taught them the game. It seemed self-defeating in the greater scheme of things, because having absorbed everything I had been taught since the age of thirteen during my grooming for senior cricket, I was prevented from being able to help show others the way and repay my gratitude for the help.

This was all at odds with the Australian system which offers an almost polar opposite outlook. Over there, you move up and down cricket's ladder from level to level, so that schoolboy crick-eters can mix with first-class and Test players if they have the ability. Throughout the generations, it's been known for Test crick-eters to maintain their associations with the clubs that produced them by playing for their grade clubs whenever they're able to do so – sometimes in the middle of an international series in which they're participating.

Australian cricket treats itself as one big family, with no one ever too big or too good to play at club level. This philosophy of making each level as competitive as possible has maintained the highest standard in the preparation of players. The step up from a grade match on a Saturday to the Sheffield Shield in midweek, while not to be underestimated, has never been as great a leap as it might have otherwise. The benefits of youngsters playing along-side better players is fairly self-explanatory, allowing them as it does to pick up decent tips and good habits, yet the Lancashire League's antiquated rules meant that only one paid player could represent each club at first-team level, and that invariably was the overseas import.

During my second season on the staff, Lancashire persuaded the league to make a dispensation so that I could feature and therefore get more cricket. Truth is, I loved playing sport in my local town. Although I have spent less time there and more in Manchester in later life, it's still a regular pilgrimage for me to see my three lads,

Graham, Steven and Ben, my daughter Sarah and the grandchildren. It was a moment of great pride to me in 2014 when one of the brood, Graham's lad Joe, made his Accrington first XI debut. It's nice to see that he's carrying on the family business I founded more than half a century ago.

CHAPTER 3

Home Sweet Dogs' Home

It was while we were on holiday at the Heysham Towers camp in Morecambe in late July 1963 that Dad spotted some news in the *Daily Express* that would change my life. There it was in black and white: 'LANCASHIRE HAVE OFFERED APPRENTICE TERMS TO ACCRINGTON ALL-ROUNDER DAVID LLOYD.'

Lancashire, this great club for whom such wonderful players as Eddie Paynter, Cyril Washbrook and Brian Statham had turned out, wanted me on their books. I was sixteen years old and Old Trafford was to become my second home. We quit our holiday that very day of 25 July to return to Accrington on the bus and discover the finer details of my contract. The terms were enclosed in an envelope wedged behind the door when we got back to Water Street, laid out in a letter from Geoffrey Howard, the club secretary.

It shouldn't have been the greatest surprise that Lancashire would make such an offer because I had been with the club throughout the summer as an amateur, playing club and ground matches on the back field at Old Trafford (which has since been tarmacked and made into a B&Q car park), bowling at the senior players in the nets and pocketing £7 a week to cover my travel expenditure. But you don't want to count your chucks in sport, and I for one never wanted to believe it was happening until that Thursday evening.

This was the correspondence that would help me fulfil my dreams and map out a career path. Given my background and lack of other passions in life, this way into the real world of working for a living proved a godsend. It allowed me to put money into the family pot while being immersed in full-time professional sport. There was also a sense of both pride and achievement that Lancashire wanted me. Imagine my surprise then that this contract to upgrade me to fully fledged status saw me put down to £6 a week. Now, you didn't have to be Archimedes to work out that things didn't quite add up here. But losing a seventh of my income mattered not a jot to me. The financial aspect was not at the top of my agenda, and my weekly pay packet was more than what my dad was getting.

Instead, there was an excitement about getting started, one which seemed to be shared by the whole of Accrington. The local pride in producing a player was quite something in those pre-motorway days when the next town seemed to be in an entirely different time zone, and the number of well-wishers reminded me of just how many people had been batting for me and made it feel akin to a collective rather than personal achievement. It was a new dawn for me in a year that witnessed a new dawn for cricket. For it was in 1963 that the distinction between gentlemen and players was abolished. No longer did those from the upper classes, who were playing the game for fun, leave the field through a gate to be waited upon hand and foot by butlers while their fellow players, who relied on the game to pay the bills, sauntered off in a different direction.

Saved from becoming a plumber's hand – a position secured with the local council through my first wife Susan's cousin, Trevor – I took my apprenticeship in cricket, as Lancashire followed the lead of football clubs in offering such schemes. That experiment ended before the 1964 season, so the theme of 'last in' from my childhood was continuing to follow me.

Once again there was a hierarchical system that required getting used to. I had only 'made it' in a provisional sense, because as with all jobs I had to start at the bottom and strive for further recognition. Only when you've earned your cap for Lancashire and the red rose is on your blazer, on your cap and on your chest, had you really earned something. In the second decade of the twenty-first century, annual appraisals tell you how the company rates you, but as a 1960s cricketer playing for Lancashire you were after one thing – because donning the red rose symbolised success.

It was far from easy being office junior. As a seventeen-year-old heading into that dressing-room environment at Old Trafford, life was tough. Suddenly, cricket wasn't fun anymore; it had lost its recreational property and became the survival of the fittest. To a large degree this is a necessary evil, going with the territory of top-level sport, but it also created bitterness and niggle between colleagues.

Do not for one minute think that when people are in direct competition for places that everyone gets on. They do not and it means that, although you're all trying to do your best for the betterment of both yourself and your employer, dressing rooms can be cruel. You share some wonderful moments of achievement – after combining in a match-winning stand your batting partner can feel like your best mate even if you have barely a thing in common – yet there is also a flip side. Whenever you throw a collection of alpha males together, it's about asserting control, and some of that comes through the undermining of others.

Mickey taking – or banter, or even #bants in modern parlance – is a natural by-product of a dressing room. There's a lot of time to fill, during which camaraderie and rapport are developed, but some of this can become quite harsh. My take on this might not align with the politically correct brigade, but I have always believed you accept it and get on with the job. Sticks and stones and all that.

You only have to consider nicknames. They're rarely flattering, are they? Unless you happen to be Vanburn Holder. I know lots of ex-cricketers who wish they'd copped Hosepipe. Like Vanburn, mine was also handed to me for physical attributes but from another part of the body, and proved considerably less complimentary.

If you and I met in the street, chances are you would think of me as Bumble, not the name I was christened. Few people question why I'm called this or what it means, they just accept that's who I am. These days, had I no wish to accept my fate, I could take my grievance to an industrial tribunal or make a case in the small claims court for loss of confidence. Suffering such an affliction may also have increased my chances of being successful in a PPI claim.

For this was the nickname awarded to me when I was accepted into the Old Trafford dressing room. Michael Bentine, one of the members of that great comic troupe the Goons, had taken his off-the-wall humour into the realms of children's television by creating a weekly series about a trio of aliens called the Bumblies. These cheerful extra-terrestrials had arrived from the Planet Bumble to learn about the workings of Earth, after their flying saucer crash-landed in the garden of an absent-minded professor of astronomy.

Such behaviour does sound like me, but it was for their looks and not their actions that I became Bumble. You see, they all had long hooters for a start and, although I couldn't see the resemblance myself, I just took the others' word for it. Some nicknames stick and this was one of them. At first, I had no idea what they were on about, I'd just heard some of the others muttering 'Bumblie, Bumble'. In a way it was a sign that this meek, unassuming lad from Accrington was being accepted and taken into Lancashire's inner sanctum.

There had been no airs and graces to my cricket education. It had been a fairly successful three years for me since making my Accrington third XI debut. Things had gone pretty well from the first time I journeyed up Thorneyholme Road, which leads to the town's cricket club, one I was to repeat hundreds of times on my bike every summer. Rather like most things in Accrington, it was functional rather than a picturesque retreat. An establishment with no more frills than a Quaker matron, it created the kind of environment to enforce principles of hard work and dedication to aspiring boys like me.

So the winter requirements of my new job at Old Trafford held no fears for me either. The club had resident electricians, plumbers and joiners, and I was seconded to the carpenters, which meant mending seats, building parts of stands, putting new doors on the toilet blocks, all that sort of thing. Having passed GCE Woodwork, it was appropriate that I was paired up with Ted, who was effectively head of joinery. The other bloke, Tom, always carried a bowl of putty around with him.

In subsequent years, after I was married, the winter job opportunities improved. To be fair, I had no desire to be a joiner's mate in the long term and so other jobs were offered. The club's idea for keeping the squad paid all year round – in those days you stopped in September and reconvened in the first week of April for a fortnight's pre-season – was that members of the committee, if possible, would employ a player. Among those committee men was a really nice chap called Richard Bowman, who was the managing director of Dutton's Brewery.

An Oxford University graduate, Richard also opened the bowling for Lancashire in first-class cricket, and did so while wearing a cravat. One of the last amateurs to feature for Lancashire, he got me a position with this brewery, which had been going since the eighteenth century, loading wagons and working in the wine and spirits department. It was flippin' hard work, which required clocking on at six o'clock in the morning. Clocking off after a couple of hours' overtime was not compulsory but became a regular occurrence.

Winter work away from the game was commonplace. If you were a county cricketer from 1963 up until the millennium, when the advent of English central contracts had the knock-on effect of counties offering ten- and twelve-month deals to players, there had to be a secondary income once frost lined the covers. You simply wouldn't survive otherwise. Throughout my career you would be summer millionaires and winter paupers, although some engagements were better paid than others and came with their own particular benefits.

Not least jobs like mine at the Blackburn-based brewery that required a great deal of discipline. If you are going to be successful on the county circuit over a fifteen-year career, discipline is essential, with punctuality being key to the functioning of a successful team. It's no good if one player turns up late for a net session, a team meeting or a bus departure time; because in that scenario, one slacker disrupts the functioning of the entire group. Dutton's had a surefire way to prevent transgressors when it came to their daily shifts: clock on even a minute late and you automatically lost fifty minutes of your pay.

Equally, you needed to be fit and I would defy any modern player who claims to be fitter than I was back then. Loading beer wagons all day so they could set off to make their deliveries to the 500 or so licensed premises Dutton's owned required the kind of physicality that would have challenged the biggest, hairy-arsed fast bowlers, let alone a slow left-armer like me. I was absolutely bolloxed by the end of a day.

Dutton's was taken over by Whitbread in 1964 and Richard Bowman's leaving present when he finally departed the company some time later was the tenancy of the Inn at Whitewell, in the Forest of Bowland, one of the best hotels in Great Britain. It ought to be; it's owned by Her Majesty the Queen.

While I was grateful to the help of Bowman off the field, it was undoubtedly Geoff Pullar, Lancashire's senior batsman, who took me under his wing when it came to support on the playing side of things. Geoff recently passed away, which got me thinking about his influence on me. When I was taken onto the staff, it's fair to say he helped me out big time, but not always in a matey-matey way because that would have done a young player entering that competitive environment no good at all. Sometimes you need tough love, and as a senior player he would discipline me with a stern word if I was showing any sign of going off track.

Geoff was a wonderful player full of well-meaning advice given generously, despite the fact that it was obvious that improving a younger rival like me could hasten his own demise. Unbeknown to me, I was being groomed to replace him in the top three in the longer term, and there are few doubts he knew it. His work to improve me as a potential top-order county player spoke volumes for the kind of bloke he was. He would give me plenty of tips in the opening weeks and months I spent as a Lancashire squad player, and the well of knowledge did not dry up before I strapped on my pads for the first time in a County Championship match.

That moment came on 12 June 1965, against Middlesex, a fixture that coincided with Pullar and Tommy Greenhough being axed following an underwhelming start to the season that had witnessed half a dozen defeats in the first eight matches. Far from moping about, or playing the Big I Am given his pedigree, here was Geoff filtering twenty-four Tests of experience into my lughole as I prepared to go out and face his former England colleague Fred Titmus.

My debut innings lasted for a little more than an hour as Titmus, one of the greatest off-spinners produced by England, was thwarted over after over courtesy of Pullar's apt assessment of how best to combat his threat. A success, you might think? Well, only in terms of delaying the inevitable.

Countering Titmus was all about getting in a good stride forward, Pullar told me, and making sure you played the ball with bat well in front of the pad to eliminate the chance of an inside edge deflecting to the posse of close catchers. It was no doubt a combination of lunging down the track and first-match nerves that led to me cramping up and requiring a salt tablet to carry on. Cramp can be bloody painful and has been known to force batsmen to retire hurt. I recall Andrew Strauss being unable to complete his innings in a one-day international versus India in Jamshedpur in 2006. He had been at the crease only a shade over two hours but it was a shade over 48 degrees, and left in no state to carry on he was escorted from the field and put on a drip in the dressing room to rehydrate.

To be fair to Strauss, he had 74 runs to his name, which by my calculations was a rather neat increase of 74 on mine, made in a climate approximately 30 degrees hotter than that of Manchester. But let's not get bogged down by minor detail.

For an hour, time and the Old Trafford scoreboard stood still. It was as if my defensive lunge was in suspended animation. I had followed Pullar's tactical missive to the letter but unfortunately, exactly as I had in my early games for Accrington two years earlier, barely played a shot in anger. Modern-day spin doctors – or the England and Wales Cricket Board's media department as they are also known – might have sold you the line that I had treble the runs I started with when Titmus finally snared me. Fair point, but everyone knows that three times nought is nought. An equally economical look at the truth would have told you that I couldn't score any fewer in future innings. Unfortunately, I didn't score any more in my next as Middlesex completed their landslide victory, this time the other 'offie' Don Bick accounting for me.

To paint the picture during that era, the Lancashire dressing room in the old pavilion was split over two floors. The upstairs was frequented by the senior players and the lower deck – or the Dogs'

Home as it was known – was the retreat of us juniors. By the time I became coach at Lancashire, things had changed and that downstairs area was given to the visiting team with all the home players changing upstairs.

Some will say that this upstairs-downstairs scenario was unhealthy; a sign that there had been little progress from the previous era when the gentlemen would look down their noses at the full-time professionals who stood alongside them on the field. It was all a bit like *Downton Abbey*.

Not that this simple lad from Accrington ever saw anything wrong with it. Contrarily, it gave me a purpose: to get up those steps into the established ranks. It wasn't as if the separation was done on a social or class basis. This was a meritocracy in which those in the Dogs' Home were upgraded when awarded the county cap. So it became a massive motivation for us rosebuds to bloom into full roses and move upstairs. It was a symbolic journey for all of us, and with it came one other significant change to our status. Namely, a big increase in wages.

It was in 1968, the year in which I married my childhood sweetheart and mother of my four children Susan Wallwork, that I was to receive my cap. I was just twenty-one. Although the financial increase that came with it – a £950 annual salary – was welcome as I began a new chapter of my life as a family man, moving up top didn't guarantee a job for life. As a county cricketer you remained subservient to the club's committee. Contracts were a standard two years in length, which meant that every other season a group of men who had not necessarily played the game but who had either good fortune, good business acumen or good contacts were sitting in judgement on your career. Your future was decided on their whim.

This committee ruled the roost. Forget any divisions existing between players young and old. There was relative civility between everyone despite the split-level changing areas. The 'us and them' analogy was a lot more accurate when applied to the players and these chaps located at the far end of the pavilion. They were the absolute gods and us their playthings. Their position at Old Trafford was dubbed the sharp end, and where we were housed was known as the blunt end.

There was a massive resentment towards the suits from us because of the power they held over our lives. They were in control of our destinies and there is no doubting the influence it had on how the game was played. Look at a lot of the scorecards from that period and they reveal a rather turgid style of cricket. The simple fact was that you were playing for your career, playing to maintain your living, so batsmen would do their utmost not to get out rather than concentrate on scoring runs.

The barriers that existed at Lancashire were eventually broken down in the late 1960s by Cedric Rhoades, whose rise to prominence coincided – as tends to be the case – with the demise of others. In this instance, it was following the resignation of the Old Trafford committee en masse. Cedric was a champion of the players when he came into office, one whose initial months as chairman were seen favourably by all parties around the club. For a while, there was no sharp or blunt. Everything was smooth.

But as can be the case with individuals who are backed so enthusiastically and in such numbers, it all went to his head. He more than slightly turned the other way from his sympathy towards the dressing room to becoming a bit of an ogre, if truth be told. Initially popular with the members – of which there were a good 15,000 in those days – for his insistence on equality, it soon became clear that he saw things in *Animal Farm* terms, and himself more equal than others. This club for all was soon becoming *his* club, a change that led to him being nicknamed Cedric Power by the players.

Cedric was a very wealthy Manchester businessman and with his level of success came a huge ego. Having made several shrewd investments in his buying and selling over the years, and then taken control of a county club, it was pretty evident that Lancashire was just another stepping stone to other more powerful committees. Soon he was on those of the Test and County Cricket Board at Lord's, ones which influenced the wider game and not only the bit played inside our county boundaries.

Rhoades was a man who would rock the boat, someone who would challenge the norm, and it was felt that he was welcomed on board by the TCCB hierarchy down in London simply because they preferred to keep someone like him close rather than operating at arm's length. This kind of attitude from him was really good for us players when he was on his way up, because he focused on providing us with anything that could help improve the team. In modern parlance, he engaged with the product and that always means the players. The more support provided, the better facilities, an increased level of backing for the captain, and the greater the chance of a team being competitive. He basically moved us forward after a period of what we felt was stagnation.

In his early days you would not only see him, you would hear him too if you popped down to Old Trafford. He was very vocal in his support of what we were doing, and displayed an almost religious devotion to getting down to every match he possibly could, business commitments pending. Talk about being hands on. He would be vociferous in the members' viewing areas and convivial in the bars at social events, often with a glass of Tio Pepe in hand.

His relationships with his captains highlighted how he operated. He had the support from the dressing room because of his pledge to 'back you to the hilt'. Tell him what you required and it was inevitably delivered because of his control over the rest of the committee. He was like a puppeteer, pulling everyone else's strings, and once you acknowledged as much you knew how to use him to your advantage. Good old Cedric Power would get sufficient nods for a majority on every major decision in those first few seasons, and it was arguably only neglect of his responsibilities at Lancashire that turned the Yes-men into Nos as the years passed by.

My own thoughts on him mirrored this. Having fallen for his powers of persuasion early on, and even used my understandings of his working to my advantage during my own captaincy years that would follow, I was taught by my predecessor Jack Bond that the way to get a proposal through an indifferent committee was to float it to Cedric a fortnight in advance. His predictable reaction would be to dismiss it out of hand in the first instance, then adopt it as his own when it came to the actual meeting, and sing the praises of the notion, promoting it as a Rhoades revelation once it had been ticked up.

You see, Cedric was so fond of his own influence that he wanted everyone to know about it, including the best plans he had pilfered from others and passed off as his own. It was this kind of behaviour, the constant striving for recognition, that altered my view of him as time went by. I could see that he was too driven by personal gratification, the shared fault of many chairmen at sporting clubs. At the opposite end of the spectrum, you have men like Sir Jack Walker, whose stewardship of Blackburn Rovers was taken from a Victorian schoolboy's book. He believed in being seen but not heard.

For the majority of Rhoades's tenure I was an admirer and supporter, but his unerring pursuit of control at the club proved a huge turn-off for me. His entrance was made when he led a vote of no confidence in the committee, a motion which resulted in such dramatic but necessary change. In the end, however, just like those he replaced, he overstayed his welcome.

Our on-field change in fortunes at Lancashire was down to several factors. I hate to use the word modernising when we are talking about those Swinging Sixties, but it is appropriate because a change in English cricket's domestic landscape really suited the characteristics of our developing team. Yorkshire – or 'that other lot from over the Pennines' as we referred to them – were invincible when it came to what they termed 'proper crick-eet', but conversely the introduction of one-day matches suited us.

It certainly made the side we were putting together infinitely more competitive overnight, because we were a collective of generally quite young blokes who had been brought up in local leagues that promoted the 'give 'em nowt' attitude. You had to work hard for your runs and become inventive at times to find the boundary. Tight bowling was backed up by tigerish fielding – there were no inner fielding circles to be adhered to, we just made it policy to form a ring around the opposition batsmen and squeeze hard to limit their singles.

When the Gillette Cup was launched in 1963, it didn't coincide with immediate silverware at Old Trafford. But once we broke the duck with the inaugural John Player Sunday League title in 1969, the proverbial floodgates were open. That trophy was defended successfully the following summer, one which marked a hat-trick of one-day trophies when we also won the Gillette Cup at Lord's.

This period coincided with Jack Bond – a great Lancashire stalwart who has done just about every job going at Old Trafford across seven decades – taking over the captaincy. It was no coincidence that under Jack's leadership we started to function much more effectively as a team and to win matches. He fostered a real team ethos and the relatively young nature of our squad bought into his vision. He was the bandleader and we played to his tune, trusting his judgements and feeling trusted to perform. Suddenly, both as individuals and as a unit we started to play with more confidence. He knew how to get people to follow him and develop the staunchest loyalty with the most gentle acts of persuasion.

The breakthrough for any batsman harbouring serious ambition is always their first hundred, and I got mine against Cambridge University. But I would not be alone among first-class cricketers in dismissing that effort as my maiden moment. It was discounted in my mind because of the standard of opposition, so even though I considered the threshold crossed on the one hand, I was still shy of it on the other. You are always striving for that elusive three-figure score in Championship cricket and for me it came against Gloucestershire at Bristol, and did so on the say-so of Jack who delayed a declaration, knackering the game up in the process.

His decision to wait for me to get over the line rather than push all-out for victory proved a magnet for grumblers as it dictated that the game would inevitably end in a draw. But the reasoning of Jack, this absolute champion father figure who we all loved, was that once I had that first one under the belt, it would really kick me on as a player. He sacrificed the outside chance of a win – maximum reward in the short term – for greater returns in the matches and seasons that followed. He considered that allowing me to get that magical hundred would lead to more of them in the future, and if that was the case the whole team would benefit.

This was an example of how Jack got blokes to play for him. A great leader of men, he so obviously cared about the team's results but more importantly the players working as a unit to achieve them. He had the attitude you would want to bottle and sell to aspiring leaders all over the world.

As a captain he was totally unselfish, and he ensured that we all had fun. He was the kind of cricketer who would fill bars rather than empty them, but what a devotion he has shown to the game. At the age of eighty-two, he was still helping part time on the groundstaff at Old Trafford. Only a serious hip operation over the winter prevented him starting the 2015 domestic season in his full capacity. In my opinion, it is evidence of the kind of unconditional love for our sport seldom few can match, and deserving of a knighthood.

He might have sacrificed that one match down at Nevil Road to further my cause, but as a reader of match situations he was without peer. For that alone, he was worth his place in the XI. His leg-spin bowling did not make it out of the nets, and he would often slip himself down to No. 9 or 10 in the batting order, particularly if we were in need of quick runs. Yet whenever we were absolutely in the mire, he would be the one to front up and get us out of it.

On occasion, he was like a wheel-on tactician and a fine one at that. In recognising his worth in replacing the lauded Brian Statham as captain in 1968, the club made arguably their best ever decision. If you require evidence of that, you need only assess the state of the trophy cabinet during his period in office. Five pieces of limited-overs silverware in as many years was simply sensational, given the lack of success that preceded the sequence.

The club I joined was one in need of a new direction; the most appropriate direction being up. For too long it had dwelt around the bottom end of the Championship. Statisticians would have told you that there had been signs of improvement, as despite a period of six years cemented in the bottom five, Lancashire finished a rung higher up the ladder every season from 1962 to 1965. Then again, they had started the sequence next-to-bottom in a seventeen-team competition, proving that statistics, like the dresses that come out of the wardrobe on Oscar night, reveal as much as they conceal.

Others without Manchester postcodes clearly recognised Jack Bond's worth too. When his playing days came to an end with Lancashire, by virtue of his decision to step aside and groom me for the captaincy, he was viewed as an asset around the shires and it was no real surprise that he was snapped up by Nottinghamshire for a season and handed their club captaincy. In later life, he became an England selector.

If Jack had fortune on his side, it was in the introduction of the

40-over-a-side John Player Sunday League at exactly the right time for the developing team he fronted. This was a brand of cricket that suited our style. Northerners like us were used to playing matches over the course of a weekend afternoon in the local leagues, so this compressed format was pretty familiar. In contrast, the stereotypical profile of a southern county team was that it was stocked full of public schoolboys who were brought up on the longer game. This was all new to them, and it was only really Sussex and Kent that adapted with any sustained success.

Stereotypes exist for a reason. Four decades on we saw Leicestershire, a county whose four-day fortunes were on the wane, reap similar rewards for embracing the Twenty20 format. Perhaps it was because the less-heralded performers on the circuit were more in tune with the 20-over Wednesday night knock-outs so popular around the Midlands. There was clearly something behind their ability to pick up a method ahead of the chasing pack and run with it successfully – three titles from five finals-day appearances in the opening nine years suggested they got it.

We embraced the change positively. The 40-over format promoted versatile cricketers who could both bat and bowl, given the eight-over restriction on a bowler. The youthful nature of the first-team squad at Old Trafford meant that sharpness in the field was almost a given. But Jack reinforced the need to sharpen up even the best among us with regular practice. This definitely had an influence on my thinking in years to come, in both my own captaincy and coaching appointments.

Despite being our most senior player Jack practised what he preached, most memorably in the 1971 Gillette Cup final at Lord's. Kent were winning that game easily with Asif Iqbal at the crease and in complete control of their chase of 225. Our old man of thirty-nine was at extra-cover, and I was at long-off, with Jack Simmons bowling, when Asif skimmed one into the covers. Bond took off like a salmon to grab the ball one handed, and a game that was dead-and-buried was resuscitated as Kent's Pakistani star departed for 89. One catch completely turned things around. It was a bit like the Decision Review System now – seconds earlier you would have been pressing the red button for us, now it was green. We went on to win by 24 runs.

Jack's big thing was to use that inner ring field to put the squeeze on during the middle-overs. He had the tools to take wickets up front in the shape of Peter Lever and Ken Shuttleworth, with Peter Lee in support. He would then know exactly when to employ the two spinners: the slow left-arm of David Hughes complemented by Jack Simmons's off-spin. He would have four fielders on the off-side to prevent the ball going through, and those two bowlers were masters of keeping it tight. It was a bit of a pre-runner to the defensive periods of modern 50-over matches that we have tried to eradicate. But in its era it was terrific, innovative stuff.

Remember, there were no fielding guidelines in early List A fare, the only restrictions being on the number of overs an individual bowler could bowl, so there was a skill at getting your fielders in exactly the right spot. This is where Jack was mustard. These days, point and extra-cover are routinely stationed on the chalk lines of the thirty-yard markings, but he would use his instinct to place fielders in the ultimate spot to both cut out singles and prevent boundaries.

He was also an advocate of keeping wickets intact when we batted to have a real dart at the end of an innings. We wouldn't try anything too risky until the final ten overs and then the policy was to absolutely smash it. Not quite to the extent of the premier teams at the 2015 World Cup, when a dozen an over became the norm, but at a fair lick for the age. Look down the line-up of that particular Lancashire team and it was packed with internationals, and those that weren't could have been. Cricketers of the calibre of Harry Pilling, David Hughes and Jack Simmons were big players in our one-day success.

My own watchful style may not have been a natural fit at the top of the order, but establishing myself during the 1968 season came against a backdrop of positivity. The heckles I had become accustomed to hearing from the regulars at Old Trafford – those who formed the infamous Pit of Hate in front of the pavilion being the most vociferous – were becoming muffled if not completely silenced by an increased amount of runs from me at a quicker tempo. Not least in the run chase I engineered to seal Lancashire's first victory of the season, when we needed a touch near seven an over for the final seven overs and got them. My success dovetailed with that of the team: the win, the first of eight from June onwards, catalysed the surge to a sixth-placed finish and cemented my place in it as an opening batsman. I was becoming an established county performer with aspirations of higher recognition.

CHAPTER 4

Red Rose Rising

The habit of winning heals dressing-room rifts and sweeps problems under the carpet. It's a fact that sprinkling a team with success has magical properties – it makes personality clashes look invisible and strained relationships look like civil ones. We were certainly a happier unit at Lancashire as the years went by, but the team that developed an addiction to silverware actually came together due to a pretty unseemly fallout between our predecessors and the Old Trafford hierarchy.

It emerged from the upheaval of 1964 when players such as Peter Marner and Geoff Clayton were dispensed with because 'their retention was not in the best interests of the club'. Jack Dyson was ditched for being 'not up to the required standard' according to the committee, who had lost patience with a core group of the club's players, both for their on-field shortcomings and their off-field attitudes. Politics has never been of interest to me and the seventeen-year-old Lloyd, D. was certainly not one to dwell on the slings and arrows of this conflict, so my recollections of this upheaval are hazy. But it's safe to say that the seismic change of that year wouldn't have happened to a winning dressing room or at a happy club.

It was a lack of trophies that had developed committee-room agitation towards the dressing room in the first place: without a Championship pennant since 1950, relations between the club's hierarchy and playing staff had become strained and, even though Lancashire had not been accustomed to success, at least the prospect of it had been retained – until that year at least. Faith in the old guard was regressing for some and it clearly caused in-fighting when doors were closed and players' abilities debated.

The upshot of it all was felt not just in the dressing room but also at committee level. Secretary Geoffrey Howard moved to Surrey during that season, and another couple of members of the committee left. Those that remained decided the time was right to remove the velvet glove from the iron fist. As well as the sackings of Clayton and Marner on what was to become known as the Night of the Long Knives, the revolution took in the dismissal of Ken Grieves as captain. It was decided that Brian Statham would oversee the first team for the next couple of years.

An outsider might suspect all this stemmed from players wanting more money and a section of the committee resisting due to a lack of faith, but that was never my understanding, which I admit was fairly limited as a teenager in my first year on the staff. Those that were ousted were just viewed as rebellious players, and one act of rebellion in particular stood out. It came in a game against Warwickshire at Old Trafford, a Gillette Cup semi-final no less, during which the visiting team put all the fielders on the boundary towards the end of Lancashire's stiff chase of 295.

The ground was full and Geoff Clayton reacted petulantly to Warwickshire's tactic – there were no fielding restrictions whatsoever in those early days of knock-out cricket – by blocking. Clayton walked off unbeaten on 19 and Lancashire lost by 85 runs. He clearly thought 'bollocks to you', probably viewing such negativity as not being within the spirit of the game. This was his way of rebelling, but he got into fearful trouble for it, and ultimately it was the action that triggered his departure from the club. This set of players would no doubt have felt downtrodden by the committee and had no voice; they might have been senior in terms of their standing in cricket, but players such as Clayton and Marner were subservient because of the discrepancies in status between management and workers. It was real blue collar/white collar stuff.

Geoff left for Somerset after that downing of tools on the job, while Marner headed for Leicestershire. Bob Barber, who was in that Warwickshire team, had departed two years previously. Not everyone was happy at this exodus of players, however, and when some questioned the committee's motives those that remained were overthrown and a new committee was formed in the Cedric Rhoades-led revolution. That uprising meant stability was always going to be a couple of years away, although there was no evidence in that decade that stability was a prerequisite of success anyway. A glance across at our neighbours and deadliest rivals provided evidence of that.

In my early days on the Lancashire staff, even the thought of playing Yorkshire would wake you up in a cold sweat at night because they were a star-studded wrecking machine. Every one of them had played international cricket and they used to give us a really good hiding. They were a fabulous team. Names such as Padgett, Taylor, Close, Boycott, Binks, Illingworth, Wilson, Nicholson and Trueman just tripped off the tongue; they were a most talented bunch of individuals who made the most of the sum of their parts. There were no overseas players among them of course, due to the then strict selection policy of picking only players who were born within the county boundaries – needless to say they rammed that fact down your throat all the time.

For us, it was a gradual process to get on a par with them before eventually winning the odd match against them. Nevertheless, the expectation from our own public that we would beat them, despite the obvious gulf in class, never disappeared. To a Lancashire supporter, the Roses rivalry was so important in the greater scheme of things that even if you'd had a terrible season but beat Yorkshire, everything was okay.

That was not something that happened very often, because this was one of the best cricket teams ever put together. They just had all bases covered: good pace bowling, an unbelievably robust batting order, a great spinner and perhaps most importantly of all an aura about them. If you doubted their dominance, they reaffirmed it for you during the intervals. At lunchtime they would delay their entry into the room so they could put their blazers on and all walk in together. It was one of the only times they ever were 'together' and this superiority complex left witnesses in no doubt that this ceremonial ritual was all done on purpose. They used to walk past us en route to their adjacent table, fixing us with a stare as they went. For a young upstart like me, it was as intimidating an experience as facing Fred Trueman in his pomp.

There were huge crowds on hand to watch them in those days too. It was like being thrown to the wolves. And they would haul you all over the county for these floggings too. They didn't just invite you over to Leeds for your punishment. They would occasionally book you in at Sheffield's Bramall Lane, Middlesbrough's Acklam Park, Bradford Park Avenue and Scarborough's North Marine Road, so the rest of Yorkshire's towns and cities could enjoy our misfortune.

To be honest, the only light relief in any of these meetings came when one of our committee men, Harry Birtwistle, accompanied the chairman Cedric Rhoades to a Bradford match. Having fallen asleep on the journey, upon arrival he was brought into the changing room to wish us all the best.

The Park Avenue facilities hadn't seen a lick of paint for years and the floorboards were all splintered. Harry had a good look round and then ordered: 'Cedric, get these changing rooms decorated and tidied up, we can't have lads changing in here.'

'We're playing away, Harry.'

'Oh, I thought it took a long time to get here.'

To be fair, Yorkshire would give us an almighty beating on the field for three days but always invite us for a beer afterwards. Just so they could remind us how superior they were, you understand. Not sure if they ever shouted their rounds, though. Later in my career David Bairstow, who was a great mate, would take us up to the Original Oak pub just up St Michael's Lane after a day's play in Leeds. They don't make cricketers like him anymore. He was so loud on the field, he wouldn't get past health and safety. He would need to be fitted with a volume control and come with some kind of warning.

It was actually a Yorkshireman who was my buddy coming through the ranks at Lancashire. From very early on, it was pretty obvious for most with a trained eye to see that both Barry Wood and I were future opening batsmen, and we were looking to make our way in the game simultaneously. Barry being a Yorkie and coming from a massive family of sisters and brothers meant we were chalk and cheese, yet we seemed to work well together from the start.

As with most opening partnerships that have developed along the right track, we complemented each other perfectly and had an understanding when running between the wickets that didn't rely too much on calling yes, no or wait. We just had a mental telepathy when it was right to run and when it wasn't. When we sensed there was a single on, we just used to go; it was like a sixth sense.

In contrast to me, Barry was confrontational as a young bloke, but there was a similarity in the way that we, as generations of northerners had before us, began with nothing and fought our way up. Pitched together at the top of the order was one way of getting to know each other, and that was extended on away trips to us rooming together too. Barry and I were typical of the group that came through, I guess, because as opposed to the sinister side of the piss-taking when I arrived in the dressing room, us lot were on a par. We were all in it together, all really great mates.

And thanks to that bloody twat John Sullivan, God bless his soul, I was Bumble. John had been the creative director in some of the nicknames along with Harry Pilling, his old mucker from Mossley. As I said, to protest or contest that I looked like these Bumblies was a zero option. Although I have thought of taking exception to the shortening of it by Neil Fairbrother, someone I played with right at the end of my career and who later became my agent. He calls me Bum on every email or text message, and I'm not sure many people would accept that.

The distribution of nicknames helps develop camaraderie and team spirit. Initially they are shared between the inner sanctum only and help create informal identities; you form a bit of a clique, an 'us and them' scenario, you're either in the gang or you're not. My nickname all the way through my youth was Sel because the foreign secretary was called Selwyn Lloyd. That's what I would be called on the school bus as well as by team-mates when playing football or cricket at weekends. In Accrington, that is how people would acknowledge me if they passed me in the street.

Now I was Bumble, while Barry Wood was simply Sawdust. Geoff Pullar, the senior batsman, was Noddy because he possessed both quite a big head and a drop-top sports car, and it was reckoned he looked just like Noddy when he was sat in it. Jack Simmons was plain old Simmo, David Hughes later became Yosser after the character in Alan Bleasdale's *Boys from the Blackstuff*, Ken Shuttleworth was Shut, then there was Peter 'Leapy' Lee, in recognition of the English singer who hit the Top Ten with 'Little Arrows'. Ken Snellgrove was Nelly, and Frank Hayes was Fish because we joked that he drank like one at the time.

Other players were known by their unusual middle names, as it gave them more distinction. So Clive Lloyd was always Hubert and another one of my big mates Paul Allott was always Wally or

Walt because his middle names were John Walter. In fact, whenever you get him and another Walter, Mike Selvey, the *Guardian's* cricket correspondent, together in a press box it's like a scene off *The Two Ronnies*. 'How are you, Walt?' 'Yeah, going all right, Walt. What about you, Walt?' 'Yeah, I'm fine, Walt.'

For young lads such as us, county cricket was like one permanent road trip and we made the most of our away days. The club allowed us a maximum of five cars for each one and that would give you enough room for twelve players and the scorer, plus all the kitbags. Now before you get any illusions of grandeur, we are talking modest vehicles – Ford Anglias rather than stretch limousines. But this simply added to the adventure.

By 1966, my first full season on the first-team stage, I had passed my driving test and owned my own wheels to boot. As a young apprentice at Lancashire, I used to run down Water Street to Melbourne Street to catch the Manchester bus. Once at Lower Mosley Street bus station in Manchester, I had to get on the Sale bus out again to Old Trafford. It stopped right outside Manchester United's football ground and then I used to have to stride along the road with my cricket bag on my shoulder. The return journey had to be made at night and so my getting to and from work in those initial days was some trek.

This all stopped though when my mum and dad bought me a light blue Mini. Over the road to our house was a little butcher's shop owned by a chap called Amos Robinson, who became a real family friend. Knowing what I was doing, Amos had been keeping his ear to the ground for news of any cars that would come up for sale. He was well positioned, for this being the local butcher's, he was subjected to chat all day. He also owned the only telephone we knew of in Water Street, which he would loan out at sixpence a call.

Sure enough, Amos got wind of a Mini for sale and the owner lived over in the next street. Mum and Dad dipped into what savings they had and bought that Mini for me for £250. Money remained tight but there were three wages coming in now and no real car costs other than petrol, as in those days everyone serviced their own vehicles, and I was no different. Whenever there was any problem, I would get it up on a ramp and check it over. Engines were pretty easy if you knew what spark plugs and distributors were. It was all about getting your timing right. Oil changes were dead simple. You just took the sump out of the bottom, changed it over, altered your filters and that was that.

What little extra money I did spend on my pride and joy proved to be a false economy. In the next street there was a battery of garages and not enough cars to fill them, so we hired one at an outlay of fifty pence a week to protect mine from the elements and house it overnight. Blow me down, if within a week I hadn't run it straight into the garage door. Of course, we couldn't afford to get the prang mended – at least not until I got my county cap and a significant pay hike.

Anyway, here were a dozen blokes setting off, heading south 95 per cent of the time, representing Lancashire. I can't get across how proud we all were of that red rose. I hope it's still the same. There was an immense pride in travelling down to places like Taunton and Chelmsford and a social aspect to it all too. You would get to know your colleagues better over a few hours' nattering, most of the time about every subject other than cricket.

Unless, of course, your travelling companion happened to be Geoffrey Boycott. Essentially, when Boycs became a British Satellite Broadcasting team-mate of mine during my commentary infancy, I became his driver. It was not part of my contract, more an informal arrangement with formal instructions. For example, whenever we were scheduled to be working somewhere in the Midlands or down south that involved only a minimal detour, he would instruct me to pick him up at such a time, making the announcement a bit like a town crier would news of a royal birth or an outbreak of war.

Then, when our journey was underway he would push back in the passenger seat, stretch his legs out and knock out a few Zs. In the days before sat navs, my natural orienteering skills were not great, so he would often wake up and check that I was on the right road before dozing once more. Stop for petrol and he would chastise me for not filling up before we departed. 'You know your problem. It's attention to detail. Preparation is the most important thing. That's why you never scored any bloody runs,' he'd tell me. It reminded me of being back at school.

Trawling the county circuit was a wonderful existence. It was like heaven, really, when you think about the fundamental aspects of competitive sport. You had huge respect for your opponents, got on with them at the end of a day's play, but were desperate to turn them over during the hours of 10.30 a.m. to 7 p.m. Every time you strapped up the buckles on your pads, your focus was on winning that game for Lancashire.

Sometimes, due to mind-boggling scheduling that would pitch us into a one-day match in Southampton two-thirds of the way through a three-day contest with Glamorgan, the intervention of heavy traffic, an accident or roadworks meant our convoys would arrive after midnight for matches that were due to start in a matter of hours. The organiser of the fixture list during my playing days was clearly someone with a sense of humour, because invariably we would be involved in a match at one end of the country one day and at the other end the next.

Some of these trips would involve multiple stop-offs for food. Particularly when Jack Simmons was in transit. Jack was a very old-school cricketer who made provisions to get through a day's play. For example, he used to tuck a biscuit in his back pocket when we were fielding so he had quick access to some snap during those lengthy afternoon or evening sessions. He couldn't go a full one without, and it was a similar story for our car expeditions. On one occasion we were heading to Canterbury and he insisted that we stopped at Chorlton for fish and chips. If you don't know the area, that is a total distance of two and a half miles from the gates at Old Trafford. You would think that would have put the big lad 'on' until our arrival, but we had to get through London to get down to Kent and he insisted on stopping at the Seashell on Lisson Grove for a second helping.

Occasionally, we would be given a coach for lengthy trips, as was the case when we got snarled up on the way to Tunbridge Wells one year. We arrived at our designated hotel at approximately two o'clock in the morning, the place was blanketed in total darkness and there was only a night porter remaining on duty. After a journey like that, it was understandable that a number of the lads were gagging for the toilet. Having disembarked, we were looking to book in with this chap, whose hair had a similar consistency to Shredded Wheat, which suggested he had been aroused from his slumbers to deal with our checking-in process. Clearly tired and already in a bit of a flap trying to sort out all our rooms, he was asked: 'Where's the toilet?'

'Down the corridor, first on your left,' he muttered.

So, about half a dozen of them toddled off in the pitch black. Imagine the collective relief to be confronted with a white wall that was pretty obviously the communal urinal. Only, it wasn't so obvious and wasn't a porcelain facility at all. They had erroneously been dispatched into the dining room. Seems like I wasn't the only one who struggled with directions. The smell of kippers was in the air next morning as we came down for breakfast. At least that's what we thought the aroma was until we realised the back wall was soaking wet.

Simmo was our travel manager, designating the driving slots for each particular trip. Getting the gig as a driver for the long-distance hauls meant you were quids in, because you were reimbursed by the club for so many pence a mile. It was lucrative enough, in fact, for some lads to volunteer to drive every week, but throughout the season Simmo would chart the lengths of journey undertaken so that we roughly got the same.

One year when I was captain, we had an away game down at Hastings, a venue that was slap-bang in the middle of town before it was turned into a shopping centre. We were given two or three days off and told by the committee that we had to turn up at the ground on the morning of the match. Unfortunately, at the appointed toss time we didn't have many lads there – the problem was simply that they didn't know how to get in. They just couldn't find the driveway that led into the ground and so they had abandoned their cars a couple of streets away and started throwing their kitbags over the walls and clambering after them. It was a most uncouth entrance, although I'm sure the locals who witnessed it just put it down to typically northern behaviour.

Further camaraderie was unearthed in the treatment room. We had various physios over the years, including Bill Ridding who was previously manager of Bolton Wanderers for nineteen seasons between the years of 1950 and 1968. Bill was in charge of the Wanderers team that went down in history for participating in one of the greatest matches Wembley Stadium has ever hosted – the Matthews FA Cup final of 1953 when Sir Stanley's lot, Blackpool, won a 4-3 thriller – as well as overseeing a 2-0 win over a post-Munich Manchester United in 1958.

Can you imagine Arsène Wenger walking out of the dugout at the Emirates for the final time at the end of a season and turning up at Hove later that summer ready to deal with Sussex's sore backs, knees and shoulders?

He had only half a thumb did Bill and we reckoned he had rubbed the other half away during his time with us. You know, a bit overworked with all his manipulating and massaging. While he was at the club, being injured proved to be something of a treat because you were regaled with all these tales of Bolton's achievements. At that time the Wanderers were a team that didn't take any prisoners, they just kicked opponents off the park.

We would sit him down, imploring him to tell his stories, such as experiencing FA Cup final glory when Nat Lofthouse scored twice to beat United. Although, of more interest to us were the exploits of the rough-and-readies who gave opponents a shoeing. Bolton were an uncompromising, physical team and the reputations of players like Roy Hartle, John Higgins and Tommy Banks went before them. Hartle and Banks, the full-backs, were a two-man demolition unit. They would clog opponents for fun. One of my favourite recollections from Bill was when they were up against 'The Wizard of the Dribble' Matthews.

'Hey Roy!' shouted Tommy across the backline. 'When you've finished kicking him, kick him over here, would you?'

No wonder rumours abounded that Matthews refused to play against them.

There was another one Bill used to love, regarding Tommy's World Cup finals duty in Sweden in 1958. With the Munich air disaster altering the plans of England manager Walter Winterbottom, Tommy was one of the players drafted in. Ahead of the group match against Brazil, Tommy had been told by Winterbottom to pay special attention to their winger Garrincha. 'I would like you to put him out of the game,' was Winterbottom's uncomplicated instruction.

One presumes he meant to lessen his impact with some astute tactical positioning, or at least the execution of some physical challenges – the old full-back's trick of letting the winger know who was boss. Typically, given the stuff we used to hear second-hand from Bill though, Tommy sought further clarification.

'Do you mean just for this match? Or forever?'

English football has always loved a hard man, in the same way cricket loves a fast bowler. It's because we all enjoy an ooh and an aah while we're watching, I guess. The thought of the pain they might inflict adds to the drama. It's not the same when you are on the receiving end, though. A crunching tackle from a Dave Mackay, Nobby Stiles or Norman Hunter is similar currency to a blow from a Jeff Thomson or a Mitchell Johnson.

As it happened, Garrincha remained on the bench alongside Pelé, with Joel preferred down Brazil's right-hand flank. But Joel didn't make it for the final group game. Far from being over, Garrincha's World Cup was just beginning, and how. A few weeks later he was one of the stars as they lifted the trophy.

Like Garrincha, Bill was bow-legged; as well as being a former Manchester United player, he had another link to that club because he emulated the most famous British boss of all in Sir Alex Ferguson. Everyone was terrified of Bill. Thankfully he had calmed down by the time he came into full-time physiotherapy, but he had a fearsome Fergie-style reputation.

Bill hailed from the Wirral and in scoring a baker's dozen goals for Tranmere Rovers in less than twenty appearances earned moves on to Manchester City and then United before injury ended his career at twenty-three. It was around this time, I believe, that he did his physio's training.

Sharing stories around the dressing room is always a primary ingredient when trying to develop a team spirit, and Bill was integral to all that. Football and cricket had a lot more in common at this time. Further evidence of that came when our pre-season fitness regime was led by Jack Crompton, Manchester United's trainer. He would come in to put us through our paces in the days building up to the first-class season, getting us fit with cross country and other lengthy runs around the streets every morning. It was only after lunch that we would get into the nets; then it would be cricket all afternoon.

All of our fitness work took place on the back field, where we would do lots of physical work such as sit-ups, press-ups and squat thrusts – what I would call natural body training. There would be no weight training whatsoever; the strength work came from all traditional exercises with plenty of repetitions and the occasional wheelbarrow race. Whatever aerobic activity we got through in a session, we always seemed to finish with a football kickabout, a bit like the England lads do now at the start of their pre-match warm-ups. For us it was always Juniors versus Seniors and if any of us Juniors were getting the better of the older lads then one of them, more than likely David Green, would get hold of you and sit on you so you couldn't move. This was a pretty harsh punishment at that time of year because you tended to be stiff as boards in pre-season.

We had a connection with our Old Trafford neighbours United in particular throughout the 1960s, and the two sports sat side by side. A lot of lads, myself included, played football to the cusp of the professional ranks, and others went all the way into the game. There was also a more natural link in those days as our footballing equivalents were a bit more normal. Let's say they operated with a lot fewer noughts on their pay packets.

That first April when Jack Compton popped up the road to drill us caused a bit of a commotion. Lancashire's established set had a fairly different attitude towards preparing for the five-month slog ahead. Skilled cricketers like Brian Statham, Geoff Pullar and Ken Higgs were used to rocking up immediately after the first daffodils had popped their heads out of the soil, pulling on their whites and netting. They always started with the cable knit sweaters on, within a couple of days removing them, and Statham typically used to declare himself bowling fit some time afterwards. So you can imagine what the senior pros made of an instruction to 'hit the deck'. As in previous years, they were fully kitted up.

'Everyone on the ground,' Jack ordered.

'We're not getting on the ground in these, they're clean for the season,' was the tone of their reply.

Not only did you have to buy our own whites, it was also the players' responsibility to wash them and ensure you looked smart whenever you walked down the pavilion steps. Your bin liner full of clothes would go home with you at the end of the week. Nowadays there are washing machines at the ground, and I suspect they have someone designated to clean everything for them.

There was an onus on you to look after your own gear because if it got ripped, scratched or broken you had to find the money for replacements. On becoming a professional my actions, of writing to a bat company asking what deal they could offer, were typical. In the correspondence to Gradidge, I explained I'd signed a contract with Lancashire and would very much like to use their bats. Nothing was dispatched on a complimentary basis, however; it was up to the company if they wanted to make you an offer and mine was a two-for-one which meant I paid £4 11s. These bats had to last because that was quite an investment for a young player on £6 a week. So out came the linseed for the start of the meticulous knocking-in process.

The only kit that county clubs supplied was your sweater and your cap. Lancashire gave us an allowance of £50 for things like gloves, pads, flannels, shirts and boots, and it could only be used at Tyldesley and Holbrook, the sports shop on Deansgate in Manchester. At the start of a season you would head down there and see Cyril Washbrook, who would tick off what you had spent on your account. This was a nice little earner, not for Cyril, who had no vested interest in it but simply worked in the shop from time to time as I did in future winters, but for Bob Cooke, the owner, who went on to play for Essex. Bob was as daft as a brush but he had his head screwed on when it came to business deals.

The upshot of Jack's grass-staining regime was the start of the tracksuit era. Modern heroes are all tied into advertising deals, whether it be through their personal gear or team-branded stuff – they have vests to keep you cool, vests to warm you up, and some that do both. They call them Skins, apparently. Well the only skin we had was underneath our pristine start-of-season shirts and off-the-peg Corby trouser-pressed pants. It was frostbitten at the start of a day and clammy with sweat by late morning. Under-armour? The only undergarments we ever wore were traditional vests – have you tried fielding at Scarborough or Blackpool when the sun has dipped behind the clouds?

We requested club training gear and it was made available to us as at a cost the following season. It was no skin off their noses, really, as we bought all of our own clobber, using a subsidy from the club to fill our kitbags. So tracksuits became the norm for all fitness work – an initial investment, yes, but a long-term saving on washing as one thrifty colleague noted.

The connection with Manchester United also meant we came across George Best from time to time, at functions and the like. 'How do you train for that cricket?' he would ask. 'Do you all just go stand in a field?' Well, some of our preparation wasn't too dissimilar from his, if truth be told. Minus the Miss Worlds and E-type Jaguars. Nothing would be thought of having a couple of beers at the end of a day's play. At some grounds there would be crates of beer or even jugs of ale on the table for lunch, and I actually had a pint of shandy while my Test debut innings was still in progress at Lord's in 1974.

That is not the only way that attitudes to batting have changed in the past four decades. Equipment, like its equivalent in golf, has improved out of sight so that mishits are now sailing over the boundary. It's no coincidence that the International Cricket Council are looking to push all the ropes back. Things have got a little bit out of hand in terms of the contest between bat and ball. What they are actually saying is that they are turning the clock back to our day. Very rarely did you arrive at a venue with a boundary rope. The playing area was the whole ground and to hit a six at some you would have to clear, not hit, the advertising hoardings.

To clear some of the boundaries you would have to time the ball as sweetly as possible. In fact, a nice firm push through the covers was almost as good. These days not quite making it all the way across the line gets you three; you might even get back for four with your wits about you, but back in the mid-1960s there were lots and lots of fives run. If you were playing on one edge of the square at Old Trafford, Trent Bridge or The Oval you would regularly have a 100-metre boundary on one side, so relay throws were the norm and you could always sneak another run on the arm given the distance. If someone pierced the infield, it felt like you were chasing it for miles.

Playing at a Test ground regularly used to rankle a bit for players like me, though, because you had to bat with these huge boundaries, whereas other lads were piling the fours up at these little outgrounds like Ilford and Leyton. The biggest boundary there might be shorter than the shortest you were accustomed to as a Lancashire, Nottinghamshire or Surrey player.

There was little doubt that my dual ability was key to winning me that first deal with Lancashire, but my progress in batting and bowling did not run parallel. In fact, although I would vouch it was my bowling that got me noticed – as is often the way with wrist spinners, good ones being so rare – things changed for me as I moved into senior competition. Fellow juniors could not handle my box of tricks, but for some reason I morphed into a more orthodox operator around the age of seventeen. A more traditional brand of slow left-arm was certainly what I sent down when I undertook my maiden second-team engagement, a friendly against Cumberland.

I should have bowled more throughout my career, but when I became captain, David Hughes, another left-arm spinner, had recently emerged and there was no real need for two of us. It happens when you're captain that you tend not to bowl yourself. Hughes had come into the team and done really well. It left me as an occasional bowler for quite some years, before working really hard towards the end of my career to get it back.

Yosser's ascent was in part down to my own misfortune, because right at the start of my professional career I got the yips. Unfortunately, it's a common problem for slow left-armers, and for a while I had no idea where the ball was going. And that was when I finally made it to the crease, because all of a sudden the natural bound into delivery and flighted guile that followed – the qualities that had undoubtedly got me noticed as a young cricketer – were gone, and I didn't know how to run up or use my arms. I was not long out of my teens and, having been signed as an all-rounder, it put an extra onus on my batting.

Eventually, my bowling came back, but it certainly took some considerable time to do so because of the gravity of the situation. Psychologically, it had been very damaging. It was like a nervous paralysis every time I was thrown the ball during the season of 1967 when things went awry. Suddenly, where previously there had been loop everything was flat.

Like most victims of the yips I fought on, almost in denial that anything was wrong. Though like most victims, I was forced to admit defeat. Few actually come back from it, and when they do they rarely reach the levels they once were at, let alone the levels they were aspiring to reach. Lancashire, pursuing their pledge to turn to youth following the crisis action of player sackings and committee overhaul the previous year, had stuck with me as a first-team player throughout 1966. But as the 1967 season developed, I was heading for the second XI. My on-field behaviour told its own story. I was petrified of making eye contact with Brian Statham, our captain, in case doing so reminded him that I was one of the blokes in his team that could bowl. Being dropped to the second XI was an inevitability and it became a case of when, not if.

I was massively anxious about things. To recap, those two-year contracts put pressure on players not to drop their standards or risk their own livelihoods, and movement from county to county was not commonplace, especially for those at my kind of level. Signing on elsewhere was not a viable option. A more established cricketer would have been a more attractive proposition and perhaps stood an outside chance – but one with a single Championship season's experience and unable to perform at maximum potential due to this bowling affliction? Not on your nelly.

If I bowled in the nets there was no problem whatsoever, but take that netting away and move into a match scenario and it was a totally different proposition. It was clearly a mental frailty. Something in my brain was not allowing me to perform as I did in practice. Perhaps I should have pretended to be Ena Sharples, from *Coronation Street*. She permanently had her head in a net, didn't she?

The mental aspect of all this was extraordinary. For some reason, as my bowling dropped off at an alarming rate, my batting improved almost beyond belief and I was able to hold my place as a batsman once I forced my way back in through strong second XI performances. It was as if cricket's scales of justice were working in my favour. After all, it was not as if I'd wanted to suffer the misery the yips had caused me or go through the mental anguish of trying to get over the affliction.

From a coaching perspective, there is little or nothing that can be done to cure this bowlers' disease, and it has ended several careers in their prime. In recent times, both Keith Medlycott and Richard Dawson were struck down not long after being picked for England. Both won the battle but not the war when it came to continuing their careers, never the same performers as they were pre-yips. Unfortunately, that is so often the case when your natural action abandons you. The only remedy is time, a commodity not often afforded to players who lose their way, and it's actually a mental rather than physical obstacle for you to get over.

The fact that Medlycott and Dawson possessed renowned cricket brains and earned county coaching positions later in life – I think the development of Dawson, whose sharp thinking was evident in his early days in charge of Gloucestershire, is showing signs of something rather special, actually – only served to highlight the intensity of the struggle.

To underline the psychological nature of the whole episode, once I had re-established myself in the first XI's top six my bowling came back to me, and I became quite relaxed about things, whether I was in the Old Trafford nets or the middle of a match on the circuit. Of course, it took a while to get back to being entrusted with the volume of overs of my first two seasons, but it was progress.

Indeed, during the 1968 campaign, my first-class victims numbered just one and I sent down fewer than twenty overs. But I was in the team to score runs and did so, stacking up 935 in all, including that hundred against the Cambridge students and earning that county cap in the process.

But the search for the potency I had shown in a rare away victory a couple of years earlier against Gloucestershire at Lydney, where I took seven wickets in the second innings to complete a ten-victim haul in the match and a 60-run victory, meant there was a gradual increase in overs bowled by me. Subconsciously, the pressure I felt previously, perhaps due to having all these great players around me, dissipated. I clearly couldn't handle it for a while.

The two big wickets of my career were Geoffrey Boycott – which I remind him of most times I see him (and that's fairly frequently you will understand, as I'm usually working just a couple of commentary boxes down from him at any given England match) – and Garry Sobers. Not the two best dismissals from an aesthetic point of view, but you always remember reeling in the big fish.

The first was in the second innings of a drawn Roses contest at Bramall Lane, Sheffield, in August 1967. Boycott, who had 54 to his name, was caught at first slip, which was not particularly unusual. Or at least it wasn't unusual until you considered that at no stage during the process of the catch being claimed, and Boycs walking off, did Geoff Pullar touch the ball with his hands. Sizing up a rank bad ball, the bespectacled one went to cut it and somehow got a top edge. Geoff, quite an ample bloke, instinctively turned his back on it during a course of evasive action and somehow the ball lodged between his arse cheeks. 'I'm not going for that,' Boycott declared, doing his best WG Grace impression as Pullar produced the missing ball from between his legs. Unfortunately, he had to. The quality of the delivery made it a harsh departure in the extreme – but all the better in another.

Sobers was actually my bunny. Fancy a player of his high class getting out to me. TWICE. Having had him held at slip by Jack Simmons at Old Trafford in 1971, when some nasty rumour-monger claimed he had wanted to get back into the dressing room to watch a televised horse race from somewhere or other, I also dismissed him in the same fixture three years later in a match with significance for me. Not only was it a rare workout with the ball at that stage of my career, which reaped four wickets, but it was during that match's course that I learned I would be retaining the England place I had won that summer when Boycott had been overlooked. My name was among the sixteen chosen to tour New Zealand and Australia that winter.

Joking aside, Garry was the best player I was confronted with on a cricket field, simply because he could do everything. There wasn't really anyone to compare him to when you considered how accomplished he was across the board. As a batsman he hit the ball incredibly hard, taking just about everybody to the cleaners regardless of reputation; then with the ball he could bowl genuinely fast or equally effective spinners and in the field he caught everything that moved. All this without ever going to sleep – a fact that while only 99.94 per cent true helped enhance his super-human image. Of course, he got some shut-eye now and again, but Garry would tell you himself that he didn't like going to bed before three o'clock – not sure whether he meant a.m. or p.m.

On the field he was indestructible with an impeccable demean-our. Strolling to the crease with a huge smile, he would make a point of saying, 'How do, is everything all right?' Well, it was for those few seconds. Next thing you knew he would be smashing it everywhere. Some cricketers have an aura about them when they walk over that boundary rope and Garry had that. Not of the same kind that another West Indies great, Viv Richards, possessed: Viv had menace but Garry was charismatic. He would be unbelievably chilled out. It was just his way of getting in the mood before taking you to the cleaners.

Imagine Sobers's value if he was on the Twenty20 market. A natural athlete able to hit balls out of the park at will – think of his carnage at Swansea when he took Malcolm Nash for six sixes in an over with a backswing you could still recognise when you walked onto the Royal Westmoreland Golf Course in Barbados when he was in his seventies. He could also take wickets by switching to whatever style of bowling to best suit the surface, and he could catch pigeons. Whether it be dollars, rupees or sterling, Sobers would be on the top shelf of anyone's auction.

CHAPTER 5

Educating Bumble

It was against Garry Sobers's Nottinghamshire that I began the practical side of my tertiary education as a full-time cricketer, making my official second XI debut in a Minor Counties Championship match (some counties' second XIs still played in this tournament) at Old Trafford a little over nine months after I had received the club offer of an apprenticeship.

There is no learning like learning on the job, and that competitive domain represented a decent classroom. This was my first experience of a dog-eat-dog environment in which everyone was fighting for higher recognition. Although, in my naivety as a seventeen-year-old thrilled to be playing full-time cricket, I'm not sure I saw the starker side of things. I was up against some experienced campaigners and some wonderful characters all told.

None more so than Carlton Forbes, a Jamaican-born all-rounder who batted No. 3 and bowled some left-arm swing. He might have been christened Carlton but everyone knew him as Cha Cha, and his sideline alongside his cricket career at Trent Bridge was that he ran a nightclub in Nottingham. Cha Cha Forbes seemed about eight feet tall and was the blackest bloke you have ever seen. Okay, I might be exaggerating on one count

77

there, but I bet he would have to stoop to get away with 6 ft 5 ins.

Cha Cha was a very amiable chap, thin, not heavy set and the first bowler to dismiss me at senior level with a big swinger. But he had associations with much more famous cricketers than me. Without being willing to swear on a bible in court, I can almost guarantee that Sobers would hardly ever have been out of Cha Cha's nightclub after he arrived in 1968. I never went in but I know plenty of lads who did, and for this after-hours association alone he was very popular.

At the top of the Nottinghamshire order was a batsman called Mike Smedley, who went on to captain them for years. He remains on the Trent Bridge committee to this day. Then there was Smedley's fellow Yorkshireman Barry Stead, another fantastic lad who bowled left arm. Barry would run through the proverbial brick wall for his captain, and was the kind of player that brought smiles to faces due to his love of the game. Relatively small in stature, he would absolutely tear-arse in, making up for any lack of inches with his huge heart. There were certainly some similarities to New Zealand's Trent Boult in the way he operated – reacting to swinging one past the outside edge with a quiet word. Nothing demonstrative, just a polite acknowledgement to the batsmen that they hadn't been good enough, in the manner and tone used by the best bowlers.

Typically of a second XI in those days, their captain was a senior hand. John Clay, a revered name on the county circuit, was then in his fortieth year and a couple of seasons into leading the Notts second XI, having previously made history when he became the first professional to captain the club in 1961, more than twelve months before the abolition of the split gentlemen and players status in the English game. As it happened, we had a captain from the other side of the fence, Bob Bennett, an amateur who would go on to be an England tour manager in future years.

Smedley and Mike Taylor, who went by the initials MNS Taylor and whose twin brother Derek kept wicket for Somerset, were among my seven victims in the match as the Old Trafford pitch took some spin. Ken Howard, our off-spinner, took five wickets in the first innings, while I backed him up with 11-7-17-3. Old Trafford was quite green at the time and this pitch was an exception rather than the rule. For spin to play such an extensive part – we won by nine wickets – was unusual at what was a fast bowlers' paradise where the pitches were as juicy as anything.

Understanding the different characteristics of grounds around the country was also part of learning your trade as a county crick-eter. At that time, all cricket squares around England had different characteristics, as you would play on the natural soil of the area. Accordingly, the behaviour of the top layer of soil determined how the pitch would play – how much the ball would bounce and how much it would deviate. In Manchester, we had grassy pitches; go to Bristol and, confronted with a reddish soil, you were served up something that was slow and low. If you went down to Mumbles at Swansea, those pitches would spin. It would be similar to Bristol in terms of its slow pace, but you would also get some turn.

People of a certain vintage will recall the quickest bowler in English cricket at that time. Jeff Jones, father of our 2005 Ashes winner Simon Jones, didn't actually play for Glamorgan when their home games were scheduled in Swansea. They just didn't see the point of flogging him in unresponsive conditions, so they just played bowlers who bowled cutters at medium pace rather than an out-and-out speed merchant. Every pitch had its own idiosyn-crasies. Headingley was a little seamer: it didn't contain express pace but it was quick enough and provided bowlers with plenty of nip, which was what skilful practitioners like Tony Nicholson loved to work with. Brian Close was also a maestro at making the most out of the assistance on offer from the pitch. Similarly, in subsequent years, it was well exploited by Chris Old.

The massive change in the game came when we got rid of uncovered pitches, because at this point standard soils were introduced around the country. We left behind the finer loams and grasses for heavier ones that would not deteriorate as randomly. Surrey loams, Ongar loams and Mendip loams were introduced into every pitch to try to get some uniformity. Instead of regional variation, the idea was that all pitches would hold together, and the ball would go straight up and down. These loams all had high clay content, which to grow grass on was not easy but gave you plenty of pace and bounce.

It spelt an end to the likes of Brian Statham and other fast bowlers mastering the conditions in an old-school way. On some pitches, they would dig a hole with their front foot where they landed. Once fully formed, it would force them to land in another spot – you never got the groundsman running on with a bucket, shovel and mallet to repair these damned craters, the bowler simply had to move to an unblemished spot on the crease, whether it be along it or back a yard.

This was an added skill within the fast bowling trade – coping with delivering the ball from another angle. There was an associated challenge for batsmen too because as a game progressed, when you waited in your batting stance, you had to contend with these holes. It meant finding somewhere comfortable to stand because even if you didn't have a boot in a fully-formed void, a pitch was rarely uniformly flat and groundstaff were not in the practice of fixing them up when the match was in progress. There would be no filling with soil or compacting, they would simply give them a chamfer shave, and then it was up to the competitors to make the best of what was left underfoot.

It was totally different when these loams came in. For a start, that landing area became rock hard and Fred Trueman, the greatest English bowler of them all, would get all curmudgeonly about the consequences he believed it had for fast bowlers, laying blame at

Auntie Olwen, me and Mum (big lady) on holiday in Morecambe.

Me and Dad with the Accrington Combination Trophy won with Cedar Swifts (Dad was the manager).

Me at the age of seven at Peel Park Primary School.

Lancashire CCC in 1965.

Some say that modern players have become distanced from the fans – there was no chance of that in 1971.

Waving to the crowds at Bramall Lane, Sheffield, in 1973, my first season as captain. Lancashire rarely got a warm welcome in Roses clashes.

I've always enjoyed my music, but I'm not sure this song ever troubled the hit parade.

Pre-season training was a little different in 1973, too, and things could go horribly wrong if your timing was out.

It's 2 June, and the game at Buxton has been transformed by snow, after we had piled up a big total. Studying it closely are (L–R) Peter Lever, Clive Lloyd, Frank Hayes, Dickie Bird and me.

When I started wearing protective headgear in 1971 to field close to the bat, it was such an unusual sight that I had to do a whole photoshoot.

And this is why it was necessary.

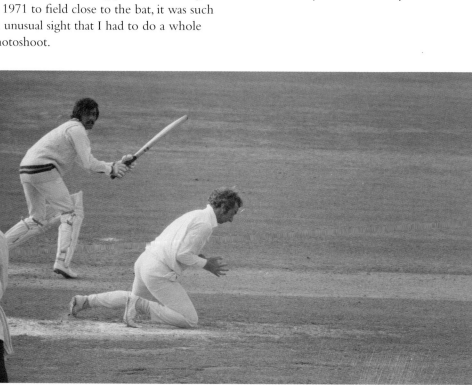

Though when 'Deadly' Derek Underwood got on a sticky wicket at Lord's, I was much safer and always in the action, taking three catches.

The pre-season photocall 40 years ago was a very different beast to today. Lining up here (L–R) are: Bernard Reidy, Bob Ratcliffe, Jack Simmons, me, Andy Kennedy and Peter Lever, all of whom had played Lancashire League cricket.

Lifting the Gillette Cup in 1975 – the only trophy of my time in charge of Lancashire. In those days, the crowd was allowed onto the hallowed turf.

There were only 24 of these moments in my Test career. My four overs didn't result in a single wicket, though I did manage to dismiss Wasim Raja in a one-day international.

Lancashire team-mate Farokh Engineer congratulates me during my career-best innings of 214 against India at Edgbaston in 1974.

Things must have gone well that innings, as I even tried a sweep shot – the height of daring at the time.

One of the most
fearsome sights in
cricket: Dennis Lillee
in full flow on his
home patch at Perth.

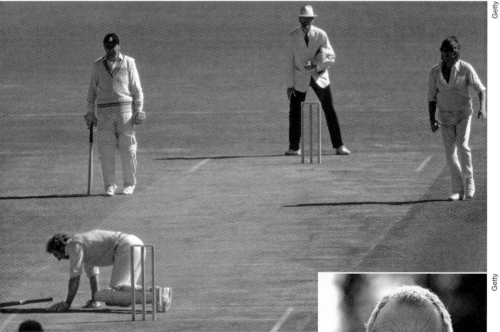

But, famously, it was
Thommo who got me in the
end – with results that still
bring a tear to my eye.

Rod Marsh looks on as I try to take the attack to the Australian bowling at Melbourne in the third Test.

Arriving back in England after the Ashes series of 1974–75, with my Test career sadly at an end.

its door for injuries, particularly those to the back, which appeared to have increased after these harder pitches were introduced. These big lads slamming down on to solid ground, he said, resulted in great pressure reverberating up the spine.

Fred talked about the dangers of indoor nets, insisting that bowlers spent too much time on concrete.

'What are you on about?' I asked him.

'These indoor nets all have one thing in common. Whatever surface is laid on top, they are all laid on concrete bases,' he said. 'So whenever you run in to bowl, you are smashing your back to bits.'

By that token, Fred would have been one of them. But, oh no. As he revealed, Yorkshire's indoor facility had a sprung wood floor. So whenever you landed in your delivery stride, there was an amount of give that effectively provided a cushion for your back. I reckoned Old Fred knew exactly what he was on about here. I lost count of the number of blokes sidelined by injury who were slamming down their size thirteen boots for a living.

Scores were generally lower on these uncovered pitches, and in that first appearance for the second XI we bowled Notts out for 85, later securing a commanding first-innings lead of 48. Our top scorer was Ken Shuttleworth, an Ashes winner and someone who was to become a great mate over subsequent years. Shut also took five wickets in the second innings.

There was also some eye-opening to be experienced for some-one with a sheltered youth like mine. For example, it was during that match that I found out why Ken Howard, a very sallow-look-ing cove from Longsight who claimed half the Nottinghamshire wickets to fall in the first innings, possessed the nickname Spout. With the use of the most inoffensive terminology I can, it was because he had an appendage which was shaped like a down spout. His party piece when the spout was angry was that he could get a dozen old pennies lined up on it.

The more serious side of my education was overseen by men like Bob Bennett and Edward Slinger, the two amateur captains under whom I featured, who have become known for other services to the game. Bob went on to become England manager while you may have heard of the name Judge Edward Slinger, as he is now known, who has regularly sat on disciplinary panels for the ECB.

They were both fantastic mentors whose guidance throughout my early career was invaluable. It's safe to say that I wouldn't have got anywhere without those two, because not only did they teach me cricket, they taught me about life, kept me on an even keel, gave me a level head and encouraged me regarding my ability.

Amateur captains became something of a feature in second XI cricket following the switch from a mixed gentlemen and players era to a professional one, and it wasn't only in their status that they were different. Because they were amateur they were no longer competing with us for recognition and a place in the first XI. That meant you had a different relationship with your captain as opposed to other players. They were no longer direct opponents, they were just there to bring everybody else on. They helped everyone through and became father figures to their juniors.

This is not to say that they were not bloody good players, circumstances had just dictated that they were ditched after the previous generation and re-engaged to bring on the next. Bob got a hundred in the first team, so that told you he could play a bit, and while Edward never got into the first team he was a very sound opening batsman for Enfield, partnering the West Indies great Conrad Hunte.

You couldn't speak too highly about those two captains, whose other duties included acting as the intermediaries between the dressing room and the committee, liaising with those making decisions on the club's future policies not only on our progress but also providing character references on the kind of blokes we were. In modern terms, they were a bit like our line managers.

There was no second XI coach, so men like these were the ones you looked up to and turned to for advice if you had any doubts about your own game. Although you knew they were amateurs, and there was always a little bit of a stigma attached with that because they were viewed on a different level when it came to ability, they offered great value.

As opposed to second XI cricket midway through the second decade of the twenty-first century, which now more often than not involves sides packed with trialists or one county combining with another to form a composite team, this was a breeding ground for the best young players in the country, a competitive stage to show an improvement, with the ultimate goal being a place on the County Championship stage.

Cyril Washbrook, one of the greatest players Lancashire ever had, and a wonderful batsman for county and country, ruled the roost at our club following his retirement. Some people would have told you he was an absolute tyrant. Whatever you called him – and he did not possess an official title – he undertook most of the judging and was effectively the first manager in English cricket. Unpaid for his service, he sat on the committee and, because of the esteem in which he was held, was unbelievably influential on playing matters.

Major Rupert Howard and his successor Geoffrey Howard, military men both, held the position of secretary during these years. However, although they held the titles, you were in no doubt that it was Cyril that ran the whole shebang. He would turn up at the second XI matches to observe, and would pick out individuals and beckon them with the curling of his index finger. Dressed in a suit, with a trilby on his head, he cut an imposing figure and so getting the finger proved a fairly intimi-dating experience.

The chat would normally start with him sitting you down and saying, 'Let's have a word.' He was very well spoken and was clearly intent on getting to know you beyond your cricket. He would ask about your aspirations, your ambitions and how you felt you were doing. It was a little bit like getting an appraisal. He wanted to know about your preparation, where you saw yourself in twelve months' time and once answered he would hit you with the killer, supplementary question: 'How exactly are you going to go about it?'

Similar processes take place nowadays with online forms, but with him it was just a chat about how you envisaged breaking into that first team, and he would store the information, not in an email inbox, but in the back of his head. At one of these meetings, he said to me: 'I've watched you and seen the shots that you have been playing. Just a word of warning – do not play the sweep.' It was a piece of advice that always stuck with me, even if I didn't heed it later in my career.

It was a little bit of a taboo stroke in those days anyway, and it was known for players to get left out of the next game if they played it in a competitive match. Goodness knows what they would have done to you if you had dared a reverse or a switch hit. I can only imagine that it would have involved a summons at dawn.

Similarly, if somebody swept you as a spinner in the mid–1960s and you asked the captain for a deep backward square leg, the reply more often than not would be 'put your sweater on, lad.' The very idea that anyone should be sweeping you was dismissed out of hand, and they certainly weren't going to encourage it by giving you protection out in the deep.

If you were a batsman who played the sweep, you were a heathen. Heaven help you if you got hit on the pad, because it was almost certain that the umpire would give you out. It was even known for umpires to raise the finger, shake the head at the same time and mutter 'shocking shot'. It was only a step up from shop-lifting in the greater scheme of things.

There were other life lessons to be learned too. Moving into that professional era we also recruited a lad called Keith Goodwin, a hard-as-nails bloke who had served in the British Army and was never shy of letting us know in his most matter-of-fact tone: 'I've killed a man.' In the pub of an evening, with a couple of pints down him, he would start singing a dirge called 'Fulwood Barracks' that could go on as long as twenty minutes.

It wasn't quite twenty minutes in length normally, it was just that if anyone stood up, or even moved from the seats where we were sat, they would be fixed with his glassy stare in rebuke and told in no uncertain terms: 'One singer, one song.' Then, he would begin again, from the start. If anybody spoke, it was exactly the same result. This military command resulted in a scrap on one occasion between Keith and Ken Snellgrove, a scouser who rarely took a backward step in his life. Rebelling against the usual order, Nelly got up to play the one-arm bandit and was immediately given the 'One singer, one song' line. The pair of them had to be separated with us young 'uns sat transfixed, almost petrified in case Keith turned his ire on us.

Life in the second XI moulded you as a cricketer. Everything about it was instrumental in your development through the ranks, and not everyone could hack it. For example, Lancashire possessed a batsman of what appeared to be immeasurable ability in the same age-group team that I featured in. Alan Thomas churned out runs like they were going out of fashion for Bolton in the Bolton League and had a reputation as the best young player in the country.

There were no debates about whether he was good enough when it came to his recruitment, it was obvious he would be signed. But he just couldn't hack it in the dressing room and ended up leaving after a year to pursue another career. If you were deconstructing the reasons for his departure to a 2015 audience, some might even call it bullying. I would suggest that it would not be the right word, because the harsh environment he rejected was character-building from my point of view.

For some, the cajoling, the piss-taking and general japes around a dressing room are part of fashioning a team and the individual players within it. You just had to survive it, and if you weren't able to, there was no other option but to walk. Playing the bully card, as someone famously has in England in recent years, was not an option.

This was just part of life in that Lancashire dressing room, although I do recall towards the end of my career colleagues of the same age insisting that the youngsters would not be put through the same kind of treatment that we were put through. People would tell you that Graeme Fowler and Paul Allott controlled the dressing room, but I didn't necessarily see them as bullies at all. They were just helping the next generation of players grow up. The Lancashire way has been passed on over the decades, and it meant that if you did get a really difficult character any problems were ironed out to ensure that the team functioned as it should. Whenever we heard of awkward characters around the country, it was often said: 'Put him in our dressing room and he'll be a difficult character no longer.' Step out of line at Old Trafford and you would have half a dozen other blokes telling you in a heartbeat: 'Don't do that.'

Later, when I became coach, someone like Neil Fairbrother would do the policing. There would be no need for me to get involved, because the senior players used to keep everybody else in check. Internationally, Mark Taylor was doing the same thing with Australia. When I was coach of England, he pulled Stuart MacGill and told him what behaviour was expected of him after he sang a derogatory song in our presence in the aftermath of Australia's 3-1 Ashes win over my England team in 1998-99.

All it took was a succinct 'we don't act in this way, mate' to

MacGill, who was what you might call a character of difference. Now these characters of difference are fine within a team, and should actively be encouraged in some ways, as long as they don't think they should be treated as characters of difference when it comes to team rules. Strong dressing rooms have strong characters reinforcing the collective ethos and not allowing individuals within to challenge that. Strong dressing rooms should always be able to handle the difficult guy without it becoming a problem that is known about outside the four walls that surround you.

Now, consider the Kevin Pietersen situation. While I have not sat in that particular England dressing room, I have been in it plenty of times, and if somebody is stepping out of line, the team is responsible for pulling him straight back in. Nobody really knows the full depth of what went on apart from those directly involved, but it all seems a little bit childish that it got to the stage it did with bogus Twitter accounts, claims that 'it's difficult being me in the dressing room', ostracisation, public character assassinations, the ripping up of a central contract following a sacking, and further clarification of his position in May 2015.

I am an advocate of sorting problems out internally, and that means sometimes if people have differences of opinion they should just let it rip. Let guys go hammer and tongs at each other in private until everything is out in the open, all differences have been put across, it's been accepted that you are never going to agree on everything and hands have been shaken in the knowledge that it's all been done in the best interests of the team. In my experience, some guys have torn strips off each other but everyone turns up the next day happy enough and the team moves on.

Unfortunately, that's not what happened in this situation and the Pietersen saga festered for years. From the outside looking in, there have been some obvious mistakes made. I would have expected a stronger leadership from the senior players in the dressing room. And better direction from those above them.

As Stuart Broad quite rightly said, there was never a need to ban Kevin Pietersen from that England team. How can you indefinitely suspend a player on the basis that he's a bit different? There's never a need to sack a player at international level, because in a meritocracy if he's not performing, not doing what you want him to do, you just don't pick him and leave it at that. It really is that simple.

If, as a management, he's not performing or behaving as you would expect, you just leave him out of the team for a couple of months. When quizzed by the media on why he has been excluded during the selection process, just tell the truth. It really is that straightforward; there should be no need for talk of a player being disengaged. If and when he does conform we will consider him again, is all that needs to be said. It was effectively what the new ECB chairman Colin Graves spelt out at the start of the 2015 County Championship season to encourage Pietersen to re-engage with our first-class game. Every player within that competition is trying to show their worth, and the currencies they are dealing in are runs and wickets.

If that missive had been sent out twelve months earlier, Kevin would not have had a leg to stand on. But he was clearly unbelievably hurt that the ECB should decide to sack him. Being dropped from a team should be enough for a player to re-focus the mind, and the brilliant ones like him want to be playing at the very highest level they can for as long as they can, because they are driven by the challenge of being the best, so it was never going to be long before he pulled his neck in. If you have been dropped, you can bleat as much as you want but unless you can give reasons to merit your selection you just ain't getting picked.

As I've already cited, Yorkshire's dressing room contained few pals, and they won the Championship annually in my era. The whole damn lot of them were squabbling, the whole flamin' time. But they were a fantastic team. They might not have liked the bloke that was changing next to them, or would never have thought about going out for a beer with the bloke on the other side of them; there would have been few that you would have ever considered to ask around for dinner with your missus, but in the workplace they had your total respect, and that one word respect is crucial in any team environment. You don't have to enjoy someone's company but in good teams you enjoy their success. If Fred Trueman got five wickets, everyone was happy. The same if Geoff Boycott got a hundred. You might have heard some of them mutter 'absolute prick' under their breath, but they acknowledged they were great cricketers. Once they crossed that white line everything changed.

One of the surprising aspects of the Pietersen affair was that it incorporated more than one breakdown in relations. He had already been given his warning and left out for a period of time for those alleged derogatory texts about Andrew Strauss sent to members of the South Africa team around the time of the 2012 Headingley Test, before being brought back into the bosom of the unit for the tour of India the following winter. For a while at least, it seemed like they had sorted things out, that he had learned the do's and don'ts, but that was because they were winning and, crucially, KP was playing a key role in the winning. He was simply sensational against India, contributing to a first England Test series victory on the subcontinent since the mid-1980s.

Unfortunately, things then broke down once again during the Ashes series of 2013-14. The fact that Strauss took over the mess as England's new cricket director and immediately stressed there were issues of trust – only hours after Pietersen had struck his career-best triple hundred against Leicestershire in May 2015 – was extremely sad. Any sport should be able to revert to its basic principles of selection on performance.

Sometimes you can have so many tiers of management that your organisation becomes cluttered. While Paul Downton – the managing director of the England team between 2014 and 2015 – was a lovely fellow, I was never convinced about his role. Why was he walking around the ground before a game? What purpose was he serving? In a winning culture things like that go unnoticed, but when a team is not winning they stick out like a sore thumb. Backslapping players and high fiving as they practice gives the illusion of togetherness when you are successful, just as it looks out of place when you're losing. Too often Downton looked a forlorn figure lapping the ground, out of place and away from the tasks he should have been concentrating on.

Throughout my playing career, there were frank discussions in just about every single season I played at Lancashire. Flare-ups are part and parcel of being in a professional dressing room. But I cannot think of an example during my time as a county player – I'm not talking about when I was coach, because that is different as you are slightly detached and view people differently – of what I would call a bad egg. Sure, people had differences in all sorts of things, and you respected that. They might not always have shared the same views but they were committed to the same cause.

On the county circuit, rooming with someone offered you a ready-made confidante, and swapping room-mates regularly avoided any associations being viewed as cliquey. As it happens, I was always an advocate of blokes sharing rooms on away excursions, and the primary reason that the practice was stopped when I became England coach was because we simply had too much kit. You couldn't get all the clobber for two players plus all their personal items in one room. It was just not possible. You would have your white kit for Test matches, your coloured kit for one-day stuff, two sets of pads and your training kit as well, which meant there was simply no room to move.

It was only when Ian MacLaurin, then chairman of the ECB, asked to see a room at the Monomotapa Hotel in Harare that things changed. I got one of the keys so he could look at the rooms and on opening the door he declared: 'My God! Never again.' He had come out to Zimbabwe to support the team and was taken aback at the standard of accommodation that we were staying in compared to the management who were housed in completely different hotels. While the Lord's hierarchy was all staying in plush hotels elsewhere on tour, those at the coal face were being shovelled into whatever was available. Usually on the cheapest rate possible, I might add.

Even in subsequent years, some lads like Andrew Flintoff and Steve Harmison would ask for interconnecting rooms where possible because they liked each other's company for support while away from home, setting up a haven complete with dartboard for amusement. On reflection, I can see the advantage of single rooms for modern international players, because at night they provide you with your own space, and time to reflect privately about things when you go to bed. Some players prepare differently to others and over the years, there will have been multiple examples of a guy who likes to go to bed at ten o'clock being pitched in with someone who is only going out at that time and not likely to be back before 2 a.m.

Mr Nightclubber comes in a bit worse for wear, chattering away, tripping over the kitbags, knocking everything off the sink. I know because I've been there. Myself and Paul Allott were on a nicely paid jolly towards the end of my career, promoting Barbican non-alcoholic lager in the United Arab Emirates. I can report that not a drop passed either of our lips but plenty of other liquid was imbibed by Walt on one particular night when I chose to turn in at a relatively early hour.

I woke with a start when this beer-battered behemoth came banging in at around 7.30 the next morning. He has always been a big lad has Wally and so he didn't half make a racket. 'What time are we leaving?' he asked bleary-eyed. 'About eight o'clock,' I told him. 'Wake me up in ten minutes then,' he said, at which point he tried to get his trousers off, putting himself into an uncontrollable spin in the process and resulting in him completely missing his bed.

Some like to get away from cricket completely once the day is over, while others will yak away all night and never leave the subject. Geoff Clayton was greyhounds mad, and became a handler at White City Dogs, which used to be a stone's throw away from Old Trafford, sandwiched between the cricket and football grounds, before being turned into a business park. The façade remained – they couldn't knock it down because it's listed – when they moved to Belle Vue, by which time I was quite into greyhound racing myself. Whenever I popped along to watch I would always look out for Geoff, known to us as Chimp because he walked like a little chimpanzee, making him very distinctive when he led his dog round to the traps ahead of a race.

Chimp was totally chilled out at the dog track. He would engage himself in chat with the trainers, liked having a bet and this world became his refuge. As a cricketer however, he was a real shop steward, and if he didn't like something he wouldn't do it, as when he refused to chase Warwickshire's Gillette semi-final total on principle.

He wasn't the only bolshie bloke in that dressing room, either. Ken Grieves was another one who left on the infamous night of blood-letting. An Australian, Ken later became professional at Accrington. Overseas players like Ken have given enormous value to county cricket over several decades, but sadly few in the twenty-first century give the service our two gems provided during the bulk of my stint with Lancashire.

If you want to assess the legacies of Clive Lloyd and Farokh Engineer at Old Trafford, then consider that they are still regulars at the ground and have remained residents in the area, adopted Mancunians the pair of them. It has been hard not to like these two champion blokes, who also happened to be two champion cricketers. Ask any long-term Lancashire member and they would tell you they are two of our own; forget the fact that they were imported from Guyana and Bombay respectively. They were certainly characters that endeared themselves to the people around Old Trafford. A sign of their popularity was that they both had successful benefit years with Lancashire despite their overseas status.

Not that everything was smooth. In fact, if things had turned out slightly differently we might have lost both early on due to teething problems. For Farokh was as likely to arrive in Timbuktu as his intended destination when setting off for an away game in those early days. He lived on the south side of Manchester and his handling of the journey to Old Trafford from his gaff was as accomplished as his glovework behind the stumps. He didn't have too many problems once pointed towards the M6 either. But the M62? He was completely stumped if we were setting off for an away fixture against Yorkshire.

Farokh was a real stalwart for us, offering us a wonderful all-round package. In addition to being one of the best wicketkeepers in the world, he was also a fine attacking batsman and we sometimes employed him as my opening partner in the Sunday League, to make use of his ability to hit over the top. 'See that Chris Old? I am going to lift him,' he would say, promising some aerial dynamics to our top order. He would say it often enough to ensure we didn't alter our thinking and slip him back into the middle-order.

'See that Mike Procter?'

'Don't tell us, Farokh …You're going to lift him?'

His explosive hitting was the perfect foil to my anchored approach, and I always enjoyed our walks out together on a Sunday. But in contrast to Clive, he was not as keen to accompany me to the nets. Clive practised, practised, practised, whereas Farokh could think of nothing more galling.

Clive arrived at the club during the same year as Farokh but only played a couple of second XI Championship fixtures in 1968 before making his mark the following season. You would have thought the club would have been moving heaven and earth to ensure that we looked after this rising star of the world scene. Oh no, they had found a cut-price deal on accommodation and ran with it, failing to view his address in the centre of Manchester, Unit Two Sauna, with any suspicion. Clive had to make do with kipping in this rather sordid establishment, until word got back to the committee that these actions were insulting to our new guest and besmirched the image of the club.

Thankfully, he overlooked this indiscretion and stuck around to become a great team-mate. The pair of us used to have real fun, telling people we were brothers by a different mother, and when it came to Lancashire he really was part of the family. Like me, he would go on to be club captain, in two stints in his case, shortly after conquering the world with his great West Indies team. But when it came to the captaincy at Old Trafford, it was my turn first.

CHAPTER 6

The New Bond

It might not have been broadcast on the jungle telegraph around Manchester, but the 1972 season coincided with an important change in my status. Although my team-mates were completely unaware, I had been chosen to work-shadow Jack Bond, having been identified by the man himself as his successor as Lancashire captain.

The grooming process, which began soon after Jack decided to call it a day, meant I spent as much time as possible by his side, so that I could learn from his methods and how he implemented certain things during his daily duties. Once you are placed in the situation of captain-in-waiting, it's amazing how much more intently you watch and how much more empathetic you become.

Undoubtedly, it altered my standing within the playing group, with those out of the know suspecting that my alignment with Bond – we got on pretty famously previously but I now spent extended periods of time in his company – was to win the captain's ear and be in pole position for a captaincy nomination as and when the change came. Even some of my staunchest pals, like Jack Simmons, saw my actions as some Machiavellian scheme. Little did they know that the club already had their captain for 1973 being groomed by the incumbent.

Lancashire's policy was for the captain of the club to be involved in the appointment of his successor, and later that decade that meant me putting forward a recommendation for Frank Hayes, who was actually a few months my senior. In this instance, though, my contemporaries might not have viewed me as a candidate to take the baton from Jack because I was only twenty-five.

My first game in charge actually came on German soil. Yes, that's right. I led my men onto the field for the first time in Mönchengladbach of all places. As a reward for another Gillette Cup-winning season, the club hierarchy rewarded us with an overseas post-season jolly. The only two catches in an otherwise well-received act of generosity were that we were not being dispatched to one of cricket's colonial strongholds and that we were required to play some cricket.

Not that we let that get in the way of our revelry at the army camp where we were based. The full eighteen-man squad was in attendance and the first night was the kind you envisage from a group high on the fumes of success. This had been the third end of season in a row that we were celebrating claiming a Lord's final trophy, and at this event there was strong German beer at hand, initially provided by the wallet of the club secretary Jack Wood and then by whoever, after a couple of pints had loosened everyone else's purse strings.

Jack Bond had made it clear he would sit out the first match to allow me to cut my teeth as captain. So, intent on taking the job seriously, I slipped off early and headed back to the military housing block where we slept to sketch some fielding plans for each of our bowlers. Prepared for each individual, I would have a word or two in their shell-likes in the morning before play to show that I had given serious thought to their best-laid plans.

Only none was there to chat with at the appointed meet time, having fallen prey to the continental draught's extra strength. To the Army team this was a crack fixture against the English domestic one-day champions, and make no mistake, they wanted to scalp us. However, there was only myself and Edward Slinger available to scalp at the time of the toss, which thankfully I won. With no option but to ask our hosts to field, I hot-footed it back to the dormitories to arouse what resembled a bunch of extras from Michael Jackson's *Thriller* video.

Few were overly eager to participate, even fewer did themselves justice and thanks to the carnage enacted on a coconut matting pitch by a West Indian fast bowler called Corporal Williams, I began my captaincy reign with a chastening defeat.

It was a great honour to be Jack Bond's choice because I had such a huge respect for his views on the game and his eye for a player. He had an unerring habit of making calls on people and getting them right, when others dismissed them as fancies of a madman, most notably when Northamptonshire released the fast bowler Peter Lee. There was nothing like a successful record behind Leapy nor a queue of suitors forming when it became public that he was surplus to requirements at Wantage Road. But Jack saw something in him that others didn't, and his faith in my credentials to become a leader in this context felt like a huge feather in my cap.

People might have thought I was still a bit green to be taking over from him, but he thought I'd had enough experience and was ready for the next career step. In one way, I was on a hiding to nothing because at the time there was no harder act to follow, other than perhaps Morecambe and Wise. I was certainly not going to be able to match his trophy haul, despite an enviable playing squad and the club's sound investment in those two crack overseas players Clive Lloyd and Farokh Engineer.

With them aboard we were simply irresistible at times, and we remained the force in limited-overs cricket for a good period. However, we relinquished the Lord's winning habit, losing there twice, which meant that the 1975 final triumph was my sole success. Clive was magnificent on these types of occasion and, having been the only man on either side to make 20 in a low-scoring defeat to Kent in 1974, took the man of the match award with an unbeaten 73 to complete a seven-wicket win over Middlesex on their home ground twelve months later. Receiving the cup surrounded by our band of travelling supporters on the outfield in front of the Lord's pavilion was a pretty special feeling. As I jumped off the podium, I let out a sigh. It was one not of relief but fulfilment.

Our one-day game plan was always to set off as if it was a normal cricket match and then go berserk at the end. That tactic did not alter through the transition from Jack's team to mine, and neither did our attention to detail when it came to fielding. Like Jack, I wanted my best two or three fielders in those key areas either side of the pitch, and so the players in question would be Clive Lloyd, David Hughes and Frank Hayes. That trio were all exceptional, as good as anything you have seen.

Despite his stooping gait and ponderous mannerisms, Clive was arguably the very best cricket has ever seen – quick, with great hands and a rocket arm. In fact, he was so unbelievably flexible that he carried a scar on his right hand to prove it. Can you believe that he would bend down to pick up the ball at pace and regularly end up spiking himself in the process? He was that supple that it caused him to cut himself several times, some wounds being more serious than others.

His agility meant he was able to do things others could not, and it caused much mirth when later in our careers he and I were doing our advanced coaching badges together at Lilleshall under the guidance of Les Lenham. One of the exercises was a fielding drill to be used to demonstrate to your charges how to pick up, turn and throw. The ball was rolled out, and we would run from the starting position near the stumps, track it down, and pick it up with your foot on your throwing hand side aligned next to the ball. You would then pivot round and return it to the person stood at the stumps.

However, Clive, bless him, could not get the hang of it. He was that good that he couldn't bring himself to carry out this simplistic exercise, preferring to pick it up in one motion and flick throw it back through his own legs. 'I know you've knocked the stumps out of the ground, Clive, but you're doing it completely wrong!' Les told him. Poor bloke just couldn't get the hang of fielding like a mere mortal, and so for the purposes of his coaching qualifications, it got to the ludicrous situation where we had to walk him through step by step. Chase, stop, turn, throw. That's it, Clive. Tick.

With cheap singles cut out, the onus was on the new-ball bowlers to take wickets. We would start off with two slips and a gully, and sometimes a short leg. If a team got 160-170 you were out of sight in a 40-over Sunday League match, while scores in the 55-over and 60-over competitions were routinely between 200 and 250, so disrupting the early innings was priceless. In fact, if you had to pinpoint the biggest change in the way the game has developed, it would be in the totals being strung together. Of course, you expect tactical changes to develop in any sport, but the way we have seen this reflected in cricket's shorter formats is something I don't believe any of us could have anticipated.

Folk will argue that it is because contemporary batsmen hit the ball further as big bats promote bigger hits, but the square was only rotated at Old Trafford as recently as 2012 and yet the only players I ever recall hitting the ball over the pavilion there, as the ground was previously configured, were Clive Lloyd and Jack Simmons. Another lad, Bob Entwistle, a player who mainly played in the seconds and was involved when I came through, would regularly hit the ball into the adjacent railway track with his forte shot, the pull. Now, the pitch didn't move in the interim and neither did the railway, but he was the only one I saw do it regularly. Equally, Frank Hayes hit one off Bishan Bedi onto what was then the nursery ground and has more recently become the net practice area. That's a really big hit.

It also went down in local folklore when Peter Marner cleared H stand with an enormous hit off the Leicestershire off-spinner John Savage, becoming the only batsman known to do so. In those days, there was no need for fancy stand names after former players, they were all just plain old A, B, C, D etc, and H had its own notoriety as underneath it was the old Draught Bass bar, a real ramshackle old thing that despite its appearance appealed to plenty with a thirst.

During the 1960s, one of the bar's patrons in particular was known for frequenting this stand, a supporter known to all of us as Draught Bass Harry. He liked his ale did Harry, and his party piece was to have a pint of Bass every time a Lancashire wicket fell. Now, even our staunchest supporters would admit we weren't a great batting side in those days, and that meant we regularly slipped to 90 for eight before lunch so that poor old Harry had slipped into the most drastic state of inebriation. On our worst mornings of the season, you would see three or four of his mates carrying Harry out.

The bars used to do a roaring trade for Sunday League matches when our attendances were regularly in five figures. Competition rules meant that you had to finish bowling the first innings by 4.10 p.m. and so, as captain, I was responsible for not allowing us to slip behind time and be punished with a loss of overs when it was our turn to bat. This is when another infamous Old Trafford regular would come to the fore. With ten minutes left, often with the opposition going well, and the ball flying all over the place because it was the end of the innings, distraction was always an unwelcome guest. All you wanted to concentrate on is which bowlers to put on at each end, where to get your field set and how to get through as quickly as possible.

But another one of our notorious hecklers, Harry

Bowker – the proprietor of the Harry Bowker Food Store in Ramsbottom and known to everyone around the members' area as Harry from Rammy – would stagger from the bar, where he'd been supping gin shandies all afternoon, at four o'clock every Sunday and ring the bell, usually coinciding with me looking exasperated, trying to work out how to protect the short leg-side boundary.

DING-A-LING!

The rest of the crowd were sent into hoots and used to respond with shouts of 'Go on, Harry!' not that he needed any egging on.

'Lloydy! Marshall your men! One more time down the line,' he would shout before making his way back to the bar in the most exaggerated stagger imaginable. This performance was as regular as clockwork on a Sunday. You could set your watch by Harry and his drunken bell-ringing.

The Pit of Hate – positioned under the clock of the Old Trafford pavilion – had its own notoriety. This was an area where like-minded fellows gathered to put the world to rights. Sat side-on to the umpires, they would provide running commentaries for those around them. They say that you can tell a Yorkshireman but you can't tell him much. It was similar with this group of Lancastrian diehards. There was not much they didn't know and they ensured that the umpires were always on their game, regularly shouting out welcome advice like: 'Watch that front line now, he's getting close to a no ball. In fact, you've just missed one there.'

The gang members in the Pit of Hate included Billy the Butcher, John the Bore, Mr Jinx, The Scribe, Rubber Duck, Rubber Duck's brother and Throbbin' Robin. Of course, their barks were far nastier than their bites and there was something pseudo-comical about their passion. Their reputations went before them – after all, how many sets of players at sporting clubs know the nicknames of a band of supporters? From the dressing-room balcony we used to be able to identify each of them whenever they imparted their public advice.

On one occasion the players got our own back when our chief prankster Mick Malone, the Australian fast bowler, dropped a rubber snake on a string right in among them as they were shouting and balling. Positioned on the balcony directly above this volatile lot, Mick lowered it into one of their pints and with a flick of his wrist whipped it back up again. 'Did you see that? It was a flying snake,' one said, after dropping his glass. 'Give me a pint of what he's drinking!' shouted another. We were all gathered behind Mick, having a right old giggle.

There was an affinity between the club's players and supporters during the 1970s fostered by the number of big matches we played and the success we enjoyed in those matches. Although the Lancashire side I took over was slightly on the wane, and Jack Bond was always going to be a tough act to follow, we still got to three more Lord's finals. Up until then, history had shown that we didn't lose these pressure matches, so it was something of a shock when that changed – in fact, it made them fairly devastating losses. None more so than in the 1973 Benson & Hedges Cup semi-final when our former player Jim Cumbes, who would return to Lancashire as chief executive in future years, came to the crease at No. 11 and helped Worcestershire secure their passage to Lord's on losing fewer wickets after they matched our all out total of 159.

Revenge came twelve months later when we won a Gillette semi at New Road via our trusted method of putting runs on the board and squeezing the game in the second innings. However, we were soon to find out that while there is no better place to win than at Lord's, equally there is no worse place to lose. The four-wicket defeat to Kent left us with the inescapable feeling that we had let the fans down. That has been a well-versed expression over the years, but during our one-day heyday it genuinely felt like you were playing for them. Thousands of folk would organise their weekends away to come and cheer us on, and it was their cup as much as ours. They expected to win too.

On Gillette Cup final day, the ground would be full in absolutely no time, the atmosphere building up well before the toss. Even entering the ground held a special feeling. We would stay at the Clarendon Court Hotel on Edgware Road, arriving on a Friday to drop all the kit off at the ground. That meant that instead of arriving on a coach as was the tradition for FA Cup finals, we would arrive on foot and saunter through the Grace Gates with the words of well-wishers ringing in our ears. The buzz of cup final morning was intoxicating.

As a Lancashire player, these occasions were not daunting; they were addictive, and full of positive memories. We knew what to do to get over the winning line. The atmosphere held no surprises, it was second nature to us. Success breeds success, as they say, and it felt like we always had one-day finals under control. Until that match against Kent, that is: a really low-scoring affair even by the standards of the age. Realistically we were never going to defend a score of 118, made from exactly 60 overs, although we gave it a bloody good go and caused more than a few jitters in reducing Kent to 75 for five and 89 for six. But once they broke into three figures, the writing was on the wall. Then, and perhaps only then, did we see that we were fallible in this new form of the game.

They were never high-scoring games, played as they were at the back end of the season on pitches that had seen better days and the light disappearing fast by the match's final throes. Yet, we never spent too much time fretting about early morning movement from any moisture that lay under the surface on these September days – I believe the mind-forged demons about the nibbling surface developed some years later when uncovered pitches had long since gone – nor the light issue.

Never was this better emphasised than in 1971 when we won a Gillette semi-final against Gloucestershire courtesy of some wonderful late-innings hitting by David Hughes. A most resourceful cricketer, Hughes offered a plentiful supply of tail-end runs throughout his career, but never were those runs to prove more valuable than the ones made in near darkness against that fabulous Gloucestershire team. When concern was expressed over the light during this late flurry, umpire Arthur Jepson offered the legendary retort: 'I can see the moon – how much further do you want to see?' Thankfully, Yosser saw us all the way to St John's Wood.

The only time I can recall a pitch being juiced up so severely that it caused a major advantage for one team over another was nothing to do with rain or early morning dew but snow. Yes, snow, in a game against Derbyshire at Buxton in June 1975, and we were the beneficiaries.

It was in glorious sunshine that we launched a batting blitz on Saturday 31 May, after I won the toss. It really was short sleeves, deckchairs and ice creams – a batting utopia. My contribution was 69, but Frank Hayes, with 104, and Clive Lloyd were the real stars of a total of 477 for five declared, with Clive's unbeaten 167 coming at a rate of a run a minute. We scored so quickly, in fact, that I was able to pull out and allow our bowlers an hour at the Derbyshire top order that evening, a short session in which we reduced our hosts to 25 for two.

The following day, we toddled off to Colchester to face Essex in a Sunday League match while Derbyshire stayed put at The Park to defeat Glamorgan. Our three-day match was therefore due to recommence on the Monday morning, 2 June. Only the curtains in our hotel room concealed an unbelievable sight. A blanket of snow covered the town, and the uncovered pitch had turned pale.

One of the umpires was good old Dickie Bird and he was his usual flappable self, exclaiming that he had never seen the like before as we surveyed the ground, the bottoms of our flares beginning to look like they had experienced a nasty bout of dandruff. All we could do in that situation was wait for the pitch to thaw.

It did not happen immediately and there was no play possible that day, but on the following morning the sun came out once more to melt any lingering white stuff, and as it did so the pitch began to steam. To be fair, Derbyshire had no chance on this sticky dog. The contrast in conditions to Saturday had – according to the Meteorological Office – been caused by a depression bringing cold air down from the Arctic. Batting on this surface was enough to depress anyone. Our quicks were unplayable, the ball pitching and darting this way and that off the seam, dislodging sods on its journey. It took just over an hour to wrap up their innings for a grand total of 42.

As captain it was my duty to walk along the splintered old floorboards between the dressing rooms, pop my head round the door of the Derbyshire one, and invite them to have another dig. On hearing the news Brian Bolus, their opening batsman, exclaimed: 'Thank you, Bumble, I can feel another desperate nought coming on.'

When Ashley Harvey-Walker, their belligerent middle-order strokeplayer, came to the wicket he took the precaution of removing his false teeth and handing them to Bird at square leg for safe-keeping. He was not without them long. This time, Derbyshire were finished off in the equivalent of two and a half hours to give us an astonishing innings and 348-run win.

We were regulars at Buxton but could rarely force results because more often than not rain disrupted us. There were at least two matches in which no play was possible for two whole days, and with the ground under water we took temporary memberships of the Buxton Conservative Club and played snooker.

That 1971 win over Gloucestershire was one of the greatest in domestic limited-overs history and a reprise of it took place in

1975, the year of my only trophy as Lancashire captain. My involvement in that latter semi-final was peripheral, sat among a crowd of 25,000 at Old Trafford, nursing a broken bone in my right hand. In a way, this injury was self-inflicted – not in the Ben Stokes way of punching a locker, but equally stupid.

We were playing a County Championship match against Hampshire at Aigburth, Liverpool, at the start of August and appeared set fair for a useful first-innings lead in reply to Hampshire's 160 all out. I had negotiated my way to 92 and everything was relatively calm as Andy Roberts came on for another five-over spell. The impudence of my next act, however, came back to haunt me. I stepped across to the off-side and picked him up over midwicket. While stood admiring this clip, I noticed Andy's eyes were almost popping out of his head.

As it was the end of the over, I was casually patting the middle of the pitch when Richard Gilliat, the Hampshire captain, walked past on his way from slip at one end to the other and muttered: 'I wouldn't have done that if I was you.' I was about to find out the consequences of riling Roberts, a magnificent bowler who could go up and down the gears at will.

The next delivery from this West Indies great reared up and hit me straight on my hand, in front of my nose, exploding my glove like a machete would a pillow and breaking a bone for good measure. The ball spiralled up into the air and was pouched by Gordon Greenidge ambling in from gully. I was out for 96, five wickets went down without the score moving off 144, and the substantial innings lead we believed was in our sights was in reality no more than three.

This injury came at a crucial period of the season as we chased a rare Championship and cup double. But Clive Lloyd took over the captaincy and the team secured a fifth final appearance in six years by three wickets, the exact same margin of victory as that classic four years earlier, and in similar circumstances with Hughes once again to the fore in the chase alongside Jack Simmons. Thankfully, my hand had healed sufficiently for me to feature in the final, providing me with one of my career highlights – lifting a trophy in front of a throng of Lancashire fans.

These Lord's finals used to attract massive crowds, with hordes of folk wedged between the advertising hoardings and the boundary rope. When they used to say that grounds were packed to the rafters, they really were in those days and sometimes the only spare seats in the house were those you bagged on the grassy outfield perimeter. There were no restrictions back then for the paying public, no heavies in fluorescent jackets rugby-tackling enthusiastic young lads and pinning them in half-nelsons.

As a player, I used to love it when the crowd invaded the pitch at the end. The comical chaos of players running off and the umpires hobbling behind always appealed to me. It was great fun and no one has shown me any evidence to suggest that players were ever endangered or anybody was ever hurt. When you had won, it was an exhilarating feeling to run back to the dressing room chased by the mob. Nobody picked a stump up by the way because there just wasn't time. Had you lingered you'd get caught up in the stampede, and like British Bulldog the name of the game was to get back to base before the chasers caught up with you. It was a good job too as those stumps were there to last all summer. You didn't have a hundred sets in the groundsman's shed waiting to replace them; you might have a spare one or two but they had to last from April to September.

The support for Lancashire throughout my playing career was incredible, partly due to a full 15,000 membership, complete with lengthy waiting list. Compare that to 2011 when Lancashire won the County Championship with the number down to around 5000 including women, who were not previously included in the figures. In real terms, the membership has dwindled to almost nothing.

The reduction in membership numbers has been one of the massive shifts I have witnessed during my time in the game, and for my mind you can no longer consider county clubs as member clubs. They still carry a membership, of course, but there is nothing like the impact either financially or in terms of support that there once was. We were made to feel that we were serving these people, and I'm not sure that is felt by our dressing room descendants at Old Trafford.

The club indoctrinated us with the idea that these Lord's final days were for the membership, to give them something back for their commitment, and I can honestly say that it made you extra motivated whenever you got into the latter stages. There was no remuneration for us, the drive to win strengthened only by a sense of duty to those who willed us on.

There would be a little bit of a bonus for winning the competition, and we had that German jaunt as a small reward, but don't get carried away with this because you weren't buying a new car. The lack of a financial carrot rankled with some of the players, because they believed the team should be better rewarded for their endeavours, given the amount of money that was washing around the game. We got a bit but to some never enough, and the money that we were effectively playing for was the sum detailed in our next contract. A cup final victory certainly gave us a bit of a nego-tiating tool.

There was no coach with a wish-list to tell the chairman that he wanted X, Y and Z in his squad for the next season; you were still reliant on blokes sat in the committee room with their gin and tonics being asked to put their hands up and vote for each player. Your future was still decided when the question 'all those in favour' was asked. Not enough hands meant you were gone. There was no warning letter, no chance for you to beg for your job back or taking the club to a tribunal for unfair dismissal. If you weren't flavour of the month with that committee then that was it, you were off. If enough hands went up, you got what you were given.

Once you got into August, and contract decision time, some of the playing staff would be chewing their fingernails. Thankfully, I never felt that I was about to be binned; I always felt that I was doing okay and would be paid a fair amount for what I was doing. I guess that was a by-product of a modest upbringing and simplistic pleasures. But there were plenty that did feel the heat and the insecurity that such a system promotes.

Things got better over the years, and when I returned to Old Trafford as coach in the 1990s contracts were upped to five years in length which previously were unthinkable. Players such as Neil Fairbrother and Wasim Akram – the Pakistani star we called The King because on the field he was cricketing royalty – demanded that kind of commitment because they were box office players. You needed to look after assets like that.

Undoubtedly, that shift from the arbitrary selection process of the committee to one of greater transparency had to happen, and it came about through the Kerry Packer era. Packer's World Series Cricket offered players like Tony Greig greater freedom and they took it – suddenly players were more aware of their market value.

The Professional Cricketers' Association – of which I later became president – had a representative at each club and I was ours. But it was not a position I necessarily enjoyed, because you had to be so careful that the club did not view you as a shop steward, stirring things up. While you were the link between the players and the representative body, you had to carry out your work covertly, like a secret agent.

There were those who were unafraid to push for the greater good, men like John Arlott, a staunch Labour supporter, and Jack Bannister, but you were made to feel like Arthur Scargill by challenging authority and asking for more or better. Here we were, PCA reps viewed as individuals who were disturbing the peace.

You were seen as activists when actually you were trying to stand up for what was right and proper, not only for yourself but for the sport going forward.

I might not have been as passionate as others, but when Jack Bond – who had been one of the twenty-nine men at the inaugural PCA meeting in 1965 – suggested I inherit the role from him I felt compelled to do it, and there was no queue forming behind me to challenge for it.

Whenever we had these PCA meetings, talk nearly always turned to strikes as a way for the organisation to gain greater recognition from the Test and County Cricket Board. Latterly, the PCA has become a very healthy, reputable body able to fund itself, as is the Federation of International Cricketers' Association (FICA) around the world, and as president I have been proud of the work it has done to help all cricketers past and present.

I have always believed in being fair. In fact, one of my regrets from my playing days was that we were not fair as a team to some of our best players. I have to say that when Peter Lever, Frank Hayes and Barry Wood opted to go on strike in a pay dispute with the club in that summer of 1975, it proved to be the most difficult few weeks of my career. The entire squad was pushing for better terms across the board, but this trio felt that their status as current England internationals merited an opportunity to negotiate a bit more toffee on top. They wanted the chance to sort themselves a superior rate befitting their elevated status. This, of course, went against any notion of an all-for-one team ethos, and there was some resentment from the dressing room that they should think in this way. Perhaps time has changed my own mind because I now feel we should have supported them. Back then, I didn't see it as an option.

That course of action could have become very messy, and as captain I already felt caught in the crossfire between the playing staff who believed they were deserving of a greater slice of the financial pie generated by our sustained success and a committee protecting the club's long-term future by keeping money for rainy days. Already pushed to the limit on getting the average player paid commensurately for his efforts, I let the talented rebels go it alone.

We didn't stay together as a team simply because we couldn't. As young men with wives, children and mortgages we felt we could not risk our livelihoods for others. If truth be told, we were scared, feeling as though we had our hands tied by the gin-and-tonic brigade. The fear of losing what we had was over-whelming. We were comfortably off, paid more than your average man on the street, and the general consensus was that was not worth risking.

So when Lever, Wood and Hayes took their public stand and withdrew their labour after returning from World Cup duty, we let them get on with it. We have come through it and we are all mates, but with hindsight we should have supported them as a group and told the club we weren't playing either on that morn-ing of 21 June.

It was the day of the World Cup final between Australia and West Indies and Cedric Rhoades, the club chairman, was therefore one of the dignitaries sat at Lord's. Their decision to pull out of this match against Derbyshire at Old Trafford at the last minute, less than three weeks on from our snow-catalysed landslide over the same opposition, was obviously tactical. From a pure cricket point of view this irked me, because we were unbeaten in our first seven matches and making a rare bid for a Championship title.

'You're letting us down pulling out at such short notice,' I told them during the frank exchanges that took place in the dressing room.

In turn, they pleaded for my support and that of the rest of the team, to no avail. The consequences of which were that our star trio sat out the game, officially with 'injuries', while those of us not in a sufficiently secure enough position to support them ventured out, Harry Pilling and Jack Simmons, carrying minor niggles, included. We began with ten men before Bob Ratcliffe, who had been out doing his Saturday morning shopping, arrived from Accrington.

Bob played his part in a ten-wicket win, claiming wickets and scoring useful runs, which served only to stir things up further. As captain, I made the decision to stick with the team for the next match against Kent, despite the England three making themselves available. Peter Lever grabbed me around the throat and accused me of betrayal when I revealed my decision in the dressing room. 'I'm not leaving blokes out who turned out and did the business for me,' I told him. Sure, we had won without them, but my stand backfired as Kent took away our undefeated status.

The conflict did not linger even though the committee suspended all three men for a few games – if it had I'm not sure I would have ended up on that podium on the Lord's outfield in early September – and my relationships with those in question did not suffer any deterioration either. If you want evidence, then consider that when I was on my last legs as captain, I agreed to the committee's instruction to appoint Frank Hayes as vice-captain and, by association, my successor.

As with all such things, this proposal needed to be put to the committee and done through official procedures. It took the form of Mr Jack Wood, who was club secretary and would later become Frank's father-in-law, extending the invitation to become my deputy through me. In his youth, Frank might not have been placed in the 'captaincy material' bracket, given his confrontational reputation, but this was an image that he did his utmost to keep rather than deconstruct. He was a bright bloke with a degree who we signed once his days at Sheffield University were over, and his gregarious nature meant he enjoyed socialising. But I certainly didn't have him marked down as a hellraiser, as others clearly did.

Although there was a caveat to him becoming my number two

in 1976 – he had to return the Samurai swords he had pinched from the Clarendon Court Hotel in London. These two ceremonial weapons, that had previously been on display in the establishment's bar, had gone missing earlier that week and the last reported sighting of Frank had been of him jousting on the Edgware Road with Mike Hendrick.

I asked Frank if this was true when I finally pinned him down. 'Yes, it is.'

'Well, where are they now?'

'We threw them in a garden about five houses up,' he said.

'You want to be vice-captain still, don't you?'

'Yes, of course.'

'Well, I think you'd better get these swords back to their rightful place … don't you?'

Needless to say, they were returned and Frank was in position waiting to succeed me when I got to the end of the 1977 season. By then I had spent five years in office and despite some nearly moments – including that season of 1975 when we headed into the final round of matches with a chance of winning the Championship pennant only to finish fourth – it was a period which delivered a solitary piece of silverware, though on a personal note I did also receive national recognition during this time.

CHAPTER 7

National Service, at the Double

A cricket career is full of stepping stones positioned to help you navigate along the path towards your ultimate destiny: playing for your country. When I started off as a spotty youth, my first ambition was to play Lancashire League and for me that meant the first team at Accrington. Then the next footing was with Lancashire County Cricket Club, and of course throughout the entire journey my thoughts were never far away from playing Test cricket. It really is the ultimate and, as it says on the tin, it is a real test.

Becoming a Test opening batsman, as I did during the summer of 1974, completed a wonderful transformation for me from the young hopeful, rummaging through the Accrington club kitbag as a thirteen-year-old to fish out its delights, to the man who was to inherit Geoffrey Boycott's vacated England place. Boycott had been one of two major obstacles in my way to the top, with John Edrich being the other. I was nowhere near the kind of player either of those men were, but I had to get past them if I wanted to fulfil my ambitions, and having them as rivals certainly ensured I kept my standards high.

Once established on the county scene, it's about demanding attention from the England selectors through consistent performances, then waiting for your opportunity. If and when that opportunity knocks, you have to ensure you're on top of your game. It's important in that situation for the two things to marry, and thankfully for me others believed they were happily wed when Boycott's omission opened up a spot. There were those who would have taken private pleasure at his rare lean patch on the international stage, but I have never had any major beefs with Boycott – a minor charge sheet containing a couple of unnecessary run-outs, a couple of heated exchanges when I was England coach and the fact that my wife Diana thinks he's essential listening notwithstanding. I simply wanted his England place.

Boycs had moved aside amid all kinds of conjecture. The rumours were of no real interest to me, however, because as an England aspirant his demise led to my rise. Reports surfaced that he was preoccupied with the organisation of his benefit and the demands of his position as captain of Yorkshire; there was even talk of him falling out with the then captain Mike Denness (only later in his own autobiography did Boycott reveal he believed the Scot had 'wanted as much to do with me as the Black Death'). From my point of view, though, everything else was immaterial – I was selected by Alec Bedser and his co-selectors as his direct replacement as opening batsman.

As far as I was concerned, he was just out of the reckoning, I had been picked, given the chance to fulfil a dream and play for my country, and everything else went over my head. I was concentrating on the business of scoring runs to better myself, focusing on that red, spherical leather object being hurled down at me from twenty-two yards – not analysing personality clashes, or the torment Boycott surprisingly suffered at the hands of the innocuous-looking swing bowler Eknath Solkar at the start of India's tour.

The chance to promote my own case against the Indians came in a Lancashire fixture at Old Trafford in May. I always felt confident against spin, had a good gameplan against it, and whole-heartedly believed I had done enough to earn a touring place to the subcontinent two years earlier because of this. So it had been something of a heartache that I was overlooked for that assignment and Barry Wood, my opening partner at county level, chosen in my place. My form at the end of 1972 had also been rich, but the hundreds I reeled off towards its back end had, according to Cyril Washbrook, the Lancashire man on the England selection panel, come too late to influence their thinking. My consolation for this near miss was a £50 fee to be a standby tourist.

However, it did confirm that I had made it onto the periphery of national selection, and showed me that the target I was striking at was only an arm's length away. As it happened, my three-figure effort against an attack including spin trio Bhagwath Chandrasekhar, Srinivas Venkataraghavan and Bishan Bedi was well positioned, sandwiched as it was between matches in which Boycott chained a succession of failures.

In four innings for Yorkshire and MCC, Boycott was dismissed three times by the left-armer Solkar and didn't make it out of the teens in any of them. It almost beggared belief that the finest opening batsman of his generation, he of the impenetrable defence and astute judge of stroke who had more than 4500 Test runs to his name, could have a problem with such an innocuous trundler whose career return on the same stage was eighteen victims at 59.44. But, when he became one of that fairly exclusive set in the second innings of the first Test at Old Trafford, I got my chance.

In truth, I had felt close to selection for a couple of years and knew the kind of figures necessary to catch the right eyes – those of Alec Bedser and the rest of the national selectors. One thing that hasn't changed over the decades is the batting benchmark of a minimum of 1000 first-class runs a season. My two previous campaigns had been the best of my career, bounties that would not be beaten as things turned out: the 1510 runs of 1972 followed by

1405 in 1973. Undoubtedly, 1972 represented my career turning point. Although it was the fourth year in a row I broke into those four figures, crucially I had begun to turn scores into hundreds. There had been only five in my career to that point, but six that season pointed to a greater maturity to my game. Confidence in my ability was abundant, perhaps boosted by my new role as heir apparent to Jack Bond, and at twenty-five you are undoubtedly at the peak of your powers as a batsman.

In addition to the 1000-a-year tally, I worked on the principle that you needed at least three first-class hundreds as the kind of form to merit selection. By the time the series against India began in June 1974, I already had two hundreds to my name for the season, including the one against the Indians in Manchester.

For some time I'd wanted to read the kind of headline printed in the *Daily Mirror* on 15 June: 'Boycott out – Selectors go for Lloyd'. Five days later, I was Test debuting at Lord's, making 46 – caught at leg gully, prodding forward – in a crushing innings victory. I actually discovered news of my selection as all players omitted or selected did at the time, via an announcement on radio. There was nothing sinister in this, it was just that the game was not as it is today, with email communication and mobile phone contact from the chairman of selectors. We are so used to our world of 24/7 connections that we forget an age when discoveries were made via television and radio. Official confirmation came within twenty-four hours.

As the debutant, I took all the telephone calls from the press men on that Sunday before the match to discuss my situation. If I was defensive about my selection during these interviews, it was nothing to do with not wanting to be cast as Boycott's Roses rival – which I can now see was an intriguing sub-plot – just that I think I was slightly taken aback still. Therefore, I didn't offer much other than the usual banalities about dreams coming true. The first thing you come to realise when you're sitting on the other side of the fence when it comes to the media is that 99 times out of 100 they want to chat to you because you've done well. They're not trying to catch you out, they're only looking for some colour to your story. But despite being in form over a lengthy period of time, my progress towards the England team had not all been one lengthy up-curve. Indeed, there had been several troughs in among my peaks.

Although I had maintained high standards for Lancashire, I kept flunking in higher company. Take the 1973 Test trial for example, a match between all the hopefuls including automatic picks, scheduled in early May, the first of its kind for twenty years. This match was down at Hove and, although I arrived in a positive mood, I departed cursing the very presence of this contest in the itinerary. I literally showed them nothing of my ability – pinned leg before for nought in the first innings, I trumped that by being run out without facing a ball in the second. I was not the first player to have suffered that fate while partnering Geoffrey, and far from the last.

Having arrived in such high spirits, I was mortified in the dressing room to reflect on such a wasted opportunity, and therefore thankful for John Snow's balm. A man of relatively few words, he suggested I forget about it 'because tomorrow's another day'. Even then, I don't think I was sad to see the back of this fixture.

When it had come round the following season, there was a hint of my place in the pecking order when I was chosen in the England XI against the Rest. Boycott and Dennis Amiss were the opening pair, with me following at No. 3. Trying to read too much into these kinds of selection can be fraught with danger, and I was unable to ascertain where I stood with any certainty thanks to another piece of misfortune.

While Boycott made a hundred in each innings of this match at New Road, Worcester, suggesting talk of his demise was premature, I was bowled by the off-spinner Jack Birkenshaw for my third successive duck in these fixtures. Even though I struck 50 in the second innings, further calamity followed when I injured a finger in the deep trying to catch John Edrich. Not only did I fail in this pursuit, he would finish with a century and a 95 as the contest petered out into a draw.

That had effectively ruled me out of contention for the first Test on my home patch in Manchester, because even if my injury had healed in miraculously quick time, Edrich had a stronger claim to a place in the top order. Indeed, Edrich took his place at No. 3 during that series, with Boycott and Amiss starting off, before the switch and my call-up for Lord's.

They say making a good first impression is crucial, but unfortunately I failed in this department when it came to my Test debut. Gubby Allen, one of the central figures in the dramatic Bodyline series of the early 1930s and a man who effectively ran English and world cricket in various capacities for the next four decades, was not someone to get on the wrong side of. So it was lucky for me then that he didn't take offence at our first meeting.

One of the aspects that *has* changed on the international scene is the arrival time of the home team before a match. Now it tends to be on a Sunday evening or a Monday morning for a Thursday start, with net practices of varying intensity in the lead-up days. In 1974, it was as late as the afternoon before, and due to my nervous excitement I turned up ahead of schedule, wearing my pride and joy – a rather snazzy yellow double-breasted leather jacket. To put this fashion accessory into context, in terms of its appeal one might consider it to be the equivalent of red trousers in 2015. Safe to say, I believed I was cooler than the Hofmeister bear in this get-up, as I strolled into the home dressing room at Lord's and put my bag down.

On entering I noticed there was this chap sat at the table, and not knowing who he was, asked: 'How do?'

'Hullo,' came the rather authoritative reply.

Although I tried to strike up a conversation, as much to help me work out who the hell he was as anything else, it was proving a bit of a one-way street, and it entered my head that he might have just been a member of the public who had wandered in. In no uncertain terms, I advised him that the rest of the England team would be on their way in shortly, hinting that he might like to make himself scarce.

'You've no idea who I am, have you?' he responded.

'No, I can't say I have, sorry.'

'The name's Gubby. Gubby Allen.'

'How do you do?' I said, sheepishly, still brimming with uncertainty.

Thankfully, he didn't hold my ignorance against me during our evening gatherings in the MCC committee room as his guests.

In contrast to Allen, who was then MCC treasurer, his successor as chairman of the England selectors, Alec Bedser, was a lot more like one of the boys. Clocking me in my yellow jacket that week, he put me at ease with the blunt inquiry: 'What the bloody hell's that?'

These days if you get picked for England, you turn up in the full suit for a Test match, what the players refer to as their number ones. Back then you were only kitted out afterwards, hence my turning up looking like a stunt double from *Starsky & Hutch*. I was yet to receive my England jacket or indeed my MCC piping blazer that I would be sporting on tour that following winter, and there was no elaborate presentation of your cloth cap as happens in public now. It was just placed under your peg in the changing room.

As it was I was quite happy in this yellow fashion accessory that I viewed as the dog's proverbials. It had been purchased from a bespoke gents' outfitters in Rawtenstall called Nobbutlads. At least, that's how it was written phonetically in our local dialect – in the Queen's English you might say Nowt But Lads.

This jacket proved something of a home comfort to me that week, and there were heaps of telegrams offering good wishes from friends and family back in Lancashire when I arrived in the dressing room to remind me of my roots too. Unfortunately, Susan and my parents could not make it down for the match, but Dad scored it in one of his books, watching on the BBC back in Accrington. Any lingering nerves were settled by my negotiation of the new ball and indeed making it back in for lunch unscathed after Mike Denness won the toss, and Dad was so very nearly registering a debut half-century. However, I was snared in the leg trap by the off-spinner Erapalli Prasanna just a boundary shy, and reaching my first England landmark was left for another day.

At that stage, it was difficult to shake the feeling that I was keeping Boycott's place warm, but the way to do so was to score runs if given another opportunity, which I duly was a fortnight later when the series moved to Edgbaston, and possibly the flattest pitch I had experienced in my life. I could not have wished for a better surface on which to play my second Test and stake a claim for a place in the touring party destined for Australia the following winter.

When everything about your game is working in unison and things are going in your favour, that's the time for you to cash in as a batsman. One match into my England Test career, I could hardly claim to be comfortable in my surroundings, but I felt in decent touch and I had now had a couple of lengthy looks at the Indian bowlers. There was nothing to strike fear into me despite them possessing a trio of slow bowlers in Prasanna, Bedi and Venkataraghavan each of whom would take in excess of 150 Test wickets.

This was a pitch on which to score a hundred and an attack that suited me, because I always fancied myself against the spinners, particularly when using my feet to hit them down the ground. I set my stall out to achieve that target. Rain washed out the opening day's play, but it mattered not to an England team with the upper hand in the series. India were shot out in no time and I was batting on Friday evening; and into Saturday evening as it turned out.

It was during that Saturday evening session that I achieved a new career high. Never before had I scored a double hundred and it was a real sense of achievement breaking that duck while playing for my country. Not that there were any over-the-top celebrations. No French kissing of the badge, beating of the chest or pumping of the fists. I simply took off my cap and held it aloft along with my SS bat to acknowledge the crowd.

Others recognised its worth, too. I got a friendly handshake from the left-armer Bedi, who I had nurdled behind square on the leg-side for the single that took me there, and another one a few seconds later from Keith Fletcher, who had hurried through from the non-striker's end. I offered not much more than a restrained smile of satisfaction and have no memory of feeling fatigued despite having batted all day. I was in the zone, in the bubble.

Farokh Engineer, a great colleague at Lancashire and a true gentleman, recognised it too, and he kept whispering over my shoulder: 'Keep going Bumble, you're in for a big one.' Do not think for one minute that this was a little soft for international sport. Had I made the mistake of lurching out of my crease at any point, those bails would have been off in a flash. Farokh played hard but fair and there is a lot to be learned from that kind of attitude.

Edgbaston had never witnessed a 200 by an England batsman before, but not everyone in attendance was impressed because as I was calmly taking in the magnitude of the moment a voice from the stands demanded: 'Here, Lloyd. How much f***ing longer?' I seemed to be a magnet for chaps like this – the one-line wits who got those around them chortling – and it always put things into context. Sport is a pastime, a bit of fun, and I was fortunate to be able to participate all the way to the top level. I finished on 214 not out after almost seven and a half hours at the crease.

As well as having a maiden Test hundred behind me, I finished that summer of 1974 with another in a limited-overs international match at the end of a troubled tour of England by Pakistan. Relations had become quite strained between the teams after the Pakistanis levelled accusations of skulduggery during the Lord's Test when Derek Underwood bowled them out. But these accusations that we were somehow complicit in the state of the pitch were codswallop.

If there was any damp around Deadly was, well, as you can tell by the nickname – deadly. Persistent showers meant water had got under the covers and left a wet patch on the pitch. He kept hitting it and they simply couldn't cope. I was stood at short leg and it was like picking cherries. Pakistan were decimated by Underwood in the first innings on a drying surface after a lengthy downpour on the opening day, and then – after we batted to secure a 140-run lead – rain struck again when Pakistan came out to bat for a second time.

It was actually on the Sunday, the traditional rest day of Test matches in this country, and Monday that London was the subject of some major downpours and when the temporary tent-like covering was removed, the pitch was discovered to be sodden. The rain had seeped through and in these conditions it was a different game altogether.

Underwood bagged half a dozen wickets with his idiosyncratic left-arm-round stuff once the match finally resumed at around 5 p.m. on the fourth evening. In plunging Pakistan from 192 for three half an hour into play to 226 all out, he took his innings haul to eight and match figures to 13 for 71.

It left England 87 runs for victory, 27 of which were wiped off by Dennis Amiss and myself before the close of play. But our efforts in ten overs against the new ball were far from the most newsworthy event that evening, due to Pakistan manager Omar Kureishi's utter indignation. Kureishi slapped in an official complaint, accusing MCC of 'negligence' and 'incompetence' in their attempts to cover the wicket. In those days, if it rained after the Test match was underway then the run-ups and edges of the square were protected but the pitch itself was exposed to the elements. On rest days, however, every effort was made to protect it, and Pakistan's argument was that they were entitled to bat on a pitch of similar condition to that when stumps were drawn on Saturday.

As it turned out, we didn't get back on. Despite the re-marking of the pitch during the final session on day five, the rain returned, and the contest, which had become more political than sporting, was abandoned to leave the match and series drawn. I failed to make headlines during these contests against Pakistan, although I top-scored in the first innings at bowler-friendly Headingley, and celebrated the news that I was in the winter tour party to Australia with 116 not out in the one-day international at Nottingham a matter of hours later.

It meant I was off to fraternise with one of the best Australian teams of all time. It was to prove a deflating experience in the middle, but there were no such feelings for me off it. I would have to say that the Australians were a terrific set of blokes. Guys like Rod Marsh, Dennis Lillee, Jeff Thomson, the Chappell brothers, Ian and Greg, and the chain-smoking Dougie Walters – revered in his own country where he averaged a touch under 58, but not so effective overseas – were all great company.

It was this series of ferociously competitive cricket that taught me the value of the post-match beer. These days it is limited to the actual end of the match, or even the end of the series, dependent on the views of the respective captains and coaches, but back then it was something that took place at the end of every day's play. Not everyone participated, of course, but the option was there to pop into the other team's dressing room for a drink with blokes who had spent the past seven hours trying to knock your block off. Unfortunately, by the end of the tour, when it came to Test cricket my drink represented one for the road.

CHAPTER 8

Felled by a Cracker at the WACA

Some great sporting careers have been ended by injury. I would not claim either that my own career was great or that the particular injury that remains synonymous with my time in international cricket caused anything more than severe discomfort overnight and a swelling that unfortunately refused to stay – but the moment that Jeff Thomson poleaxed me with his cracker at the WACA was the one that told me I had scaled my peak. After that it was all about the descent.

It was mid-December 1974 and my Test life was only six months old, yet being helped from the field, forced to retire hurt, is what most people talk about when they recall my nine caps. I averaged over 40 and scored a double hundred, but I was not quite up to coping with what Australia hit us with during that winter. Neither, in fairness, were the majority of my battered and bruised team-mates.

In some ways, the blow I took to my particulars in Perth was self-inflicted, as I was not in any position to play the ball in question with any authority. You see, some injuries are directly related to others. For example, a back injury and hamstring trouble often go hand in hand. My problem during the 1974-75 Ashes – apart from struggling to see the 90 m.p.h. thunderbolts Thommo was launching, sometimes generously delivered from as far away as twenty-two yards – was that a bulging disc in my neck prevented me getting into my usual side-on position at the crease. Instead, my stance was contorted, and its open nature invited danger to the body if I made the slightest error in judgement.

Arguably, I shouldn't have been playing because of this neck problem. But once you have got an England place you don't relinquish it lightly, and after the frustration of missing the first Test at Brisbane due to a fractured finger there was little going to get in the way of me adding to my international appearances. I wanted to be out there feeling the heat – and how I felt it.

Recall this gladiatorial era of uncovered pitches when facing the planet's best fast bowlers – such as West Indies' awesome foursome of Malcolm Marshall, Andy Roberts, Michael Holding and Joel Garner – to get a picture of how intimidating life could be as a top-level opening batsman. It was a bit like break-dancing on the M25.

Of all the blows I ever took out in the middle, however, never was I in as much discomfort as that day during the second Test in Perth, when my genitals were returned to me after being found on the other side of what the manufacturers claimed was a *protective* box. Let's run through some facts here: the litesome in question was pink and plastic when I needed something more befitting the Valyrian steel armour worn by combatants in *Game of Thrones*.

I might as well not have been sporting anything between my legs, for the good this so-called protector did on impact with the leather sphere hurled at breakneck speed by Thomson on Australia's quickest and bounciest pitch, during an England second innings that began minus the injured Brian Luckhurst and in a match in which we were struggling to make the rampant hosts bat again. It was simply not fit for purpose. In fact, I'm not sure it would have stayed intact had you dropped an average-sized bar of soap on it in the washroom. Come to think of it, it looked awfully like those pink soap trays you used to get in pub toilets.

Nowadays, batsmen are much better protected around the groin, but this thing turned into a kind of medieval torture implement when it split. Full of breath holes, it splintered into several shards and rearranged itself around my orchestra stalls. The initial pain struck me as the ball hit the bullseye, a nanosecond before it clamped its plasticky jaws around my tackle. No wonder that I sank to my knees and jack-knifed straight onto my head in the most extreme pain. Just thinking about the moment makes my voice ascend an octave or two.

Thankfully, Bernard Thomas, our tour physio, was soon on the scene to assess things. Now looking a chap's nether regions was not the kind of task he had signed up for, I'm sure, but boy was I glad for his handling of a delicate situation. Imagine a cactus growing the wrong way out of its pot. Apologies if that was too graphic, but it's the best description I can provide of the landscape when, once I had been helped from the field, my trousers were removed in the dressing room.

All this because I was in the wrong place at the wrong time – for the particular delivery in question rather than my location I mean, although some might suggest the wrong place on both counts. I simply got myself too square-on and immediately knew there was trouble looming as I prodded lamely down the wrong line. Without doubt the ball would have passed above stump level, but unfortunately it wasn't given the chance as it clattered into muggins here.

That pain in the neck – which had plagued me for the much of the tour and got worse towards the end after I damaged two vertebrae taking evasive action at short leg when Bob Willis was bowling against New South Wales, ruling me out of the sixth and final Test – had led to more pain elsewhere. To show how much the game has moved on, there were no chestguards, armguards or double thigh pads, just a rolled-up magazine or an old pair of socks shoved down your trousers if you felt extra padding was necessary. Ducking and swaying were essential to survival, but I had lost some of the agility necessary.

Being struck amidships is not something you forget. There are few things that leave me completely speechless but that is one of them, and there was nothing I suffered in my cricketing career to compare to that blow from Thommo. Mike Selvey, who was brisk rather than rapid among the fast-bowling fraternity, did double me over in a county match at Lord's once by shaping one back into me. Concerned he might be fretting over my well-being post play, I considered the most responsible course of action to be a visit to the Middlesex dressing room to put his mind at rest. 'Don't worry, Selve,' I grinned. 'Compared to Thommo, you were a pleasure.'

You know as an England opener in Australia that you're going to cop some, and the crowds can turn pretty vociferous when aroused. They like to see their Poms barbecued medium rare, and during the Perth Test when I was batting alongside the recalled 41-year-old Colin Cowdrey the crowd-baiting turned to applause for every over we survived. Of course, it was laced with sarcasm. It wasn't support for our efforts. Sadistically, they just wanted to prolong the misery.

During the first innings of that match, we were fairly well placed at 99 for one before the rot set in. Cowdrey, who had been flown out in an emergency (following my fielding practice-induced finger break as well as John Edrich and Dennis Amiss being crocked at the Gabba), became my room-mate and we were reunited for over an hour, repelling over after eight-ball over in stultifying conditions. However, when the pitches gave Lillee and Thomson any kind of encouragement they proved an awesome pairing, and once we were parted the team plunged from a decent-looking position to 208 all out.

The hellish demands their speed and bounce placed on you stopped short of frightening, but it made you extremely wary, particularly when facing someone as rapid as Thommo. The Australian tactic of targeting the body of batsmen was reminiscent of Bodyline, but all well within the laws and therefore a decent one.

The hairs stood up on the back of your neck walking to the crease anticipating a serious 'do' from them, and the exaggerated lift that a Perth pitch offered – it has always been a venue where batsmen have been able to leave on length on off-stump – made life uncomfortable when the ball was straighter, and there were plenty of bumpers, as Cowdrey was so fond of calling them.

Although I was not overly prolific on my return to the side, in my defence there were very few scoring opportunities against a backdrop of chin music, and in addition to top-scoring with 49 in the first innings, the six hours seven minutes I remained at the crease across the match was longer than anybody else managed.

I had spent another hour or so in the company of Colin, the equivalent of cricket royalty, after we marched out as new opening partners trying to erode a 273-run deficit on first innings. Days shy of his forty-second birthday he may have been and twenty years since he made his England debut, but there was still a touch of class about him. He turned up on the tour looking rather lavish in a pinstripe suit, every inch the archetypal gentleman. He even smiled at the young autograph hunter who verbally abused him at the end of a day's play. 'Marvellous,' he said, signing the lad's book, showing the unflappable nature and restraint we all needed to imitate in the face of such provocation.

On arriving in the middle for this WACA warfare, Cowdrey introduced himself: 'Mr Thomson, I believe. How good to meet you.' The reply he got was rather uncouth, comprising the words 'piss off' and 'fatso', befitting the image of an archetypal Aussie hoodlum.

But Colin lived to a certain standard and was not one to let those standards drop. I had found that out to my cost as a young Lancashire player some seven years earlier during a County Championship match against Kent. Back in that era, county teams did not always travel with a twelfth man in tow to away matches. So in instances of injury, a substitute fielder was borrowed from the home team at a cost of a pound. That was the equivalent of doing a day's overtime for very little effort and therefore not to be sniffed at. In the majority of cases, you stood a bit like a statue at mid-on and mid-off. Unfortunately, however, this was exactly what I did when Kent came to Southport for a County Championship match in 1967. Summoned on to the field for what was a relatively short passage of play, I promptly dropped two catches – one in each position.

'Tell me about your twelfth man,' Cowdrey diplomatically said to Statham later that evening. 'What *exactly* is his role in the game?'

My role in this second Test match had been to remain in unison with him as long as possible, but we were separated with the score on 52 by my tickle on the tackle. Colin was dismissed soon after-wards, and so when I returned to the crease early next morning at 106 for two it was Mike Denness, the captain, that I resumed alongside.

I could cope with the anticipated pantomime jeers and showed some determination to outlast Denness and another couple of partners until I was sixth out. But there was a limit to what I could contribute to the total due to the discomfort from my existing ailment, which required treatment before just about every match on that tour. It undoubtedly handicapped my strokeplay because my head was set in a crooked position, and standing almost chest on meant that I effectively closed off the off-side, negating the majority of shots on that side of the wicket.

It was very hard to turn at the crease and I was frustrated and angry that I couldn't actually do what I wanted to do with a bat in my hand. So, although the blow I took in Perth was well doc-umented, an equally significant one had been dealt to my ego.

The reality was that despite a couple of fighting 40s I never made it to a half century, and numbers are the proof of your qual-ity at the highest level. While never the kind of batsman to take an opposition apart, even in my most carefree days, had I been able to grind out a hundred against this top-class attack, I would have made a case for retention beyond that winter. Instead, that tour dished out the harsh reality that despite my best efforts my career as a Test player was in jeopardy of being terminated sooner rather than later.

Having failed to convert my opportunities, albeit in the tough-est environment of all, it offered others their shot. I guess for the short time I had my own spot in it – often wedged in the dressing room between like-minded fellows such as Bob Willis and Mike Hendrick – Boycott was the elephant in the dressing room for me, even though it would be a while before he returned to the England side.

Confirmation that I'd be going on the trip came in official cor-respondence from the Test and County Cricket Board, penned by Donald Carr, in late August. At that stage, I did not even possess a passport. All the paraphernalia for the tour followed in one leather cricket bag: the England tour blazer, MCC cap and sweater, shirts and trousers all tucked inside. When we landed in Australia we arrived in a cloud of smoke. Do not misconstrue this and imagine sixteen prize fighters sauntering down the runway steps in a box-ing-style walk-on. It was just that in those days long-haul flights were dotted with folk with fags hanging out their mouths.

It made me chuckle when I saw an Instagram photo posted by Kevin Pietersen when he returned from Australia's Big Bash League in February 2015 – he had pulled back his eye mask and taken a selfie on what appeared to be one of those reclining beds, surrounded by personal gadgets, no doubt with click-your-fingers waitress service thrown in. The only luxury we could expect shoved at the back of the big bird in economy would have been some cough mixture to counter the spluttering and wheezing. Upon arrival we had to make do with very basic accommodation, two to a room, with hotel gyms and splash pools not even a twinkle in that other David Lloyd's eye.

The previous England team that had travelled to Australia in 1970-71, under the captaincy of Ray Illingworth, had returned victorious, of course, a truly historic win for an England team down under. John Snow was a key figure in that victory, and he had really riled the Australians with his refusal to back down in any contest. Unfortunately, this time he was not in our party.

From the moment we arrived, Australia were determined to show they were the better team and that they would avenge that defeat by Illingworth and Co four years earlier. And it is fair to say that we were caught on the hop by a combination of their initial Test line-up and an overwhelmingly comfortable warm-up period on the pitch, incorporating two wins and two draws against the state sides ahead of the first Test.

Despite this, there were problems. We landed in Australia in late October 1974, and were involved in four four-day games between 1 and 25 November. Given all the travelling logistics such a huge country provides, this was a gruelling schedule, and it was made especially so for our bowlers, who were not accustomed to bowling eight-ball overs.

Four decades on, armed with high-energy drinks, diet and nutritional advice, and directed by strength and conditioning experts, an England touring party is light years ahead of where we were. There is no doubt we were a fit bunch, but had we been tested I'm sure we would all have been flirting with the danger zone when it came to hydration as we fielded or batted.

While we understood the need to get fluids on board, there was nothing like Gatorade (apologies for the product placement, other sports drinks are available but come less readily to mind). Sure, we drank whenever there was a break in play, but what we drank was extraordinary by contemporary standards. It was called a brown cow. A brown cow, would you believe, was an intriguing mixture of Coca-Cola and milk. Meanwhile, back in county cricket, strength and conditioning would have amounted to an arm wrestle with your mates at the lunch table, while being careful not to knock over the beer bottles clumped in the middle – because for each home county match at Old Trafford, crates of Watney's Red Barrel would be passed around.

Our kit wasn't ideal, either. It was furnace hot and we were sporting these bloody great socks, made from thick wool that would have come in handy had Test cricket reached the Arctic Circle. The tour jumper was wool too – thick, cable knit. Not a thought was given to the damage the sun could do us, either. We would go sunbathing on our rare days off, sleeves rolled up and shirts unbuttoned to top up tans; a few would cover their heads with sunhats, but others would be slapping on low-factor tanning oils, such was the world's general ignorance when it came to skin cancer in that era.

Unsurprisingly, the tour physio Bernard Thomas had his work cut out. His daily duties included stretching the fast bowlers, which entailed the likes of Bob Willis and Mike Hendrick putting the back of one of their heels up on Bernard's shoulder, and Bernard raising up on his toes to extend their hamstrings. This, of course, was more acceptable physical contact with one of the players than the incident in Perth when, during his examination of me, I pleaded with him: 'Can you take the pain away but leave the swelling?'

I hope Bernard agreed a good overtime rate for that tour, as our chastening on-field experiences during that 4-1 defeat gave him plenty of work. It was a reprise of the bouncer war that Illy won on the previous tour. Things had not gone well for any of us, almost from the moment we landed in Darwin. Denness, our captain, suffered from pleurisy in the early days of the tour, and was absent for a few weeks while in recovery. Then, there was the range of injuries to contend with: my little finger broken in fielding practice, John Edrich broke a bone in his hand in the opening Test of six and later broke a rib in Sydney, while Dennis Amiss also fractured a finger in Brisbane.

What began as an adventure of a lifetime – a first foray overseas for yours truly – soon had the excitement sucked out of it. I had never been on a plane, other than a light aircraft flight over Blackpool on an early childhood holiday, so going on a trip like that was fairly daunting. The roar of the take-off was otherworldly and held an excitement all of its own.

Yet, for a cricketer with aspirations of an international career, there had been several moments to relish ahead of the epic journey, not least toddling off to the Stuart Surridge factory to select my two tour bats. When we got to Australia, we undertook all the usual tourist photos – posing, cuddling koalas under gum trees or in front of a family of kangaroos, or pretending to fish in Sydney Harbour.

However, this was going to turn out anything but a jolly. Of course, we were quite confident about our prospects given our performances against India and Pakistan at home that summer. But results in our own conditions against that kind of opposition didn't necessarily tell us where we were at compared to the team Australia was putting together. We arrived feeling that we would be very competitive, and this feeling was reinforced by our early results.

Unfortunately, as several eminent Australians later reminded me, I had made the mistake in the build-up of claiming I could play their attack with my manhood. From what we had seen, it was hardly a bowling line-up to strike fear into an international opening batsman. How those words would come back to haunt (not to mention hurt) me, and given what was to happen, I should perhaps explain why I said it in the first place.

First of all, few anticipated Dennis Lillee being declared fit, and when he was, on the eve of the series, it undoubtedly gave the Australians a boost. The main thrust of the pre-series talk had been that Lillee was not going to play. He had suffered a serious back injury, spinal fractures that had caused him to be set in plaster from his backside to his shoulders for six weeks earlier in 1974, and he was rumoured to be behind schedule in his recovery.

In his absence, there appeared to be little to fret about, and if anything Australia's bowling stocks seemed thin. Gary Gilmour and David Colley, with a handful of caps between them, shared the new ball for New South Wales against us ahead of the first Test.

And the name Thomson that kept recurring held little fear for us. As well as this beach bum Jeff, who had gone round the park for a ton without success versus Pakistan a year earlier, there was Victoria's Alan Thomson, otherwise known as Froggy because of the way he sprang to the crease and bowled off the wrong foot. He had featured on England's last visit four winters previously, but hardly covered himself in glory with figures of 17-0-85-0 against us for his state this time around. Unfortunately, it was the man who would forever be known as Thommo who would force us into a rapid reassessment.

Thomson had only recently arrived on the scene, and proved a potent weapon for Australia not only due to his slingy action, which made the ball nigh-on impossible to pick up until very late, but because of his indefatigable spirit. He just charged in all day long and provided no respite. Mentally, countering him was made tougher by the fact that in Australian first-class cricket they were still using eight-ball overs. You would get through four and then realise the job was only half done.

Queenslander Thomson had looked nothing like the ferocious beast unleashed for just his second Test appearance, when he lined up on his home ground for the tour fixture with England just a few weeks earlier. His tactical coasting was on instruction from Australia captain Ian Chappell, who was keen for his new tyro to get a look at our batsmen but deny them a proper study of his true self.

Occasionally, you are pitched against bowlers who make it more difficult for a batsman to be able to do that because of slight quirks in their actions. With Thommo it was almost impossible, because he didn't let you see the ball at all as he wound up to wang it down. With other people, you knew where their hands were going and you could watch the ball all the way because it was visible. But with him, you just never saw it because the way his arm dragged behind him, with his body tilted backwards before uncoiling like a giant spring, meant it remained behind him until the last possible moment, and then it was coming at you with frightening velocity.

So unrefined was this hoodlum from out in the sticks that he didn't even have a measured run-up when he first started his professional career. During net sessions, he just shuffled up and slung it down, which is probably why he overstepped so often. There were thirteen no-balls from Thomson in that first Test and plenty of others we reckoned too. Word had it that Chappell was on his shoulder after the first couple, realising that his inexperienced paceman was struggling with his stride pattern.

'How many paces do I do, skipper?' Thommo asked him.

'What do you mean? I've no idea. Don't you know?'

'Nah, I've always walked back to where the tree is at this end – but they've cut it down!'

This one-man sonic boom, as someone rather aptly coined him, was such a pure talent that it had never occurred to him to get the tape measure out, as is the contemporary tendency for the fast men. These days a measure and tape, plus some white spray to mark initials in the grass, are essential accessories in a player's kitbag. But marking out meticulously just wasn't in keeping with Thommo's maverick style.

So when that most wonderful of fast-bowling combinations came together for the first Test, we were taken by surprise. We had fallen for the local propaganda that suggested this gruesome two-some were by no means certain of starting the series. Lillee, possibly a yard slower than the bowler the world had witnessed in the 1972 Ashes, was the artist and Thomson the artisan.

And how the great Tony Greig made us pay for his actions too. No Test cricket series possesses so rich a rhetoric as the Ashes, and the war in this chapter was started by the Poms, according to Lillee. For it was Greig's decision to bounce Lillee in the first innings of that first Test in Brisbane that got the blood pumping below that hairy chest and medallion.

As Lillee regained his feet and brushed past Greig, having been caught behind attempting to hook, he said to his adversary: 'Just remember who started this.' Now, forget who picked the fight, there was no question who finished it, although at the same time Greig for one never shirked any sign of confrontation.

In such an arena things can get fractious to say the least, but there was no talk of bringing the game into disrepute, no physical gesturing or in-your-face ranting, after this quiet verbal exchange. The Australians played unbelievably hard but they were fair, and to his credit Greig never lost his showman image in the heat of battle, signalling his own fours whenever he opened those big shoulders of his, much to the chagrin of his Australian adversaries. It all added to the drama. Not that the wonderful new-ball crafts-man Lillee appreciated it when Greig uppercut to the fence and then dropped down or leant forward to wave his right hand to the audience like a music hall conductor.

It was actually fairly extraordinary that the opening defeat took place at all, because in the build up to that Gabba contest the weather had been horrific. All kinds of storms had hit

Queensland and the ground had been under water, but the mayor of Brisbane stepped up his efforts to get the game on. The great Richie Benaud told a television audience he feared it would be a 'mud heap' following the most controversial pitch preparation in Anglo-Australian history, after the use of a heavy roller led to fears that this had caused a dangerous ridge at the Vulture Street end. You see Alderman Clem Jones, the mayor in question, doubled up as groundsman, one of the stranger job shares you will come across, surely.

Having sacked the local curator, he had taken over ground duties himself, and there he was slaving away in a cork hat, pair of shorts and vest by day before switching into his chains and robes to host the two teams at an official function on the evening before the series began. So sodden was the square, in fact, that as the clock ticked down to the first ball, it was difficult to ascertain which strip the match would be contested on, and it only became visible on that penultimate day.

These fears about the pitch proved misplaced. However, the match was full of short stuff from both sides as the bowlers tested out the underprepared surface's bounce. Six Australian batsmen were out hooking or pulling after Ian Chappell won the toss and batted first, a decision that spoke of his assessment of the surface.

Australia scored 309 and a 44-run first-innings advantage was more than handy on a pitch that was bound to deteriorate as the sun dried it out. For those of us who had questioned why we should be fearful of a bowler who had taken none for a hundred and plenty in his only previous Test, we found out during that first innings as Thomson bowled frighteningly quick – into the wind!

The thunderbolts proved even deadlier in the second – which courted controversy when the debut umpire Robin Bailhache ordered Ian Chappell not to bowl him and Lillee on the fourth evening as he was concerned that with a storm brewing it was not acceptable light for their three-bouncer-an-over policy. Thomson took six for 46, figures he would never better in Test cricket, we went 1-0 behind and, after what had just unfolded, were destined to discover the quickest pitches possible at each of the other established Australian international venues.

Several England batsmen received painful blows to their person during the series and it wasn't like we hadn't been warned. The whole of Australia knew what was coming courtesy of their television coverage. Every evening there seemed to be an interview screened with one Australian player or other during which they spelt out how they were going to marmalise the Poms.

Arguably, the most memorable was when Thomson declared: 'Truthfully, I enjoy hitting a batsman more than getting him out. It doesn't worry me in the least to see the batsman hurt, rolling around screaming and blood on the pitch.'

As an opening batsman you are bargaining from a position of weakness, but I always liked to keep relations with those hurling that leather sphere down at me at the speed of light on an even keel. Dennis Amiss took the same approach, and so the pair of us tried to maintain a certain friendliness, for self-preservation as much as anything else. We were united in the opinion that dealing with short stuff on those encouraging surfaces was an inevitability, so why antagonise our opponents into sending down any more.

Others among the touring group were more feisty, including Essex's Keith Fletcher, whose enthusiastic response from gully at a Greig bouncer clattering into Dennis Lillee's elbow was: 'Well bowled, give him another.'

Lillee's response was to turn his head in Fletcher's direction and warn: 'It'll be your f***ing turn soon!'

In case Gnome was in any doubt that he was on Lillee's hit list, he was reminded in the post-play interviews when the interviewer alluded to relationships between the two teams.

'The Poms are a good set of blokes, I get on with all of 'em,' he said, before looking down the camera lens. 'Except that little weasel Fletcher, that is. I know you're watching, Fletcher, and you might as well know I am going to sort you out.'

True to his word, Lillee roared in to him whenever he came to the crease and, having received a painful blow on the elbow earlier in the tour, he was now dodging bouncers helmetless as Lillee sent down the full artillery in Sydney, culminating in one that failed to get up as much as the rest which took a chunk of bat and struck him straight on the head, flooring the England No. 5 batsman in the process, and careering the ball to Ross Edwards in the covers.

'Blimey, he's only gone and knocked St George off his 'orse,' gasped Geoff Arnold, in reference to the emblem on the front of the MCC caps, as we sat in the dressing room watching the drama unfold.

The tour may have meant misery in terms of results, but I did not view the whole Australia experience in the same vein. Sure, it would bring my Test career to a shuddering halt, there was the nagging neck injury to contend with, but as a young shaver on tour it was an eye-opening adventure whenever we ventured into the bush away from the cities.

My only England tour was also an environment for making lifelong pals in some cases and strengthening friendships with others. Because of the number of established pros in the group – men such as Cowdrey, John Edrich, Fred Titmus and Brian Luckhurst – there was something natural about my 27-year-old self's gravitation towards the younger clan. Tony Greig was the gregarious leader of every party going, a real life-and-soul charac-ter, while Bob Taylor, Bob Willis, Chris Old and Mike Hendrick all offered great companionship.

It wasn't that I disliked the combative nature of the competi-tion – contrary to opinion elsewhere, sledging didn't exist, at least not when I was on the field, and I was for four of the six Tests. I knew Ian Chappell, the Australian captain, through Lancashire League cricket and his brand of leadership was tough and uncompromising for opponents. Crucially, however, it never passed the threshold into abuse. My only beef from a cricket perspective was that I couldn't do better.

Greig was the one with the character best suited to stand up to the Australian bravado, his wonderful all-round ability notwithstanding. Alan Knott's nuggety style also had its merits when England came under the cosh, which is something Lillee and Thomson and a troop of wonderful batsmen ensured we did on a regular basis. There was the languid strokeplay of the Chappell brothers, big contributions from Ross Edwards and Ian Redpath, and the irrepressible Doug Walters, who smoked like a chimney but had the talent to be dubbed the new Don Bradman, and emulated the Don by hitting an Ashes hundred in a single session at Perth.

Only once when the series was alive, in the first innings of the drawn third match – Melbourne's maiden Boxing Day Test after the Australian authorities rearranged their fixture calendar to accommodate a six-match affair – did we manage a lead on first innings. And even then only by a single run. It was not the first time that Knott top-scored with a useful contribution towards the end of an innings.

For its even-contested nature alone, the match in Melbourne was by far the best of the series, and offered the prospect of all four results as it concluded. Set 246 to win, Australia headed into the final fifteen overs with 55 runs required and five wickets intact, but were contained by our Steptoe and Son combination of Fred Titmus and Derek Underwood before Australia made a late dash against the second new ball.

Despite some powerful hitting, Tony Greig, who had caused typical crowd uproar with his theatrical pointing to the pavilion upon dismissing Rod Marsh, was given the ball by Mike Denness and when it ended up in his captain's hands at cover when nine runs were needed from three balls with three wickets left, it kept the series alive. Our chances of victory remained to the end, but Australia finished on 238 for eight, eight runs shy of their target.

My personal experience of the Australian crowds that winter was that the banter that flew about was mainly of a good-hearted nature. The infamous Bay 13 at the MCG was marvellous actually, although not necessarily if you were the one positioned on its boundary edge, as Derek Underwood happened to be on one occasion during that Ashes series. They broke Deadly pretty quickly, to the point where he protested about fielding there.

Typically of the man, Greig said he would go down there and take the verbal slingshots. True to the old adage, the words never hurt him, but it was a ritual for the Bay 13 lot to start throwing sticks and stones once into a mild state of inebriation. This lot could be loutish when stone cold sober, and in the absence of actual sticks and stones would use anything else they could get their hands on. The bombardment normally began with lumps of ice. More often than not it went from single ice cubes, to handfuls of ice, finishing with the final assault of the remnants of their cool boxes. Tony was not one to walk away from confrontation, so he naturally started lugging these frozen missiles back with interest.

Dennis Amiss and I had shared a century stand at the MCG, and I followed my 44 there with 49 in England's first win over Australia on the tour – the one-day international arranged on New Year's Day 1975, immediately after the Test had concluded, and organised because of the success of the hastily carded corresponding fixture in 1970-71.

From a personal perspective, I'd had my strokes of luck – caught behind in Perth on 17 in the second innings, Australia failed to appeal, then Ian Chappell sportingly owned up that a catch had not carried in Melbourne – yet also departed to a couple of blinders during that series to Greg Chappell in the gully and Jeff Thomson in the deep. All part of the swings and roundabouts of Test cricket, I guess.

A draw and a win in Melbourne was undoubtedly a balm to our spirits and we headed to Sydney with greater belief. Unfortunately, the pendulum of power had swung only temporarily and another roasting meant the Ashes had gone. At that stage, my average for the series remained on the right side of 30, but a pair of single-figure contributions in the Australia Day Test in Adelaide sent it south. Like the team I was representing, I was not good enough and those scores of four and five were to be my last in the Test arena.

Aggravation of my neck injury in our second meeting with New South Wales did not prevent me turning out at the Adelaide Oval, but it became clear that it needed rest so, as the sixth and final Test opened in Melbourne, I was preparing to fly home early. The law of the sod was on hand with another cruel twist of fate: their endeavours over the series had taken their toll on Thomson, who also missed the match, and Lillee, who contributed only six overs before limping out of it, and without them it was a totally different ball game.

England, in my absence, stacked up 529 – comfortably more than we had made across two innings at the Adelaide Oval – the tour ended in a run-fest, a victory and the saving of both face and Test places for some. I was on a different path. My Test chance had come smack bang in the middle of my career – nine years after debut, nine before retirement. I was privileged to answer Donald Carr's invitation to tour Australia in the affirmative, but I was realistic enough to reflect that for all the high praise about my ticker when under siege, I was operating at full capacity to hold back the dam. It had burst and there would be no more tours.

CHAPTER 9

Jack of all Trades

Intuition told me that I was soon to become an ex-Test cricketer, and when you're willing to even consider that prospect there is only one way your career is realistically heading. At least that's what I thought in those initial months after returning from Australia, for it later became apparent in fits and starts over the next, and final, nine years of my career that there were other goals, albeit lesser ones, to achieve. I had reached the zenith of my career that previous winter and there was contentment in doing so, just as there was frustration that I was now returning to the rank and file of county cricket.

It would be wrong to suggest that I didn't have some enjoyable times during this period; for example relinquishing the captaincy at Old Trafford provided an instantly liberating effect on my individual game. Some time later, the national selectors would call once more, and in the twilight of my career I was nearly the restorative Mike Brearley figure. I may have been dwelling in the international wilderness, playing just once more in the 1970s, but when England were looking for a leader at the turn of the next decade, I had some conversations which offered hope that it might be me. Had I made a better fist of things, that legendary 1981

Ashes might have had a different protagonist trying to get the best out of Ian Botham.

Some of the pizzazz was lost from the international stage during the late 1970s due to the emergence of World Series Cricket, which meant that many players were unable to play in Tests for a while, but that didn't dilute the ambitions of Englishmen when it came to playing for their country. My efforts were rewarded with a single call-up, for an appearance against Pakistan, between travelling home from the 1974-75 Ashes and the start of the 1980 summer. So despite scoring two Benson & Hedges Cup hundreds – against Derbyshire and Scotland – and an unbeaten 90 in a John Player Special League win over Gloucestershire as an opening batsman in the fortnight building up to the international curtain being raised, a recall at the age of thirty-three was a surprise.

Yet that was not the full story because they wanted me to be the experienced head down the order, the hinge at No. 7, and if I acquitted myself okay, I would be under consideration to lead England in the near future. At the time there was an issue over who should be captain, and a strong feeling that there was too much responsibility on an all-rounder like the 24-year-old Botham.

So while they made him captain for that summer, they also primed some older candidates, like myself, Keith Fletcher and Mike Brearley, that an opportunity might present itself in the not-so-distant future.

For the previous five years, I had come to terms with being a former international batsman – that solitary limited-overs match against Pakistan in 1978 being very much a call out of the blue – but any cricketer with pride never entirely gives up hope of forcing their way back in.

However, my last life as an England player spanned just two days – the length of a weather-interrupted opening match of the Prudential Trophy at Headingley. West Indies had made 198 in their 55 overs on a day of interruptions for rain and bad light. We had closed on 35 for three after gritting it out for 23 overs against their lauded pace attack. Resuming the match next morning with the required run rate at five runs per over for victory, the end of a brief Botham flurry signalled my entrance to face Malcolm Marshall.

It was to prove a painful reintroduction as an England batsman. Marshall pushed off out of the pile of sawdust, charged down the slope and let go one of his customary searing deliveries that comfortably defeated my defensive prod off the back foot and imprinted a Duke tattoo on my right forearm. Despite the pain and embarrassment I actually carried on, although not for long, my ignominy completed when I was bowled by Gordon Greenidge – yours truly his first and only international wicket.

The swollen arm was a memento of my final time in international action, preventing me playing in the next match at Lord's. However, worse was to follow as it wasn't the impact that caused most discomfort in the aftermath. Once the swelling had gone down in my right arm I resumed playing for Lancashire, but greater and greater discomfort developed in my left one and would not go away. Initially, the medics thought I had tennis elbow and so administered a cortisone injection that didn't make a blind bit of difference.

X-rays later revealed an astonishing conclusion: on the ball's impact with my right arm my left jarred down awkwardly, causing a piece of bone to dislodge inside. There had been some reverberation through my neck and all the way down into my left elbow; surgery was required and to this day I still have a rather extensive scar as a reminder. If there was a funny side to any of it, it came when Mr Glass, my Manchester surgeon, offered me a sherry before, with the aid of four blokes to hold me still, he administered a cortisone jab.

It was the end to a sobering experience and one that probably should not have taken place. Although I had orchestrated a successful one-day county team, I should not have been picked again. Indeed, I should not have retained realistic hope of a recall once I'd been overlooked for the 1975 Ashes, which was shortened to four matches due to the presence in the calendar of the inaugural World Cup. A sign that I wasn't too far back in the pack was given when I was chosen in the MCC representative team to take on the Australians.

I had returned from Australia with continued discomfort in my neck but with a determination to rail against the feeling that my number of Test caps would not reach double figures. Although I put on a century stand with Graham Gooch, the new kid on the block and as yet uncapped, it was he, not I, who was picked for the first Test at Edgbaston, where he made an infamous pair. So good was his England record in future years that it was hard to believe he had started with nothing.

Lancashire went well enough under my stewardship that year and threatened a first Championship triumph for a quarter of a century, before dropping off at the business end. That meant we had only the Gillette Cup to show for our season's efforts. I say *only* because such was our proficiency in one-day cricket that we could be forgiven for becoming blasé about success in that competition. In contrast to the team's results, however, my own form was sketchy and my batting lacked fluency.

There was just one hundred to show for it, against the champions Leicestershire in Blackpool, when I scraped to three figures in the 100th and last over of the innings. Competition rules that year restricted first innings to this 100-over limit and it took a horrible slog and equally horrible dropped catch from Raymond Illingworth for me to secure the two runs to take me off 98.

Afterwards, Illingworth wasn't the first Yorkshireman to suggest one of mine was the worst innings he had ever seen. Richard Hutton was not very complimentary about one of my innings in a Roses match, although at least Raymond's dismissal of my efforts followed a first-class hundred. One of my career regrets was not to make one against the old enemy.

There was some talk about my stepping down towards the end of the 1975 season but I didn't necessarily link my productivity, or lack of it, with the bat to the leadership of the team, and the speculation in the *Daily Mail* that I was to quit was dispelled when just a fortnight after getting my hands on that elusive first trophy as captain, I was reappointed for the following year.

The following two winters I did get tour places, but unfortunately these comprised only the Derrick Robins XI's venture to South Africa, which spanned five weeks, and a place on the plane as an ex-Ashes participant for the Centenary Test against Australia. Qualification was four Tests and I had squeezed in, just. The South Africa tour held a real thrill for me, because I had been chosen as captain and Ken Barrington, my hero as a youngster, was the manager. They say you shouldn't meet your heroes but Ken was an exception to this rule, as he proved to be one of the finest blokes I've ever met. A great player, averaging 57 in Test cricket, he possessed even greater humility.

A subconscious admission that my career was winding down was also made in this period, as I tentatively began accepting a clutch of after-dinner speaking engagements. Despite feeling comfortable behind a microphone and with a television camera pointed at me at Sky Sports, to this day I cannot say that I've ever enjoyed getting up and speaking to a drunken audience that demands that you make them laugh. Getting those laughs was generally not a problem, as I found out over many years, although my inherent shyness stopped me relishing these occasions.

Back on the field, I spent the majority of the 1976 season down the order to accommodate Andrew Kennedy at its top, but returned to opening with a measure of success by making 82 against the touring West Indians in mid-June. The hostility of the

West Indies appealed to my love of situations when the odds were against me: in adversity I played some of my best innings.

After the highs of the previous years, however, this offered something of a low: next to bottom in the Championship, we also tasted a rare defeat at Lord's when Northamptonshire took the Gillette Cup off us. I'm sure some of the cleaning staff thought we had been robbed that following winter, as they had become so used to seeing the cup in the trophy cabinet.

Even in defeat, however, there was fun to be unearthed in the Lancashire dressing room thanks to the wonderful Farokh Engineer. No matter that it was a Lord's final, he was once again at his persuasive best, with the opposition's opening bowler the subject of his well-loved 'lifting' negotiation.

John Dye – known to us as Dr Dye, the Queen of Seam, a bloke who had a Bobby Charlton sweep of hair flopping on the breeze – would saunter in on an angle from another postcode with the wrist of his bowling arm cocking up and down along the way. Farokh insisted: 'I can lift this man, Bumble.'

Having been given his opportunity to prove it, he got bowled through his legs for nought, having an almighty hack. He was spitting feathers when he got back through the Long Room and into the dressing room.

'What's up, Farokh?'

'The arsehole Dye bowled when I wasn't ready.'

'You what? This bloke runs in forty yards!'

One of the other amusing idiosyncrasies of our wonderful over-seas recruit was his adoption of the fast bowlers' chunterings, or his own pidgin versions at least. For example, Peter Lee and Peter Lever might greet an inside edge for four with a shout of: 'Well, f**k my old boots.' In contrast, Farokh, in his distinctive Indian lilt, would mutter: 'F**k, old, boot,' every time a ball flew over the slips or dropped just short. We used to kill ourselves laughing.

If you talked about the great wicketkeepers of the time, the conversation would have started with the names of Alan Knott, Bob Taylor and Farokh Engineer, and not gone much further. Here was a natural player who hated practising but had these wonderful hands and a great eye. One of his cameos with the bat resulted in him scoring 96 versus West Indies – before lunch. Farokh was a real showman behind the stumps, an extravagant, exuberant player.

He used to get me in on the act too. Being left-handed, I would be at leg slip to the spinners Jack Simmons or David Hughes, and Farokh would tell me to flick the ball back quickly whenever I could. It became second nature to dive away to my left and return it in one motion, and Farokh would shimmy the bails and lob it to slip all in one movement. It used to draw a real reaction from the crowd. However, when he was missing one week playing for India, it meant Keith Goodwin took his place behind the stumps. Of course, I produced my usual party piece and Goody happened to be looking the wrong way when the ball struck him flush on the ear lobe. Cue a chain of expletives from our former army man, one of the most frightening I've ever met. Thanks, Farokh.

After the drought of 1976, the summer of 1977 was so wet that it ruined the season and dampened my love of the game. Best estimates suggested we lost twenty days of Championship action due to the elements, and there was no real enjoyment when we did make it onto the field. The way I felt was clearly shared by the team. We just weren't enjoying our cricket as a collective anymore, and it was obviously time for me to quit as leader. I handed in my resignation as captain that October.

Ironically, following erroneous newspaper reports that I was to pack in altogether twelve months later, this is something I did actually consider at the end of 1979, only to be talked out of it by the club, who persuaded me to sign a new two-year contract. I'm not certain they would have had the appetite to do so had Barry Wood not moved on at the end of his benefit year.

Thoughts of quitting opened my mind to other careers. I had dabbled in loads, yet – although it was true that the Old Trafford I once loved had lost its appeal and work became a chore –– none of the alternatives had sufficient appeal to entice me away. Cricket is what I knew best; what I had once loved and would come to love again. But for a time, life as a professional player took on a different veneer. What I had once viewed as adventures around the circuit, meeting up with familiar adversaries, became a monotonous trek to take on the same old faces. The county beat was losing its appeal.

There were several reasons that I developed a more negative view. Jack Bond was now back at the club as manager, but in my thirties I was not as much help to him as I had been a decade earlier, and on more than one occasion I was dropped as injuries bit and my form dipped. There's no doubt that once you become an established player you feel immune to being overlooked in selection, and it therefore makes it all the more painful when it happens, as it does to 95 per cent of players.

As so many discover, the ageing process does not help. My biggest problem was my eyesight and my refusal to acknowledge that I was struggling to see the ball as the decade drew to its end. Indeed, it took me a long time to wear glasses as a cricketer, because I felt doing so would jeopardise my chances of winning new deals at the club. Once it was made public that I was struggling, I thought that would be the end for me. I kept putting myself in the place of a committee man considering my future: 'This bloke can't see, get rid.'

Fear of being binned made me very wary of admitting any such problem existed, so this period was laced with frustration. The one thing I could see was that I wasn't picking the ball up early enough when batting, and when I eventually got my eyes tested it revealed that I was actually seeing an oval ball rather than a spherical one. Even then, being self-conscious, sometimes I would wear the specs I had been given and sometimes I wouldn't. I had recently started to wear a helmet, of course, and because of its clunkiness, glasses and helmets didn't really go together. It all felt a little bit alien.

However, the prescription coincided with a general upturn in my fortunes. So much so, that 1982 represented something of an Indian summer for me – a mountain of runs and a first-class average in excess of 40, the first time I had managed such a feat since 1974, the year of my international debut. If only I had gone to the optician's sooner to address a natural deterioration, I might have scored a few more runs in the interim.

Towards the end of my career, there was some fun thanks to the emergence of Graeme Fowler, another Accrington lad. He and I proved inseparable, and he introduced me to all sorts of riotous music. I had never heard of Bruce Springsteen before. Then there was Southside Johnny and The Asbury Jukes. Travelling in the car together, music blaring, we would be singing like good'uns. He even got me listening to Meat Loaf, and I wasn't the only one in cricket that was ignorant of this man's work.

Lieutenant Colonel John Stephenson, the secretary of the MCC, was a fine old stick who cycled into work daily with the bottom of his trousers in bike clips. One day, he revealed that Lord's had received an approach from an American popstar to appear at the ground. 'We met the man in question, and his representatives,' he said. 'And I didn't know whether it was appropriate to call him Mr Meat or Mr Loaf.' Quite.

Despite the age gap, because of our backgrounds Fowler and I were thick as thieves, and when he broke into the first team I took it upon myself to look after him. He made a fine start, scoring a hundred batting at No. 7 on his home County Championship debut in 1980, a victory over Nottinghamshire at Old Trafford. He was one of the most boisterous blokes you could meet, and he was bouncing around everywhere after that start. Unfortunately though, he couldn't maintain it and after that initial effort he simply wasn't getting any more, causing me to ask: 'How long are you going to live off that, then?' He burst into tears.

Of course, he went on to become a fine batsman for Lancashire and England, and I was soon to become an ex-batsman for Lancashire and England. By my mid-thirties, it wasn't only the recurring neck injury that was doing my head in. There didn't seem to be any respite, solution or suitable treatment for that. It was a case of me having a bit of infra-red and a rub, but never did it go away. I also battled through rehabilitation for two slipped discs in my back, courtesy of Paul Allott who put me in touch with an osteopath from Wilmslow. He would tie me in knots, give me a bit of a kick, and make me scream. Then, it was a case of, 'Arise, take up thy bed and walk.'

Transformed from a fit, young bloke to one plagued by these aches and pains, which prevented me doing what I wanted to do, meant I eventually had enough. I missed half of the 1983 season recuperating from debilitating pain down my right side stemming from my neck and woke one morning with my mind made up – my eyes and body were telling me the end was nigh as a professional cricketer. I was packing up.

In my absence, Lancashire had unearthed some exciting young talents – including a much more dashing left-hander, Neil Fairbrother. The club did not appear to need my services any longer, so it was a pleasant surprise that after I informed them of my decision they continued to select me. Even more pleasing was that I went out in style.

My final Lancashire appearance, at Wantage Road, saw me open the batting with Fowler. We both hit hundreds in a drawn match with Northamptonshire. After twenty seasons' service, there was no better way to go.

The question of 'what next?' now surfaced more strongly, and it wasn't as if I was short of options. I had experience in a raft of off-season jobs while on the Lancashire playing staff. One was with Associated Tyre Specialists, in Burnley. I wasn't so great at changing tyres, but I did pick up the mechanic's gift of the gab. 'New valve and balance, Sir?' was the standard question, because that's where your money was. Every time you did one, it was something like 150 per cent profit. Incredibly, customers nearly always said yes. It involved putting a bit of lead on the wheel and spinning it. To all intents and purposes, these tyre valves had a lifetime guarantee, but you would always ask the question.

For a while, I worked for Croft Roplasto, a Preston-based double glazing company with an outlet in Moss Side. This was rather ironic, I felt, as rumour had it there were few windows intact in Moss Side, certainly not with glass in them anyway, and I cannot recall seeing any evidence to the contrary. This, like another job I later undertook with the Wilson's Brewery in Newton Heath, was effectively one of selling, and it was clear to me from the start that I was never a salesman. That came to its end when the workforce called their bosses' bluff one time too many with strike action and the place shut down.

For me, it was a bit of a relief because the job I was engaged for involved going around the pubs and clubs persuading them to take Wilson's and Webster's drinks. They were trying to use my sporting background as an attraction for new customers. But 'Hello, I'm David Lloyd, of Lancashire and England' didn't always work, and as well as feeling an embarrassment at trying to sell myself in this way, I also lacked the capacity to cope with the social demands.

At every stop-off you would be offered a drink – that went with the territory and because there were no real drink-drive laws at the time, I could see this becoming a problem. Being offered drinks by establishments non-stop all day from 11 o'clock in the morning struck a fear into me that I could become an alcoholic if not careful.

This was a really hairy time for me because, after two decades at Old Trafford, I had left cricket, or full-time cricket at least, and yet I kept finding myself returning at the slightest opportunity. If I had an hour spare and I was close enough, I would just bob in and think nothing of sticking my head into the dressing room or sitting suited and booted on its balcony. As soon as you have retired, there is a harsh lesson in store: you no longer have a right to be there. Once you've left, you've left, simple as that, and it's no longer your domain. Once yours, it now belongs to others.

No one ever said anything on these drop-ins because they didn't have to, looks were sufficient to confirm it. When an ex-player pops in, it triggers a silence that speaks for itself. You are left under no illusions that you have outstayed your welcome and need to back off. That's not necessarily easy to take, and I was neither the first nor last to find it difficult. But I can totally understand why so many ex-players have a hard time adapting once their playing careers are over. Being part of a team environment offers a great lifestyle – all your mates, all the scrapes, the laughs, the despair you have been through together. For a while you've shared everything, then suddenly you're out on your own in the outside world, and it can contain some grim reality.

There are no guarantees of anything, and there are dozens of cases of ex-cricketers who have been unable to cope once it's all over. Thankfully, the Professional Cricketers' Association, an organisation of which I am president, are well on top of this these days and anyone who does fall into difficulties, or gets themselves into trouble, tends to be helped out a bit. Supporting your old pals is always a start, and the mainstay of our 1970s team get together now and again for a well-received catch up.

My refuge came in speaking at those dinners, which offered pretty lucrative rates of pay, and continuing to play cricket at weekends for Accrington. Going back to my roots proved a real saviour. I threw everything into my return to Thorneyholme Road, helping to spruce up the clubhouse and raise money to improve other facilities. Some people walk away from the first-class game and never pick a bat up again, but I knew I wanted to play league cricket. Being back as a player at Accrington for six years – initially as the club's professional, combining it with Minor Counties duty for Cumberland – just felt right. By that stage in life, my eldest lad Graham was coming through the club's junior ranks, so it was nice that I could be up there with him.

When you leave a dressing room for the final time, no one is showing you to your office, helping you into your chair at your new desk and asking you if you would like your morning cup of tea. I simply found another one and became pretty hands on in drumming up interest around the town.

There were other links developed with cricket at this time. For one, I got myself onto the reserve list for umpiring. That meant I was effectively on trial for a while in a bid for a second career. I was learning the trade as I went along, and over the years when I officiated, three of which were on the full list, I thoroughly enjoyed it. I might not have known it from the start, but the reconnection with Accrington and keeping my hand in with umpiring in the first-class arena was leading me towards a stint in coaching.

My interest in sports shops, stoked by working odd days in Bob Cooke's Manchester store over the years, meant I put my name to one of my own in Accrington. David Lloyd Sports became a rival to the other sports shop in the town, Gibson's, where Mum and Dad took me for my first bat a quarter of a century earlier, and Mr Gibson was pretty peeved about that. The big seller in our shop was darts and all its accessories. We were innovative because we had a dartboard up in the shop and encouraged blokes from the Working Men's Club to pop in for a game. We would sell dye tungstens in all different weights, with a variety of flights – unicorns, rainbows, skull and crossbones, the lot.

Immersing myself in Accrington life once more, as I had done as a boy, suited me just fine. I was never any good at courting. In fact, I've only ever had four girlfriends – which is unusual, I suppose, given my incredible charm. I can name each one of them: Eileen Stanton, Christine Marshall, then my first wife Susan Wallwork were all from the Methodist Church. Then, there is Diana, my second wife, the only out-of-towner of the quartet.

Typically, I always wanted to get back to Accrington. All four of my children were born there and only through marriage to Diana in 1999 has the connection with Accrington dissipated, as time has been shared between Cheadle Hulme, Cheshire and Coxwold, North Yorkshire. Even then, because all my immediate family remain in Accrington, it means I make regular trips there when I'm not overseas.

It's a bit like the majority of town centres these days in that it's run down and could do with some reviving. But just move slightly away from Accrington town centre and there are some absolutely beautiful places. The scenery and architecture are simply stunning.

Accrington always used to be a pretty tight-knit community and the cricket club reflected that. You have to remember that as well as me, the town produced Bob Ratcliffe and Graeme Fowler. There were lots of other cricketers from our small enclave of Lancashire who made it into the Old Trafford dressing room. Bernard Reidy was from Enfield, Jack Simmons came from Great Harwood and then there was Russ Cuddihy, who is still involved in coaching around the area, and Alan Worsick, a truly fantastic player who broke records at both Rawtenstall and Accrington. Eddie Robinson, a top-quality spinner, was one of the best cricketers I played with at any standard and never got further than the Lancashire League.

When I returned in the 1980s, there were some great characters to catch up with, and some naturally talked a better game than they played. Take the semi-final of the Worsley Cup in 1989 when we were drawn away at Todmorden, whose overseas professional at the time was the Sri Lankan all-rounder Ravi Ratnayeke, a handy cricketer but hardly one to put the wind up us. So we remained unperturbed about facing him at Centre Vale.

However, Ratnayeke was absent when we turned up and the sight of a beanpole West Indian strolling across the ground caused a stir. It turned out to be none other than Ian Bishop, world cricket's new fast-bowling sensation who had made his Test debut within the previous twelve months. With Ratnayeke injured, Todmorden had hired Bishop from Derbyshire for the day – a very handy piece of transfer business indeed.

Our opening pair of Nick Marsh and Andrew Barker, elder brother of Warwickshire's left-arm swing bowler Keith Barker, resisted manfully to keep Bishop at bay during his new-ball spell. Todmorden did not separate them until we had 63 on the board, in fact, and that put our wicketkeeper Billy Rawstron on the verge of going in. Now Billy had been confident enough to declare in the privacy of our own dressing room that, in his estimable opinion, this new pace sensation was not as quick as others were making out. He even shunned the idea of wearing a helmet despite others, including myself, trying to persuade him otherwise. Furthermore, if Bishop bounced him he would, he confirmed, be taking on the hook shot.

Of course, this was just asking for trouble and at 71 for two, Billy's predictions were about to be put to the test. Bishop hurtled down said bouncer and it struck Billy flush in the mouth, causing the batsman to career into his stumps as a result. Not that Billy was backing down after being brought round with a whiff of some smelling salts.

'I can't be out like that,' he declared. 'I'd completed my shot.'

'Billy, you hadn't even started it. Now let's go and see a man about some teeth,' I told him, as he was escorted from the field.

But he was nothing if not brave, Billy, and despite his predicament he refused treatment until he had completed his duties with the gloves and we had secured our place in the final via a 51-run win.

Another team-mate of that era was a lad called Neil Jones, who would chance his arm on any number of schemes to make a bob or two. One of them was with a company called Racal, one of the first suppliers of mobile phones. Remember the ones that looked like bricks but were twice as heavy? He was often late for games but would usually turn up with great levels of enthusiasm if he had shifted a phone that week. His deal with Racal meant he received something like 10p in commission every time a phone call was made on one of these devices, and in no time he and his brother Howard were raking it in. He ended up living in Darling Harbour, Sydney, with Nicole Kidman as a neighbour. Then there was Ian Birtwistle, who took nearly 1,000 Lancashire League wickets with his gentle swingers, a tally that belied his frailty – there was so little of him he wore supports on his wrists to help him lift up his bat.

Characters like Billy, Jonesy and Birty have contributed to a compulsion to help the cricket club whenever I've been able to, by any means viable. So, at the age of sixty-one, following an extraordinary general meeting that was called to stop it going down the gurgler, I was persuaded to come back for a third playing stint with the club as part of a drive to keep it alive and garner other interest.

There was no money to work with and it required several of us to put a financial stake forward to ensure that this cricketing nursery that has been home to dozens of Test cricketers over the generations – think Hedley Verity, Bobby Simpson, Wes Hall and Shane Warne for the depth of history – continued to offer the opportunity to follow in their footsteps.

It was the intervention of Mr X – as he wished to be called at the time – with a five-figure donation that actually secured the club's future in the short term. Peter Barratt, our late chairman, informed the rest of the crisis group of this sum being pledged and asked that I go down to the clubhouse as this mysterious figure wished to meet me.

The chap in question turned out to be Ilyas Khan, a local man who made his fortune as a London financier. I didn't know him from Adam, or so I thought. However, his willingness to help his hometown club dated back to the 1980s when I had devoted my own energies to its cause through its youth players. During that period, as I was putting my coaching skills to the test, I ran nets down at the local sports centre for budding cricketers. It cost £1 for any child who wanted to be involved, and regularly this little lad turned up and stood watching at the door. He never had his quid on him but I always shoved him in for a bat and a bowl. Now this little kid was sat opposite me all these years later, paying us back in spades.

We discussed what we could do to attract more publicity and, with Graham still playing, it resolved my determination to accept the challenge thrown down to me. I got fit and declared myself available for selection. Dave Ormerod, the captain, gave me what amounted to a couple of trials, and after the green light at my second net I was selected for a comeback match against Haslingden, the team that pipped us to the Lancashire League title in 1989, my previous season with the club.

It was a fairly dramatic entrance as I walked in with my lad Graham at the non-striker's end and Steve 'Dasher' Dearden, at the end of his mark, on a hat-trick. A salvo of abuse from short leg greeted my arrival: 'He was no f***ing good twenty-five years ago, he will be no f***ing good now.'

'Well, you obviously know who I am. I'm afraid I have no idea who you are,' was my retort.

I was incredibly nervous, boxed clever by taking guard outside the crease and got right forward, negating the chance of being lbw. That first ball crashed into my pads – outside the line thankfully – and there was a good half hour of the Lloyds at the crease. Getting out caught at deep square leg provided great amusement for Graham.

'After all those years you told me never to sweep,' he chuckled, shaking his head.

We lost that game by a dozen runs but had the last laugh the following season when on 13 September, its final Saturday, we stole the title from them. Cruising out in front for 95 per cent of the 2009 campaign, Haslingden fell apart on the home straight and it meant we had a chance to finish top if we beat Lowerhouse away. I know now how tail-enders feel, waiting for the moment to be the hero.

I was itching to have a bat as we set off in pursuit of a 174-run target and pleaded with 'Dibber' Ormerod to get me in with every falling wicket. At No. 9 I felt too low, but after we lost momentum in mid-innings, got my chance with nine required. It was getting tense and at the other end was Paul Carroll, who had been swinging like a sixties suburban key party for the past couple of years. Nerves were eased when he nailed one into the car park, causing me to consider giving him a mid-pitch glove punch. A momentary lapse of concentration, I can assure you, and I refocused my energies into chopping one away for four. To hit the winning runs was dead special. I had served my purpose of getting Accrington Cricket Club back up and running, and the final stroke in the fiftieth season after my debut had sealed the title.

Half a dozen years later, thanks to Ilyas and a small band of other committed souls, the club has much better practice facilities. His money stabilised us for a while but more was required, and so we successfully applied for a grant from Chance to Shine. I made up the rest. People will ask why I did this, and there are certainly lots of other things in life I would like to spend my money on, but I felt an obligation to help out. This was the club that started me off, and for that I owe them a great deal.

Like other northern clubs, we took out a brewery loan twenty-odd years ago, and allowing the interest to build has hit us hard. Our arrears now total around £80,000 and need paying off. What we have tried to do is get people to loan the club £1,000 each, but getting that kind of financial commitment has been very difficult.

I feel the same obligation to Accrington Stanley and go up weekly if I can. Whenever you stroll into the offices at the Crown Ground, there are always three or four people working their nuts off, putting their heart and soul into their jobs, and yet the club, like its cricket equivalent, is still in dire straits. I proposed a similar thing for Accrington Stanley during the 2014-15 season when for the umpteenth time its very existence was seriously jeopardised. Surely, I thought, there were 250 people worldwide who would donate a grand to have their name on a Wall of Honour outside the ground? Unfortunately, I have to report that on the evidence of the initial uptake, there are not.

For all the enjoyment they give me, I have to try to make others feel the same way. When Ilyas Khan footed a £308,000 unpaid tax bill to keep the club afloat, I became more involved with promoting its cause, mainly by supporting Peter Marsden, the new chairman, as a non-executive director. From my perspective, all I'm doing is publicising the club on social media at every opportunity. I see myself as a bit of an ambassador: a relatively easy job for me because I'm a supporter, a spectator with passion, and it's a real thrill to watch them play.

On Twitter, I keep the name of Stanley to the fore by tweeting about them around every match. One of the disappointments that we cannot seem to overcome is that when we were in the Conference we were getting crowds of 3,000 and yet within ten years, having got to our promised land of the Football League, we are down to 1,200 or so. We have no idea what's gone wrong, but obviously we need better facilities to go with our fantastic playing surface, the pride and joy of a local hero made good. Martyn 'Buzzer' Cook, the groundsman, is a recovering alcoholic who was brave enough to speak up about his problem and given the job to help him rehabilitate. It's great to see a local man like him thriving in his job, and the grass is definitely greener now for everyone.

John Coleman, the manager, and his assistants Jimmy Bell and Mick Newell, a Premier League winner with Blackburn no less, are three more of the good guys. Others work at the club without pay. Some of my frustration is for them. I just cannot understand why the people of Accrington have not shared our pride in having one of the ninety-two Football League clubs. If you see the lads who stand behind the goals, the Stanley Ultras, they are banging drums and singing their hearts out. I just wish we could bottle that passion and soak the rest of the town. There is a supporters' club of 180 people trying to raise £25,000 to better the facilities for the players. At the moment they change in portakabins – something that didn't go down well when future England manager Roy Hodgson visited with Fulham in the FA Cup in January 2010. His Premier League prima donnas changed in the team hotel before arrival, claiming there wasn't enough space to do so in our dressing rooms.

In order to keep functioning we need people through the turnstiles, and the reality is that means double our crowd as 2,000 is our break-even figure. We have almost been robbing Peter to pay Paul for a decade. We are the smallest club in the top four divisions and that leaves us vulnerable. The battle is to remain in that fourth tier, although my ambitious nature means I would like to see us push for League One.

Part of my Twitter drive has been to uncover a millionaire, an entrepreneur; even a bull-shitteur will do as long as it's one with readies. The challenge is: give us a million pounds and it can be your team, your club. Let's see what we can do with a million pounds in the bank. Why do I do all this? Because it's about the community and community is important to me. The amount of work Accrington Stanley do in schools through the club's Trust and Academy is incredible, yet it's not having the desired knock-on effect.

It's a unique club, the club that wouldn't die, and to that end I could not resist tweeting Russell Crowe when it became public that he might be interested in buying Leeds United off Massimo Cellino, after he'd bought his beloved South Sydney Rabbitohs rugby league club when they were on the brink. We haven't got rabbits but I know a few folk who keep ferrets, if only he would get back to me. Stanley, I told him, were tailor-made for him. 'Stick two fingers up to Yorkshire and tell them you are coming over to Accrington,' was the gist of it. I thought our gladiatorial nature might appeal to him too.

While out in Australia for the 2015 World Cup, I happened to be in a restaurant in Woolloomooloo, the suburb in which Crowe lives. I tried to lure him out, with messages like: 'I know you're at the end of the road. Why not come out and have a curry?' He must have been away filming because he didn't reply. I would happily have treated him to some poppadoms. If he had bought Nicole Kidman with him, I might have even stretched to a bottle of Prosecco.

My love of watching Accrington burns as strong now as it did in 1953 when my dad took me to my first game and stood me on a brick so that I could see. Football always carries the potential frustration of losing, but crikey, our lads give it their all to avoid such an outcome. They don't leave anything out there on the pitch, as they say, and not one of them rolls around on the floor. You see some of these Barcelona lads go down if a hair gets knocked out of place and fear they will be in intensive care all week. It gets a little bit more feisty in League Two than it does in El Clasico, or as we call it in Lancashire, t'derby.

As well as passion, there is a history to cherish. We believe we've got a wonderfully named football club, a club with great tradition. This town, with a population of 35,000, provided one of the twelve founder members of the Football League. These days the place is quite different to how it was in 1888, but regardless of the era, community is everything to me, and clearly to a man like Ilyas Khan too.

My affinity for the area played a part in my turning down the chance to move down to Essex, at the age of thirty-six, to become their second XI coach. While the job appealed, because they were one of the most successful clubs around, I felt it was probably just a bit too close to my playing career, and uprooting the family to move 200 miles away just didn't feel right. Accrington is where we were from, and so I continued to plough on with my work both at the club and with the local youngsters.

I would continue to play for Accrington for the next six years but knew it was time to call it the day when I snapped my Achilles tendon while batting against Rishton. By now, I was combining playing at weekends and a couple of days with Cumberland in midweek, with umpiring. While I had no great desire to spend my next twenty years as a man in a white coat, it did give me the chance to keep a link to the county game that had been my home for so long. A telephone conversation with Lord's, to assess my chances, returned a favourable result, as although they had no space on the full list, they made me a reserve, meaning that I could expect university matches as well as last-minute call-ups in case of illness and injury.

However, when David Evans was sidelined on a permanent basis midway through the 1985 season, I found that my part-time role was a thing of the past. I could now consider myself to be back on the county cricket circuit permanently. To get on the umpires' list of 2015 involves a much more exhaustive process – interested candidates have to prove their commitment over a period of time in local cricket before they can even make it as a reserve. So it might be a surprise to learn that thirty years ago there were no such demands, qualifications or training required.

Lengthy service in the game as a first-class player was seen as a sufficient apprenticeship.

As an ex-county captain, I possessed an added advantage. I knew how a game should be conducted and, having been on the other side of the fence as recently as two years earlier, knew how players thought. As an official, getting on the same wavelength is so important. Knowledge of the laws is one thing, but I always found the understanding of the struggles that can exist on the field, the frustrations it can entail, while maintaining a sense of humour, were essential ingredients of the job.

That sense of humour came in handy when I stood in my first match. It involved Essex, the club I had recently turned down, in a fixture with Cambridge University at Fenner's. John Lever, the former England bowler, whose practical joking could prove almost as devastating as his left-arm swing, opened from my end and his first ball caused a real commotion as a relatively slow half-volley literally exploded onto the bat of the Cambridge opener. Only it wasn't a ball at all; the silly sod had sent down an orange. Some might not have taken it that well, but I was never an officious type during my three years as an umpire and had to laugh.

Naturally, there were others who I didn't see eye to eye with, most notably Peter Roebuck, who gave me a mark of one out of ten during his duties as Somerset captain. It came at the conclusion of a match at The Oval in which I gave a rare rebuke. With Surrey batting, he left the field without informing me of his desire to do so, leading to an exchange between me and the twelfth man who replaced him, and me dispatching the poor bloke back to the dressing room with a message to his captain to request his leave of absence before walking off. It led to Roebuck gesturing from the balcony that he had hurt his hand.

Generally, I was happy to be on the road, even though it meant long hours and poor pay, because it offered a reprise of my previous career. Some of my colleagues found ways to make their devotion more cost effective, with Ray Julian employed to do odd jobs at Leicester's Grace Road during the winter, and others such as David Constant and Alan Whitehead travelling the country in caravans to avoid the cost of hotel bills. Thankfully, remuneration is better now and Graham is carrying on the family tradition, having been upgraded to the full list from its reserve for the 2014 season.

My only grievance with the modern method of umpiring is the 65-years-old age cap that dictates officials are forced to retire. While I understand the reasoning – to help the development of their younger colleagues – someone like Peter Willey is too good a man to be lost to the game, as he appeared to be on losing his appeal to continue. He has an incredible depth of knowledge from half a century in the game, and during the flux in English cricket in early 2015 I considered him to be an excellent candidate in any new regime. Here was someone who has seen the county and international games at first hand, as both a player and umpire, and over the past decade had kept a close eye on the best emerging talents of the county scene. In my view, he would make an excellent selector.

Although not flush during the 1980s, my public speaking bookings were bringing in a few quid, and I was also earning fees as a commentator on early satellite television coverage. There were some irregular bookings with BBC radio too. I found this stimulating and rewarding, moving in a slightly different direction in my life but retaining my association with cricket. My jack-of-all-trades working life had taken me down another avenue.

Being back on the county treadmill meant I kept in touch with some significant characters of my playing past, most notably Keith Andrew who along with Les Lenham had run the advanced coaching course at Lilleshall during my off seasons with Lancashire. Keith was not only the national director of coaching at that time, he was also chief executive of the NCA, the body responsible for all non-first-class cricket. I was already putting my coaching credentials to the test with the up-and-comers of Accrington when Keith asked me, in a phone call out of the blue, whether I would be interested in coaching at some of the NCA's junior sessions.

Keith, an old-school wicketkeeper with a notorious ability to talk batsmen out during his time with Northamptonshire, was known to me earlier in my career because, as a son of Oldham, he had served on the Lancashire committee during my captaincy tenure. I willingly took up his offer, but at that stage I could not have imagined that he had just set me on a pathway that would result in me becoming England coach a decade later.

In those early days Keith, who was based at Lord's, would turn up to spy on my sessions – literally so, as his party piece would be to put the rolled-up newspaper he habitually carried to his eye and focus on me behind the stumps or on the batsman at the other end. Soon, I acted as a floating coach, supplementing the four permanent national coaches that the NCA employed, and was instrumental in trying to break down the clunky, archaic barriers that existed between the NCA and the English Schools' Association. Change was so evidently necessary but, as in most examples when this is the case, it was met with reticence.

Arguably, what broke it down was the launch of Kwik Cricket, an innovation that also raised my profile in terms of coaching. Keith and I shared the belief that there was no hook to pull kids into our sport and this version of the game would hopefully change all that. The Kwik Cricket road shows took the sport around the country to primary schools, with the initial target being to visit 500 schools a year. With more and more becoming affiliated, however, it was pretty obvious that this would no longer be a part-time passion and I was therefore in effect now an employee of the TCCB.

Another extension of these links was that I suddenly became

closer to the England age-group teams. Initially, the Under-15s became my primary focus. That is an age when young boys become men and there were some very mature players in terms of their physicality – Marcus Trescothick being a standout. By that stage, courtesy of his love of sausages and crisps, he was on the way to earning his nickname Banger. Arguably, the best player I encountered was Robin Weston, a batsman who none of his peers could dismiss and one I felt would go on to play Test cricket. However, his progress reminded me somewhat of Alan Thomas, the mega talent of my youth who failed to fulfil his enormous potential. Weston just didn't appear to have the motivation, certainly not to the level of Trescothick, and although a subsequent move from Durham to Derbyshire did suggest he was giving it a go, his career came to a premature end.

Involvement with the England Under-19 team showed me that while there was huge talent it was not always matched by the same levels of application. Our young cricketers, like their contemporaries in other fields, were as concerned with enjoying themselves at night as they were at gaining recognition for their performance during the day. While it needed a culture shift for these attitudes to change, being a father myself helped me recognise that these lads were no different to any average teenager. They would make mistakes and when told off look at the floor or stare into space.

Only once did a transgression result in anything more serious. It was on the 1996 tour of Zimbabwe, when we all hopped on the bus for a drive to Harare, only for the hotel manager to abort our journey before it began. There were, he said, some unpaid bills. That could be rectified soon enough, if only he would share the names of the individuals concerned. Unfortunately, neither Mick Jagger nor Cliff Richard, or Archbishop Desmond Tutu for that matter, happened to be on board that day, and so myself and Graham Saville, the tour manager, forced the entire squad back indoors to discipline the transgressors. As is often the case in this kind of situation, one lad who shall remain nameless took the rap and was warned about his future conduct. But the threat of being sent home, although directed at him, was made to the entire team.

Meanwhile, back in England, the combination of all these varied posts – which since 1993 had included the position of first-team coach at Lancashire – and the demands they took on my time led to the unfortunate but inevitable breakdown of my marriage to Susan. Time has healed, and thankfully we all remain on friendly terms but such were the demands of work that it literally took over at the expense of everything else. It was a dreadful chapter of my life, and the worst part of it on a personal level without doubt.

I left the family house in Accrington and had nowhere to go. So there I was, Lancashire coach and homeless. With nowhere to live, it meant I dossed with Pete Marron in the groundsman's house at Old Trafford for a fortnight before I got a flat. I was almost itinerant; trapped in a vicious circle. To get through the anguish of it all, I just immersed myself in work; every hour I was awake I was working somewhere. Punch drunk, if truth be told, but I reasoned that was the only way.

CHAPTER 10

Flippin' Heck

Montego Bay will hold special memories for hundreds of Brits who have ventured to the Caribbean for some winter sun. It retains its relevance for me because it's where I was offered the chance to become England coach. There are worse places to be told.

Naturally, this is not a job that you plan for. After all, it carries a fair amount of exclusivity, being the only job of its type in the country and one not to be treated lightly. Additionally, it had never really occurred to me that I might even be in the running for it, until the day in January 1996 when I picked Michael Atherton up from the airport following England's disappointing tour to South Africa.

Atherton, with whom I enjoyed both a personal friendship and professional relationship as his coach at Lancashire, told me in no uncertain terms that I just had to get involved in reviving the national team's fortunes. It was not a period in which I dwelt too much on future plans because the present needed plenty of attention – the breaking up of our family unit hit hard, particularly for our four children, and I felt responsible for the upset I had brought to their lives. It seems a lifetime ago now, but it would be wrong not to acknowledge it was wretchedly tough piecing things back together.

When I returned to Lancashire as coach, I had been away what seemed like an age, and I think that helped. The young players I was asked to work with had an idea who I was but there was no baggage. I knew what playing for the club meant, and I wanted to transfer that into the team. I tried to make it our style that anyone who came to Old Trafford was going to find an aggressive team playing for the badge, the red rose. It was a policy that paid off, and my CV included the 1995 Benson & Hedges Cup final victory over Kent at Lord's and fourth-placed finish in the County Championship that year. All this while losing as many as half a dozen players to England duty at any given time.

My affection for the club meant that the move back to Old Trafford in the winter of 1992-93, to replace Alan Ormrod, and share team responsibilities with David Hughes, who became manager, was a happy one, a reflection that contrasted with the disillusionment I felt during some of my final seasons on the playing staff. As back then, one-day cricket proved our forte, and given the quality of players like Wasim Akram, Atherton, and John Crawley, not to mention 1992 World Cup finalist Neil Fairbrother and other highly under-rated performers such as Mike Watkinson, Peter Martin and Ian Austin, it was no wonder.

I was so proud of this team, and when it didn't get the credit I felt it deserved in defeating Kent in that B&H final, I flipped. For some reason, although we won, Kent's Aravinda de Silva was selected for the man-of-the-match award, which might not have irked me but for the post-match press conference when the general theme appeared to be of his wonderful 112, and the fact you would never see a better one-day innings.

As Lancashire coach, and a victorious Lancashire coach, all I wanted to focus on was how good we were. I was in the privileged position of knowing exactly how we had planned that game tactically and it worked to perfection. Yet all I was hearing was 'Aravinda this, Aravinda that.' It caused me to become a bit bristly. 'He played really well, it was a wonderful innings,' I agreed. 'But when he came in they wanted under five runs per over. When he left they needed six and a half.' That showed how we had done. Some will say that is bad sportsmanship. Not a bit of it. I was just pushing my team, wanting them to gain recognition for executing their plans so efficiently. We controlled a terrific player even though he was in great touch, and when he chipped Austin into the deep on the leg side it was game over. Here was a sign that as a coach I would always be backing my team.

That match, which resulted in a 35-run win, was always under control, aside perhaps for a very short period during which John Bower, our chief executive, left his convivial meet-and-greet in the Lancashire box to pay a visit to our dressing room. I caught sight of this red rose suit approaching when I was out sat on the balcony. I was in my office, in the zone, as it were, concentrating on what was unfolding in front of me.

'I say coach, we have to get this chap out,' he said.

'John, you're right on my flight path,' I told him.

'I see,' he said, sober enough to realise it was time to turn on his heels.

During this period Micky Stewart, the then England manager, used me on occasion as a pair of trained eyes to assess potential international players and even pitches that England were about to play on. Up until then, my only other link to the very top level of cricket was in developing players like Michael Vaughan for the English Schools side, and the likes of his Yorkshire colleague Anthony McGrath and Marcus Trescothick for Under-19 series. Soon, I was asked along to help at some full England get-togethers.

The build-up to my appointment comprised a period of volatility in which Stewart, whose contrast in attitude to his captain David Gower was well documented, moved aside for Keith

Fletcher, a quite brilliant county coach with Essex, who was subsequently removed himself in the aftermath of the 1994-95 tour of Australia.

That led to England employing Raymond Illingworth in a joint role as team manager and chairman. Not to put too fine a point on it, Raymond ran English cricket on his own for a spell, albeit with John Barclay in support on the administration side. However, while things appeared fine on the surface – a 2-2 draw with West Indies was no bad result given the standard of opposition, and the following winter was no disaster either when looked upon from a statistical point of view as South Africa were deadlocked until the final Test in Cape Town – it concealed concern from at least one protagonist, Atherton, whose Herculean batting efforts alongside Jack Russell against the South Africans maintained the 0-0 score.

Yet I had no idea anything was amiss until this airport conversation with a man three years into his England captaincy. During his tenure, Atherton had worked under two managers and two chairmen and was of a belief that combining these roles was neither desirable nor practical. He did most of the talking on that car journey but my limited response was not down to a lack of interest. Although I cared passionately about the England cricket team, and that has never waned, any notion of getting involved was fanciful stuff. Quite simply, the position to suit my skills did not exist within the set-up.

There was no time to change things before that year's World Cup, which was only a matter of weeks away, but after the disaster that unfolded in their performances in India and Pakistan it became clear that Atherton, using his influence as England captain, began lobbying for me. The embarrassingly one-sided quarter-final defeat to Sri Lanka led to inquests. No matter that they went on to win the whole damned thing the following week by shocking Australia in the final. Within days of England's return, Illingworth had relinquished the managerial half of his job share but announced his intention to remain in charge of selection.

Then, a single move by the Test and County Cricket Board improved my chances of employment in a heartbeat. They made it public that they no longer required a team manager for England – what they wanted was a coach. So, it happened that while on Lancashire's pre-season camp in Montego Bay in early April, I was invited to become England coach, initially on a six-month basis. I flew home to sort out the details of my contract with AC Smith, then in the final throes of his stint as TCCB chief executive. The offer – £25,000 for six months' work – did not come without complication.

For a start, what was to happen at Lancashire in the interim and what if, on pledging my commitment to the national team until October, things didn't work out? Where would I be in six months? In a generous act of support, Lancashire, through chairman Bob Bennett, agreed to keep my position open throughout my 'trial' period.

I wanted to get the England team to win. I've always liked the idea of teams playing cricket with smiles on their faces, but it's pretty hard to smile when you're losing, and England hadn't won much for a sustained period of time. It's hard to look happy when you're coming second. There were lots of droughts to address – for a start there had not been a victorious Test series abroad for five years.

Illingworth proved a surprisingly supportive chairman of selectors who did not allow a challenge to his position by David Graveney – knocked back by Graveney's employers, the PCA, due to a perceived conflict of interest – to affect the functioning of the selection committee, of which Graveney was to become a part, or the reduction in his overall responsibilities to affect his relationship with me. In fact, despite the upheaval he appeared more than happy in our working environment for the twelve months he held the position. For my part, I found his autocratic image did not match his private persona.

Dour but sharp-minded as a cricketer, he had dismissed me as an on-field adversary in his typically gruff manner during his playing days with Yorkshire and Leicestershire, but he clearly had a higher regard for my coaching credentials. I found him sociable at the end of a day's play, and as well as open and honest, more mischievous in private than he let on publicly.

Of course, I was aware of some of his conflicts with the players in previous months, not least Atherton, and more infamously his confrontation with Devon Malcolm in South Africa, but this I dismissed as going with the territory when you put a Yorkshireman, and a successful one at that, in charge of a team. If his name was going to be on the results sheet, he wanted to put his stamp on things. I also found that like me, particularly in those days, he could be sensitive to criticism. Men who take on a coaching role across any of England's sporting teams and are not so, are few and far between.

The one big shock to me on becoming England coach was the process of selection. There was nothing particularly scientific about it. In fact, it was done over dinner, with glasses of wine on the table, and felt like a throwback to a bygone age. Rumour suggested that in these meetings Raymond would be the one to get his way, but in my experience this was simply untrue. It was rarely, if ever, the case.

Initially, I was a part of this process. Only later, having taken stock, did I take the decision to come off the selection panel. As coach, doubling up as a selector – and only one voice of five – meant there was an obligation to justify decisions made by the group as if they were my own. This caused some discomfort for me in dressing-room situations. Players who are left out naturally wonder which of the selectors have lost faith in them, and if the coach is one of the five this carries unnecessary tension. An example of being placed in a compromising position – supporting the decisions of others even though they contradicted my own view – came in the Caribbean in early 1998 when I wanted Mark Ramprakash in the XI for the first Test versus West Indies but the other tour selectors were firmly opposed to the idea.

The buck stopped with me to justify a decision not mine in the making. It would have been improper to let on the truth, so I was forced to act as if I was behind it. Ramprakash was a player who needed to feel backed by his coach, and even in this instance when he was being backed, it did not appear so from the outside. During my time, the panel reduced in number from five to three but then increased to four once more, the common number since.

My feeling as coach was that selection should be the remit of a single man – a system that would promote clearer accountability. In football, a manager picks his team and sends it out to do his bidding. On match days selection is his domain, yet through the week he may have a cast of thousands on the training ground feeding back advice. As the millennium approached, this was the system I believed cricket should adopt.

My thirty-eight months in charge of England offered arguably my greatest challenge. While there was some progress made in stopping the rot, most notably when we won our first five-Test series for a dozen years against the touring South Africans in 1998, the fact that we were still only a mid-ranking side showed what a big job was on our hands. It certainly wasn't one to be completed in the space of a year or two, and would take long-term planning.

But putting strategies in place was not easy. With Lancashire I had been used to arriving in my 'office' at Old Trafford not long after sunrise in early season, preparing for each working day by chatting to groundsman Peter Marron over a coffee. Pete, who sadly lost his battle with cancer in 2015, was the best ally one could wish for and someone who would do anything for you. I knew if I wanted anything, he was the man to ask – but it was also important not to upset him. He was a tough man. You didn't mess with him. Sat behind my desk in the converted toilet block tucked behind the dressing rooms in the pavilion, I would scribble notes on players and pitches and plan training schedules. This was my working environment as a county coach, but my routines for England were quite different. Surrounded by blocked off urinals I might have been, but I knew what I was working with at county level. But with England there was no such regularity when it came to 'office' work. There was no staff to call on and not even a settled squad. I had big plans for England but not necessarily the financial backing to put them into place. That much I found out in my first few months in charge when, having discovered funds were available for certain schemes, I was stymied by counties unwilling to loosen their collective purse strings.

At that time, I wanted all eighteen clubs to invest in technology such as a universal video system that had first been introduced in New Zealand rugby. All this seems par for the course now in an age where players walk from the field to watch their dismissals and other highlights of an innings instantly, either on their personal laptops, tablets or smartphones. As well as giving physical evidence of their performance, and any evidence of faults in technique, this particular video system offered footage of opposition players, highlighting their strengths and weaknesses and what one might expect when confronted with them.

In the late 1990s, this was all cutting-edge stuff but English counties appeared to contain no appetite for it. It might shock cricket followers au fait with the Decision Review System gadgets like Hawk-Eye and Snicko and virtual reality practice devices such as ProBatter, that some of the counties baulked at the idea of forking out £23,000 each so that every ground in the country could share this video system and build a national library of footage.

The area of English cricket I believed I could advance the furthest was our one-day game, if only I could break down the stigma of selecting specialist players suited to the shorter format rather than the traditional style player. There was lots of potential for improvement, as England's recent record in 50-over cricket had been poor, culminating in a limp World Cup effort. Unfortunately, that has been echoed across a couple of decades because as a nation we have always tended to pay lip service to big one-day tournaments.

Progress was made initially in 1996 and 1997 but later hit a brick wall. Through the influence of David Graveney, who took over from Raymond Illingworth as chairman of selectors on the eve of the 1997 Ashes, we tried to get one-day specialists selected – the kind of players rather short-sightedly dismissed as bits-and-pieces men whenever we didn't win but some good cricketers like Vince Wells, Matthew Fleming, Ian Austin, Dougie Brown and Mark Ealham. These were people with good one-day records. However, a lack of continuity damaged our efforts. We had a history of picking Test players to play one-dayers, particularly on overseas tours, and the team development we planned was occasionally hit by not having the right kind of personnel to hand when on tour.

Like a magpie I tried to adorn our own nest by pinching a tactic off Australia. In a bid to add a sprinkling of dynamism in the field, I asked the team to buzz the ball back to the wicketkeeper whenever they picked it up. I liked the energy it gave off and left the opposition in no doubt they were in a game. If I had an influence with selectors, it was that whichever kind of player they were looking at, be it batsman or bowler, if they got into a toss-up, I let it be known the successful candidate should be the best fielder. I didn't want a load of donkeys. Sure, there would be a few who would not be overly athletic and there was no need to change them because it was for their primary skills that they had been selected. Others were electric in the field and one of the very best never got any credit – Mark Ealham was quicker off the mark and a better fielder than most folk thought. In fielding drills, he was always very good at hitting the stumps with his throws.

The potential of the team was highlighted when in the space of a few months we beat Australia 3-0 and then won the Champions Trophy – a four-team tournament in those days – in Sharjah. During that period, Adam Hollioake proved himself to be an inspirational captain, a true leader and a brilliant one-day player who England could have got more out of in the longer term. His best qualities were that he kept things simple while being a great innovator. He just had the feel for one-day cricket, with his slower balls and power hitting. These days, they talk about funky fields and changes of bowling on a whim. Well, he was about fifteen years ahead of his time. He did everything on instinct. Also, if it needed someone to come in and give it a thump he would be the one putting his hand up. His other ingredient was the essential one for a captain: all the other players wanted to play for him.

People would tell you that Adam Hollioake was not quick enough to be considered as a serious bowler. People would tell you that he was not good enough to be considered as a top six first-class batsman. In fact, I myself wouldn't have put him down as a Test match player, but what I do know is that he would be box office in the Indian Premier League right now. He would be earning an absolute fortune. In fact, I don't know why he doesn't get himself fit, stop his cage-fighting and get himself on a plane. While I was commentating there in the spring of 2015, I came across a leg-spinner called Pravin Tambe who was still turning out for Rajasthan Royals at the age of forty-three. Brad Hogg was rolling out his chinamen at forty-four.

Back then, Hollioake always wanted to fight. You could probably tell in the way he played his cricket. When he first came on the scene in 1997, he had this reputation as a battler and Shane Warne stood at the end of his mark shadow-boxing in taunting fashion. 'Don't upset him,' was my immediate thought, because

Hollioake would have dropped him like a stone. In 2014, at Twenty20 finals day, he was still seeking some rough and tumble on duty for the ECB as a crowd entertainer. Michael Vaughan happened to be the mystery competitor in the mascot race and when Hollioake got wind of what was going on, he came over to ask me which one he was. At this stage, I had no idea why he was asking but having told him it was the squirrel, I watched in horror as Hollioake, in best shirt and shoes, charged after these furry friends, picked Vaughan out and rugby tackled him to the floor.

Poor old Vaughan – who barely has a leg to stand on these days, given that post multiple operations his knees are held together with bits of old sticking plaster – took considerable time to get to his feet after Hollioake hit him so hard that it sucked all his breath from him. With his victim laid out in shock, Hollioake beat the ground in convulsions of laughter.

I always considered Hollioake to be a loveable wild man. After winning the Champions Trophy, he saw the British journalists gathered in the foyer of the team hotel and from his position a couple of floors up decided to make his own fun. He picked up a plant pot and dropped it from 60 ft, shattering it into fifty pieces right in the middle of them. Pot and soil flew everywhere. A few yards either side and one of them was in serious trouble – A&E kind of trouble. He was absolutely crackers.

On a trip to the West Indies, he devised some training activities to beat the wet weather. We were staying in some villas in Jolly Beach, Antigua, and it had poured down for a week. It was literally monsoon weather, and with no grass to work on, we ended up practising on the concrete pathways where we were staying. The players took it into their own hands to create other routines too, as I was to discover when one day, a bloke came over to me and asked who the group of blokes were stood across the way. I told him that they were the England cricket team and they were with me. 'Well, can you tell them to stop throwing tomatoes at my yacht. That's my yacht there,' he said, pointing over towards the water. For fielding practice, Hollioake had been purchasing pounds of tomatoes and was taking aim trying to hit specific targets on this vessel. I couldn't fault him for his ingenuity.

We fell short in the 1999 World Cup, not because we were a poor team but for a number of external factors. Hollioake, who had suffered a loss of form and no longer justified previous optimism in him as captain or indeed an automatic place in the team, suffered one moment of madness too many when he stopped off on a road trip to Southampton to barrack a village green game. He had already been given a warning for a disciplinary misdemeanour in the warm-up match versus Essex, and this after Graham Thorpe had been fined £1,000 for failing to attend a reception put on by our tournament hosts, Kent. Timing is everything, and had Hollioake's running commentary come when we were winning it would have been received rather differently, I'm sure. But we were not winning.

Distractions and ill feeling were everywhere we turned. On 12 May, two days before the World Cup's opening match, ours against Sri Lanka at Lord's, I was invited to a dinner with the ECB's senior officials. It put me in a room with Brian Bolus, a man who I suspected to be a source of several newspaper stories about my removal as coach, for the first time since his appointment as chairman of EMAC, the England Management Advisory Committee. During this dinner, I put it to him that I thought he was nailing me behind the scenes, but he denied this and suggested it was someone else on the committee, a man I trusted and always liked, who wanted to sack me. I didn't disbelieve Bolus but neither did I want to accept any suggestion of betrayal. It did not help my mood.

In addition to struggling to get as many specialists on the ground on tours, it was difficult to break hard-set English thinking on how to approach 50-over cricket from a strategical point of view. There was never a doubt in my mind that maximising the first fifteen overs, when the ball was hard and the field restrictions were on, was paramount. Then, look to be busy in the middle overs before launching at the back end. For those that watched the 2015 World Cup, this policy might seem familiar. Frustratingly, although the concept was simple enough, we either made a Horlicks of it too often or didn't have enough people buying into the need for speed at the top, to the point that we took the hard decision to drop Nick Knight, who was in sketchy form, and in the absence of the injured Michael Atherton, use Nasser Hussain as a top-order anchor.

We beat the holders Sri Lanka, and the minnows Kenya and Zimbabwe comfortably, but were victims to a large degree of Zimbabwe's upset victory against a South African side who had been clinical in their defence of a 226-run target against us. An appalling rain-affected performance against India over two days was a humiliating way to end an international coaching career.

On reflection, we were just too stuck in our ways. We had tried to be brave with Knight and Ali Brown at the top of the order in previous years, but it was un-English, and any new ideas were generally frowned upon. The enigmatic Graeme Hick remained an automatic limited-overs pick despite his fluctuating Test form which had seen him dropped on several occasions over the year, and I strongly fancied him to be a major influence on our World Cup campaign. One of my policies for that tournament would be to use a flexible batting order – if it's good enough for the best teams at the 2015 World Cup it would certainly do for me sixteen years earlier. It was something I raised in team meetings in the build-up to the tournament. Such a tactic requires full commitment from the entire group of batsmen, but Hick was one of those reluctant to buy into it, insisting he should be assured of batting in his preferred position of No. 3.

His argument was a bit old school: even when it took him time to get going, once set he was a good bet for a big hundred. I countered that if he took that time but got out, we were missing the chance to make merry in that important 15-over period when the fielding restrictions were in place. Just three years earlier, before I had become coach, Sri Lanka had shown the merits of an aggressive attitude during the first part of an innings and their momentum took them all the way to the trophy. In the end Hick came round, but he took some persuading in private and even then I'm not sure he fully agreed with the scheme.

It was in Hick's native Zimbabwe that the episode for which my England tenure will best be remembered took place. I wasn't long into the job; only a few days of 1997 had passed in fact when I became the focus of some sensational headlines and an official reprimand from my bosses for my behaviour. Not for an abject defeat, nor an horrendous performance but for allegedly being graceless in reaction to a drawn Test match with Zimbabwe, the newest of the Test-playing nations at that time.

In my defence, I felt they had pushed the spirit of the game to its limits with their tactics; we had played all the cricket and they had done no more than play the role of spoilers by pushing the interpretations of fairness to the nth degree. Others in my situation might have kept tight-lipped but I refused to, and my suggestion that 'we flippin' murdered them' will stick with me forever.

We flew into Harare on that tour and were to stay at the Monomotapa hotel, one known to me as it had been a base on an Under-19 tour in the not so distant past. I did not favour it and made that known to my superiors, suggesting that Meikles or the Sheraton, two higher-class establishments in the city, were decent alternatives. In the build up to the tour Medha Laud, one of the best sports administration staff you could wish to have working for you, went out on a recce and reported misgivings about the place but Tim Lamb, the then chief executive of the ECB, dismissed them and argued it was a suitable establishment.

Interestingly, though, when he arrived later in the tour he ventured to the Sheraton. We were due to stay here for quite some time, and while not expecting silk robes and plunge baths I considered the comfort of the team to be a priority. Ian MacLaurin, the board chairman, later revealed his horror at the standard of accommodation we were being asked to stay in while serving our country. He could not believe that 'pokey' rooms, lacking air conditioning in 100-degree heat and with barely space to house one grown man let alone two, were suitable at all. Comfortable it was not. South Africa checked in that winter and immediately checked out. It didn't improve spirits when a member of the Zimbabwe Cricket Union warned us that Harare had its problems with crime – warning against wearing jewellery in public and of predatory prostitutes in a country where sexual diseases, particularly AIDS, were rampant. It didn't give off the best impression of Zimbabwe as a country.

Our feelings of being unwelcome only increased when the Harare Sports Club, the capital's Test venue, prohibited us from even conducting fielding practice at the ground. It meant that what practice we did have took place at the adjacent rugby ground, goalposts and all. On the mornings of match days, rubbish from the home dressing room had found its way into ours and no effort had been made overnight to clear it. General debris and remnants of the previous day's lunch littered the floor and my daily routine on that tour began with a sweeping-up mission. Despite the soaring temperatures, there were no showers to freshen the players up after hot, sweaty days and that meant dashing back to the hotel immediately after stumps.

If I made a mistake it was keeping all this detail to myself, something I did to avoid looking as though we were ungrateful, grumbling guests. Only later did I realise that putting up and shutting up was the wrong course of action. I even came to view the uncomfortable environment created for us as a tactical ploy from the Zimbabweans, who were coached by Dave Houghton. It may have been. Equally, it could have been mere coincidence. Houghton, a man known to the English media through his time with Worcestershire and someone who has worked in the English game with Derbyshire, Somerset and Middlesex since, has become a good friend and someone whose knowledge of the game I respect.

At the time, it felt like our travelling press corps was only too willing to seize on any negativity that we might exhibit and cast us as aloof and superior. Meanwhile, wherever we went, there were mutterings about how England had not supported Zimbabwe's case for Test status. But that was a decision taken by the suits at Lord's, and nothing to do with me or the players out there representing their country. If we became insular on that trip, it was with good reason. Some suggestions were that we had spurned Zimbabwean hospitality on more than one occasion, but other than an invite to Heath Streak's family farm, which the entire squad attended, I cannot recall another event to which we were asked along.

Our entertainment was therefore of our own making, with cards, chess and Balderdash, a board game for bluffers, all played in the team room at the Monomotapa. Amid all the criticism appearing in the newspapers back home and faxed over to us daily, suggesting that the players had become reclusive and uninterested, I took the decision on behalf of the team to turn down an invitation to spend some of Christmas Day with the British press pack. I was told that there was some tradition in sharing a drink or two and for the scribes to put on their version of a pantomime. But I just felt that to share in festivities with those who had been overly critical of us on a daily basis would have been hypocritical. This was not supposed to be a jolly.

Harare has few delights. In terms of the Test circuit, it's a city among the most dingy and depressing, and also smacked of the worst excesses of the old colonial days. During play, from our vantage point in the away changing room, we could see members of the Colonial Club adjacent, sat in the stand drinking beer from bottles served to them by black waiters. Every time one was emptied, it found its way onto the grass between the stand and the boundary rope, where one of the waiters was expected to venture to collect it. It became a demeaning game, taking on the image of some racist ceremony, as more and more bottles made their way into this area, the majority of which were thrown while one of the waiters was in the vicinity picking up. At one point, I made my way out to pick one up myself and return it to the hulking neanderthal who had thrown it. The whole booze-fuelled group went berserk, and although I was a little nervous because of my actions, I was pleased I had made my point. Some of my dearest friends in cricket are black and to sit in silence was to do them a disservice.

This was an unseemly and disturbing backdrop to the cricket, and although I wouldn't use this as an excuse for our poor performances, I would argue that it puts into some context our state of mind. To be frank, although we didn't do ourselves justice with the white ball, our Test cricket was not as bad as it was portrayed.

Rustiness undoubtedly contributed to us losing a warm-up match, the first of the tour, to Mashonaland, and our lethargy extended into a one-day defeat to a President's XI. Despite beating Matabeleland, we then proved woeful in losing the first ODI by two wickets despite reducing Zimbabwe to 106 for seven in their chase for 153.

To add to the discontent, we were then given early morning notice by the match referee Hanumant Singh that we were being fined for sporting oversized logos on our bats, a threat averted following contact with his boss, the ICC chief executive David Richards. Hanumant was fastidious by nature and a little bit of an oddball. Some of our players thought he had been given his comeuppance one day when, having entered our dressing room, it was noted that he had bird shit all over one shoulder of his ICC blazer. The giggles were cut short, however, after the ex-Indian international referred to his new fashion accessory by claiming it must stay there all day in order to bring him good luck.

It had not been an ideal build-up, but then there rarely was one when it came to touring at that time. You travelled with limited resources, and we were thin on the ground from a playing perspective with just fourteen to select from, with Dominic Cork absent on compassionate leave and Ronnie Irani having injections in his back.

Still, we headed into that fourth-innings chase in Bulawayo on 22 December 1996 with every chance of winning. Nick Knight had played absolutely brilliantly to get us to within striking distance of our 205-run target. But after Zimbabwe resorted to bowling balls you wouldn't have reached with a yard brush – artfully varied with one outside leg followed by the next outside off – the equation became five runs required from three deliveries, and then three from the final one.

With the one television monitor in our viewing area on the blink, I had made my way to the boundary edge near the sightscreen to assess the Zimbabweans' liberal interpretation of what constituted a fair delivery. Arms folded, lips pursed, anyone who knew the real me would have recognised I was ticking.

Heath Streak sent down a low full toss that Knight drove out to deep cover. Unfortunately, Darren Gough was at the non-striker's end. Had it been Linford Christie, my infamous 'flippin' murdered 'em' outburst would not have made it into English cricket's pantheon. As it was, our whole-hearted fast bowler from Barnsley was left short of his ground as Andy Flower collected the throw from the deep and whipped off the bails. Result: match drawn with the scores level.

'England finish tantalisingly one run short,' Bob Willis was telling the live television audience. 'Controversial tactics from

Zimbabwe as they fired the ball wide either side of the wickets. We have seen one-day finishes all over the world, but we have never seen a Test match end like this.'

Nick sloped off disconsolate. The rest of our lads were perched just outside the tented area in front of our dressing rooms. I was seething. I've always been passionate about winning. But I felt we had been on the end of some sharp practice. It was not the way I thought the game should be played.

My emotional response was a reflection of my personality – passionate and patriotic. The players were emotional too, and they were my players. As a coach, my primary responsibility was to them. Contracts can say whatever you want them to say, but the one constant in any that you sign is that you are the custodian of that group. They had been denied a special moment – Test wins are to be treasured and it was an era in which we didn't claim too many. I knew how much they wanted to win, and it was my belief that their quest for success had been stymied by gamesmanship.

In my view, only one of the two teams had been trying to play the game properly, and I stormed into the umpires' room to take up the issue of wides with them. Steve Dunne dismissed me in a flash and so I marched off to see Hanumant to discuss what constituted 'the spirit of the game'. He had referred to this in the build-up to the series, but now he only suggested that was something for the umpires to interpret.

Upon the conclusion of the presentation ceremony, I was involved in an exchange with a few locals, including the parents of Alistair Campbell, the Zimbabwean captain. Starting with taunts like 'you couldn't even beat us', their tone and language became increasingly inflammatory and loud. It was later said that in losing my cool I gave them a two-finger response. For clarity, the salute I gave consisted of a single finger but it should not have been raised.

Back in the dressing room, Ian Botham, our temporary bowling coach, tried to calm me down before I went to the press conference. It gave me time to think about what I was going to say, but even then, with a few minutes to cool off, I could not hide my true feelings.

I was certainly good copy for the travelling press pack that evening. 'We couldn't reach half the deliveries but that's the way it goes,' I told Charles Colvile in an interview with Sky Sports later. With me in that mood, however, pseudo diplomacy was never going to last long: 'We've absolutely hammered them and they know it.'

I was not one to bite my tongue and so when Colvile playfully commented 'terrific game of Test cricket there' it slackened my jaw. 'It would be, to be a draw in the end, and everyone to be on the edge of their seats. That's a moral victory for us. When you have got nine people on the boundary at the end of the game, you are not in the match.'

'England would have done the same in that position?' Colvile wondered.

'Probably would have done. Probably would. If you want to play that way, carry on.'

Then, I gave a slight variation on the views I provided in the written press's post-match conference: 'I am sure it would have been compulsive viewing. It looked marvellous, getting so close. But we have murdered 'em, hammered 'em. We know it and they know it.'

This, along with the more roundly quoted 'we've flippin' murdered 'em' comment, was a figure of speech. The kind of language you might use to your mates down the pub. Colloquial, earthy, no more than a sound bite. But crikey, did it cause a reaction.

Of course, those resident in Zimbabwe saw this quite differently, with one newspaper suggesting it was 'distasteful' that I should have made such 'loutish and unsporting remarks'. Another writer suggested I had mistaken myself for the head of the Barmy Army, which at least made me chuckle.

Those in authority had contrasting views: Hanumant Singh, in his capacity as match referee, dismissed it, but Tim Lamb, the ECB's chief executive, did not. On a visit to my hotel room, Lamb reeled off a charge sheet of complaints that he said had been formed after consultation with journalists he respected and members of the crowd. It was a surreal experience, listening to my direct boss relay observations and accusations about my behaviour, jotting down what he said on the back of an envelope. That face-to-face meeting was the equivalent of a yellow card. It was followed by an official letter a fortnight later, after we had moved on to New Zealand, reiterating that some of my conduct had not only tarnished my own reputation but that of the team. Before signing off, he added, rather insincerely it seemed to me: 'This particular episode apart, let me assure you that you have the absolute support of the Board.'

We travelled to New Zealand after wet weather washed away our chances of pushing for victory in the second Test. We had started poorly but were well on the way to completing a turnaround. But we were underwhelming in the 3-0 defeat in the one-day series, and our habit of taking time to get into our stride in matches, often starting poorly as a result, threatened to limit our prospects against the Kiwis. We probably should have won all three Tests but settled for victory by a slightly narrower margin and could have even have been pegged back to 1-1, which would have been a massive injustice in my book, on the final day of the third Test.

But for Danny Morrison, a batsman notorious as the worst on the international stage and a holder of a record twenty-four Test ducks, holding us up for three hours alongside Nathan Astle as a nailed-on win in the first Test was transformed into a draw, that series finale would have been a dead rubber. That was another tear-your-hair-out moment for me but we got through it, and at the end of a chastening winter, to borrow the captain Michael Atherton's much-used phrase, winning is all that matters.

People said I had eccentric methods as England coach, but I wouldn't concur with that at all. I wanted us to be proud representing our country on the world stage. A 'we will fight them on the beaches' spirit. That refusal to surrender represented the kind of attitude I wanted to instil. On the team ghettoblaster I played anthems such as 'Jerusalem' and 'Land of Hope and Glory' in a bid for patriotism and commitment to the cause.

Never was commitment to the cause better demonstrated during my three years than in the 1998 series win over South Africa. The microcosm of that summer was provided at Trent Bridge, the scene of one of the great fast-bowling/opening batsmen duels cricket has witnessed. To set the scene, we headed into the fourth innings needing 247 to win. Allan Donald was bowling around the wicket to Michael Atherton, who was our rock in these run-chase situations, when a short ball appeared to hit the glove on its way through. Atherton – as was the trend of that era and incidentally remains so, even with the introduction of the technology-driven review system – stood his ground and Steve Dunne, the neutral umpire, clearly doubtful contact had been made, turned down the caught-behind appeal. It was a decision that clearly incensed Donald.

A flurry of verbals followed as Donald stood and glared at his opponent. Atherton, often stirred into his best innings by confrontation, remained outwardly impassive but did make eye contact with the South African. Here were two unbelievably proud blokes standing their ground. It was gladiatorial, raw, tense. It was theatre.

This had echoes of a seismic scrap from my playing days between another South African, Mike Procter, and my dear pal Clive Lloyd in a second-round Gillette Cup match between Lancashire and Gloucestershire at Old Trafford in July 1978. Due to a rain intervention the match spilled over into a second day, and having resumed on 7 for one, we were soon 33 for three, in pursuit of a 267-run target. We were struggling and in need of a big partnership for the fourth wicket.

That's exactly what we got thanks to Procter flicking Clive's switch. The Gloucestershire man was bouncing back to his mark, full of beans, in the belief that they were going to get a rare one over on us. Despite being a very good side we were their bogey team and used to nail them, usually securing victory after an epic contest swung this way and that. Almost invariably, our meetings with them were the best matches of the season.

He walked past and said to the pair of us: 'You ain't f***ing winning this one.' That certainly got Clive's competitive juices flowing. Procter, bowling from the Stretford End with the wind at his back, bounced Clive, who got in an almighty tangle but managed to get just enough bat on ball to spiral a top edge over fine leg for six. While it sent Procter into a rage, I soon discovered the incident had altered Clive's mood too as we met in the middle of the pitch.

'This man, he vexing me,' he told me.

'Pardon?' I asked him.

'He vexed me, man! I'm going to hit him into the pavilion,' he informed me.

I caught his drift but not as well as Clive caught this one particular delivery. He had this wonderful front-foot pick-up and he smashed him into the stands during what would have been a marvellous spectacle for the crowd. Proc, who never failed to get the home crowd going as a visitor, absolutely steamed in. On occasions, he used to remonstrate with people, seeking a barracking just to get him going.

Meanwhile, at the other end, Gloucestershire had a left-arm swinger called Jack Davey who I simply could not get away. I kept persuading myself to get forward because he was not quick, but every time I played a shot I kept clunking it, jamming down on yorkers. Until that is, Clive, immersed in the contest, offered some advice.

'Stop coming forward. Go back,' he advised me. 'Just open up and put him over midwicket.' It's a fairly recognisable shot now in Twenty20 but not necessarily one I played. But on Clive's word, I just hopped onto my back foot, waited for the ball to come to me and drop-kicked it over the infield on the leg-side. The full length I was struggling with had effectively been turned into a half-volley. Now, Procter as Gloucestershire captain had another problem. If he was putting a man out there, where was he getting him from? Other gaps appeared and by the end our unbeaten fourth-wicket partnership had swelled to a record 234, still the biggest for this wicket in English domestic competition.

That great West Indies team played for Clive and I shared their respect for the man. He was just a top bloke, and one of the saddest things for me is that Michael Holding, another dear pal, has fallen out with him over recent West Indies politics. They were an awesome outfit in their day. Forget all this contemporary sledging, shouting and bawling, which takes place against a backdrop of claims that 'we know where to draw the line' from players. What line? There wasn't one when you played West Indies.

Draw whatever line you want, it might as well have been the Siegfried Line if you started abusing that lot. You would be running home to your mammy for tea. Come up against Colin Croft, Holding, Andy Roberts, Malcolm Marshall, Wayne Daniel and Joel Garner and you didn't say a word. They didn't have much to say either. Nor their successors Courtney Walsh and Curtly Ambrose. They would stare at you and that was enough. I, for one, wouldn't have wanted to have got them any more agitated.

Equally, Atherton drew admiration from his team-mates for the way the heat of a battle inspired him to his best. That week was one of his best as an England player, I would suggest, coming out as he did victorious in that contest with a pumped-up Donald and the match itself. That particular episode actually showed the desire to win on both sides in an enthralling series. From an England point of view, we had not won a series of five matches in length since 1986.

That was a long wait and the opportunity to overturn it all came down to the final morning at Headingley, when South Africa needed just 30-odd with two wickets standing. That it had come down to this was thanks to a fine team effort but notably Atherton – who had shown remarkable resolve since relinquishing the captaincy earlier that year – along with his successor Alec Stewart. Atherton's runs in Nottingham had hauled us level, but those he made alongside Stewart in a double-century alliance in Manchester a fortnight earlier prevented the tourists taking a 2-0 lead. It was unmissable cricket that evening when Robert Croft and our No. 11 Angus Fraser, who told me that Donald would have to knock him through the stumps to dismiss him before departing the dressing room, rebuffed their efforts. Unless, of course, you had a vested interest in it all, and really would not rather watch your last man in combat with a fearsome pace attack. One of two leg-before shouts while Gus defended those stumps could easily have been given. But we survived and the only score on the board was South Africa's landslide victory at Lord's.

There had been talk of the public losing interest early in that series, but there were signs to the contrary on that final morning when Yorkshire left the gates open and more than 13,000 wandered in to witness what proved to be an historic win. It showed how much winning Test matches and Test series still meant to people in this country. The mood inside the dressing room pre-play was that we weren't losing. It's called a Test because it tests your resolve, your nerve, your character. Had we got it in us to come through and deliver? Had we ever. Positivity flowed through the team that final morning to complete the last rites of a series you simply couldn't take your eyes off. To come from 1-0 down to win 2-1; it doesn't get better than that.

It had been tetchy at times and South Africa expressed post-series ill feeling that they had suffered badly at the hands of the umpires. Unfortunately, our mood was to turn sour at the end of the summer when we hosted Sri Lanka in a one-off Test match on a pitch described as 'scruffy' and liable to 'turn big time' by Graham Thorpe, who was a decent judge given his experience as a player at The Oval with Surrey.

There was no time to dwell on our fantastic achievement against the South Africans, no sense of reflection on a fine adver-tisement for our national team. Instead we were pitched against the Sri Lankans on a surface that suited them perfectly. We had been up against hostile pace all summer, and from nowhere sud-denly we were thrown into battle with the world's new spin threat Muttiah Muralitharan.

Murali is someone I have become friendly with in recent years, but at the time he wasn't well known to English cricket followers. Inevitably, people were asking questions about his action as a result, and I was one of them. In my view, both he and fellow spinner Kumar Dharmasena breached the woolly laws as they stood, in that they partially straightened their arms in delivery. Back then it was open to interpretation in that an umpire should call no-ball 'if not entirely satisfied with the absolute fairness of a delivery' and that such a delivery was illegal if dispatched from an arm that 'partially or completely' straightened. Only since have we replaced this arbitrary process with a scientific one and the world become accustomed to the fifteen degrees of leeway bowlers have been afforded.

Quite a few things became apparent in subsequent years after video analysis was applied. Watching him deliver the ball with the aid of slow motion proved mightily revealing. Most significantly, Murali was well within the fifteen-degree limit. But he also possessed one of the strongest, if not the strongest wrist, of any spinner in the game's history. His wrist action was simply magnificent – almost as other-worldly as those trademark eyes.

At the time, the majority of the cricket world, myself included, were ignorant of all this and having expressed my concern to Simon Pack, England's international teams director, prior to the triangular one-day series that preceded this Oval match, I was advised to put them down on paper after a subsequent telephone call to the International Cricket Council, which was then based across London at Lord's. My letter was acknowledged by the match referee Justice Ahmed Ibrahim, of Zimbabwe, but nothing further was said until a BBC television interview I did with Simon Hughes at tea on the fourth day, *before* Murali cleaned us up with nine second-innings wickets to complete a sixteen-victim haul for the match.

I really tried to watch my Ps and Qs, and said he was unorthodox, and if that was legal we should be teaching it. It was meant at face value – I didn't want to call him a chucker on live TV, but I obviously retained some reservations as per my correspondence with the ICC. I did no more than express a degree of doubt about his action's legitimacy. It was up to others to judge, but my comments were seen as inflammatory. Neither did it help in the post-play press conference when, asked if I had made any feelings on the matter known to the match referee, I blatantly lied and said 'no'.

Within a few hours I received a memo from my bosses at Lord's, asking me to explain my comments. This was not the first time they had taken this course of action. But surely they had done their research? If they wanted me to be England coach, then their homework would have told them where I was from and what I was about. They only needed to go to Accrington and have a look at where I grew up. If someone kicks you once, it's obligatory to kick them back twice, and preferably twice as hard too, just to stay in credit. You fight your corner; you scrap for everything.

I am from a community where it pays to be forthright; one in which people call things as they see them. During my three years at the helm, I was desperate to get away from the nicey, nicey, stiff-upper-lip Englishness we were showing and had always shown. Sometimes there is a time for straight talking, so forget this idea of showing the other cheek. It reflected the way I wanted the game to be played. If someone was coming at us, we were going to give it them in spades.

In the job description they made a point of emphasising the need for a higher profile when it came to the media – I think I gave them that. But my reaction to Geoff Boycott's comment on the final day that England would be better served with a coach 'who could keep his mouth shut' triggered the kind of publicity they were eager to avoid. It may not have been the wisest course of action in the circumstances but, in keeping with my beliefs, I confronted Geoffrey outside the commentary boxes in an area I took to be a private place. Unfortunately, although we parted amicably enough after I got my point across that I would prefer anything he had to say about me to be said to my face first, it had clearly reached someone's ears, and a summons to a meeting with Tim Lamb and Simon Pack followed later that week in a conference room at Lord's, at which we discussed the issues from The Oval.

This didn't take the form of an informal chat, even though that's what I had been anticipating on my train journey south. There was even an HR representative in the room (just who she was representing I could not fathom). Tim confirmed he had no issue with my TV interview with Hughes but with what had been said in the subsequent press conference. Now this was news to me, as the media manager Brian Murgatroyd had raised no concerns in our debrief upon its conclusion. In launching my defence of my public utterances on the Murali issue, I got Simon to acknowledge that I had lodged my concerns formally in a letter to the ICC, which he duly did.

But it was the Boycott altercation that they focused on and, after agreeing to disagree on whether this took place in a public or private area, I was shocked to discover following a brief recess that an ECB statement had been prepared in advance of our meeting. I argued quite forcibly that this was no way to treat an employee and that any such statement should be softened. They agreed they would contact me during my journey home for clearance to release a revised version. However, with no great discernible difference in its tone as the new version was relayed to me on my mobile phone, I lost my cool, told them to do whatever they wished and terminated the call.

The statement, which made reference to 'inappropriate comments' about Muralitharan and an 'altercation with a television presenter', continued: 'David Lloyd has been reprimanded, warned about his future conduct and left in no doubt as to the responsibilities that go with such a high profile position.' It finished with the standard clap-trap line: 'The matter is now closed and David goes as coach to Dhaka and to Australia with our full support.'

However, this had stung me so badly that in the immediate aftermath, I questioned whether I had the desire to lead those tours. Those within the bosom of what I believed was a strong team unit – people like Alec Stewart, the captain, and Wayne Morton, our feisty physiotherapist – urged me not to do anything rash. So, by the time I received an official letter from Lamb – effectively a final warning after the Zimbabwe affair – I had resolved to commit fully to the remaining eleven months of my contract.

On reflection, my treatment was a case of a sledgehammer being used to crack a nut. I had skirted around the periphery of the Murali issue and told another ex-player what I thought of his own comments. It was neither the last time Muralitharan would raise suspicion – indeed we were the opponents later that winter in Adelaide when the Australian umpire Ross Emerson's calling of him led to Arjuna Ranatunga's walk-off protest – nor that Boycott would provoke a reaction from someone within the England team. I have come to accept that is a consequence of straight-talking in the pundit's role – a pre-requisite of the job.

There were more important battles to be fought across those three years for me than re-engaging any Roses rivalry with Yorkshire's most-famous bespectacled man. Not least when we were trying to turn the tide of Ashes results in the summer of 1997 and allowed a 1-0 advantage early on to be overturned. Unlike my successors Duncan Fletcher, Andy Flower and Peter Moores, I had no real control over who played when or how often in county cricket during that six-match series. Once a player hits the Test team these days, their shire writes off their availability for evermore. By contrast, the only way we would ever get them a rest period was to dispatch chairman of selectors David Graveney cap in hand.

Ludicrously, we had to beg to get our crackerjack cricketers recuperation time, or even adequate practice for an international fixture. By the way, we rarely won a battle in this regard because the counties could not see the bigger picture. A £1.9 million annual handout and compensation for England calls on top has certainly helped alter thinking, but back then all players were remunerated by their counties, and in some instances that actually made the players develop a club-first mentality, a bit like what exists in top-level football.

A shift towards the England team taking priority only occurred after Fletcher took over in 1999. This came through the introduction of central contracts, and a cultural change that was necessary. Anyone involved in the game has to accept that it is international cricket that underpins the domestic structure. Previously, it could feel like players would turn out for England if and when they were free.

Dual commitments led to some players turning up 'fit' but

barely fit for purpose on occasion. Bowlers would rock up with jelly legs and need to recuperate rather than net with their colleagues once it got beyond midsummer. Thankfully, the medical monitoring has improved beyond recognition. Now, counties liaise with the ECB, and information on strength and conditioning and overall fitness is shared. If a player is summoned to the National Performance Centre in Loughborough for any matter, off they go.

Contrast that to when I was coach and arranged a team-bonding camp – a three-day get-together at the NatWest training premises in Oxfordshire – on the eve of the 1997 season. My aim was to develop a 'unity', concerned that whereas rivals like Australia and South Africa appeared tight, we were thrown together from the length and breadth of the country and dispatched on an overseas tour.

The subsequent reaction of Graham Thorpe to this summons showed the difficulty the players were under. Thorpe, one of the finest batsmen England has produced, on being asked to give up three days outside his cricket schedule, refused, citing it as a family time, and informing us that he would resume cricket activity closer to international matches. He turned up, following an assertive phone call from Tim Lamb, but I for one could understand the pressure these players were under at home. They weren't being paid to be there, and we were relying on them eating into their home lives.

I arranged for the squad to be addressed by Frank Dick, the former British Athletics Federation's director of coaching, who was carving out a reputation as a motivational speaker. The players were asked to think about their own personal landscapes. Were they mountains or valleys? Mountains were the individuals striving upwards and achieving, while the valleys would allow their performances to dip on occasion for an easier life. He spoke about the recipe for a good team ethic – collective trust and a willingness to be considered as a single entity, not as individuals. This proved a stimulating exercise during a very productive three days. Our mistake, I concede, was in trying to build on its success with other team-bonding jaunts in schedule gaps. Sometimes less is more.

What I certainly was looking for was positive thinking, and one of my initiatives was to create video montages of each individual player's best moments with their favourite music as an accompaniment. It took some diligence but I wanted them to acknowledge their good points. To complement this, I made a bloopers tape of the Australians. I wanted to dispel their immortal image.

There was certainly an air of confidence about us when the Australians arrived in 1997, and by the end of the Texaco Trophy that preceded the Test series, the nation was believing in us too. The 3-0 victory in those one-dayers could be accurately summarised as a trouncing.

A real energy ran through our team in that whitewash, exemplified by the way our lads threw themselves about in the field. A mobile team is always pleasing on the eye for a coach, and in the second match at The Oval, four of the six wickets we claimed were run-outs. Brought up under Jack Bond's tutelage, even in my coaching career I continued to emphasise the importance of fielding to the highest standards.

The inclusion of the Hollioake brothers, Adam and Ben, was invigorating for this team. They might have had Australian backgrounds but they showed they were neither uptight with nor weighed down by the attention and expectation this carried. They really energised us. Adam took a couple of wickets and then raced us to our target with an unbeaten 60-odd in the first of the three matches, at Headingley, while Ben's precocious talent was first witnessed on the international stage a few days later, with the series already settled, at Lord's.

Because of his tender years, in the pre-series media gatherings the presumption was we would be looking to slip Ben down the order and break him in gently. This was never our intention, though. We had selected him on ability, not age, and we had chosen him to bat No. 3. How refreshing it was to witness a young England player express himself fearlessly, driving Glenn McGrath down the ground and hoisting Shane Warne over deep midwicket for six. It may only have been two decades ago, but 63 off 48 balls was still a fair old lick in terms of a scoring rate.

Ben Hollioake was a really exciting player. Here was a true athlete, a talented sportsman, who had chosen cricket for his career path. Never did he consider failure as an option; he played purely on instinct. We wanted to expose his talent, not muzzle it. To his credit, the following year it was Alec Stewart as captain who really pushed for Andrew Flintoff to be in the England team. The assumption might have been that it was me because of a Lancashire bias, but not a bit of it. This selection of Ben was another example of faith in youth, and what a tragic loss to cricket it was when he died in 2002. Naturally it has led to thoughts of how good England might have been at one-day cricket with a side containing both Hollioake junior and Flintoff in their prime.

Seldom is there a correlation between what happens in white-ball and red-ball assignments, but beating Australia in any format provided further evidence that they were not impregnable in that summer of 1997. The previous winter I had chatted to Bob Woolmer, who had just been engaged in a series with the Australians as South Africa coach, and he reported that despite defeat he saw that this team could be beaten.

Unlike the disastrous decision to base the England team in Canterbury two years later for the 1999 World Cup when I had requested to be positioned in Leicester, a central location easily reached from north and south, the decision-makers at Lord's scheduled the start of the Ashes that summer perfectly. Birmingham is a great place to open any series with its patriotic crowd – that Eric Hollies Stand is as partisan as any in the country when it's at full capacity. Their vocal backing is equal to an extra man on the field.

Additionally, the conditions can be challenging for batsmen from overseas, even if they have enjoyed a decent period of acclimatisation, because the ball tends to nip around first thing in the morning. One of the strengths of that particular England side was the new-ball acumen of Darren Gough and Andrew Caddick. The reintroduction of Devon Malcolm for the first time since the spat in South Africa with Raymond Illingworth provided an injection of pace in reserve. Extreme speed is the one entity that can trouble even the finest batsmen, and Devon was not to be underestimated in this department.

We couldn't have started any better. The first morning was like a dream as the ball talked. Gough was the protagonist as eight Australian wickets toppled before lunch. Having made the most of the atmospheric assistance, the anticipated Australia fightback proved a fleeting one, and a near-triple century partnership between Nasser Hussain and Graham Thorpe put us on course for a win inside four days.

Even though Australia got to 327 for one next time around, the gulf was too wide to be bridged. The public reaction to us chasing down our modest fourth-innings target on the penultimate evening was memorable. Spectators pouring onto the outfield evoked memories of Lancashire's Gillette glories.

Unfortunately, this only served to stir Glenn McGrath from his slumber. During my time as England coach, there was not a pace bowler that provided more problems than McGrath. He was neither an out-and-out quick nor darn-right nasty with his bowling, he didn't seam or swing it lavishly, but his uncomplicated, repetitive action and nagging line meant he was a constant threat. Such a bowler preys on errors of judgement or loss of concentration by his opponents. Few have worn the Baggy Green with such distinction.

McGrath routed us with eight for 38 in the next match at Lord's, one that with rain as our ally we crept out of with a draw. However, our optimism was swiftly pricked over three consecutive defeats. It was an authoritative comeback that might have been stopped in its tracks but for an uncharacteristic miss in the slips by Thorpe when Australia were 50 for four. It denied debutant Mike Smith a maiden Test wicket and allowed Matthew Elliott to progress from 29 to 199.

Smith, Dewsbury-born but a prolific left-armer in county cricket with Gloucestershire, was selected for his ability to move the ball through the air and had taken ten wickets in a recent County Championship match at Headingley. This was a decent horses-for-courses pick and, despite suggestions to the contrary, was not at the behest of chairman of selectors David Graveney, a Gloucestershire man. There was scepticism from Atherton, the captain, as to what Smith would do if the ball did not swing due to his lack of height and speed, but all reports suggested that he got it to go like clockwork, and so we even entrusted him to choose our ball from the box presented to us by match referee Cammie Smith. Unfortunately, he didn't get it off the straight and we were all left to rue that life for Elliott.

One thing we do know about Australians is they hate losing to England, and so I was infuriated when our victory in the fifth and final match was deemed inconsequential because of alleged dead-rubber status. In previous series, England teams had lost 4-0 and not looked like winning games. Yet this time we had beaten them twice and there was still a sense of embedded failure to our performances. Undoubtedly, we deserved more credit.

It just so happened that we caught them on an Oval pitch that suited us – or certainly a pitch that suited Phil Tufnell. It was particularly pleasing to see Phil do well, because Mark Waugh had done an interview in the build-up to that Test match in which he questioned his ability. He spoke too hastily because Tuffers got him out with two absolute beauties.

Unusually, there was a decent build-up into that match and we got home in a tight game as Tufnell and Andrew Caddick shared 19 of the 20 wickets to fall, the former claiming match figures of 11 for 93. Yet when Australia, who took a 40-run lead on first innings, then dismissed us for a second time for just 163, we appeared to have as much chance as them winning the Eurovision Song Contest.

But there is something about chasing small targets that plays tricks on batting teams – for some reason batsmen start doing things they would never usually dream of, or alternatively they stop playing their shots altogether – so on a crumbling pitch and with a fervent crowd roaring the bowlers on, the theory was put to the test.

When in the mood, Tufnell and Caddick were both top-class performers. With confidence up, impishly skipping into his delivery stride, Tufnell got plenty of revolutions on the ball, and this was a tailor-made surface for his kind of artistry, as it fizzed from his left hand rather than rolled as was the case whenever he wasn't doing so well. Caddick had lots of similar attributes to McGrath and could be devastating when everything clicked into place.

In contrast to the boisterous post-match celebrations was Tufnell's reaction: so often the bar-room reveller he sat, towel draped over his head, for a period of quiet reflection. There was some to be done for me too – earlier that summer on the back of those Texaco Trophy displays, optimism overflowed. Unfortunately, we couldn't handle the opposition's spinner, Shane Warne.

We were not alone in this, of course, and analysis of what Warne did to opponents is fascinating. He did not overwhelm with a repertoire of variations – in fact, although he possessed one, he rarely bowled googlies. With him, you might get one or two over the course of a day's play. But his genius was in his relative simplicity. Most adversaries were set for what was coming – if you weren't sure how much the next leg-break was going to turn, he would do the decent thing and tell you – yet they just couldn't handle it. He possessed a great flipper, superb control and an ability to really rip the regulation leg-spinner. To me, the latter quality was key. Warne was different to other leg-spinners because of the sheer number of revolutions he managed to get on the ball, and the result of giving it such a significant rip was a deadly dip towards the leg-side before it spun the other way. Even after retirement, when he gave a Sky Sports masterclass during our Test match coverage in 2012, you could still hear the fizz of the seam as the ball made its way down the other end. Other leg-spinners might have got it to turn nicely; he got it to turn nastily with his strength of wrist. To be able to get the ball to shape in before spinning away was a God-given talent. You simply cannot teach someone to get that many revs on a ball.

Although in our planning meetings we discussed the need for an aggressive game plan to try to throw Warne, executing it was easier said than done when you had a once-in-a-lifetime bowler to contend with. Nasser Hussain's attempt to be proactive resulted in him being comprehensively stumped. But that was an isolated example because no one else had the confidence to go after one of the world's greatest ever bowlers.

Throughout the late 1990s, whenever we talked about balancing sides, we came back to a belief that we needed a five-man attack. But what we saw with Warne, and subsequently in Graeme Swann's career with England, was that with a world-class spinner in your team you needed only four. If you work on the theory of having to bowl ninety overs in a day, that leaves 25-30 for your controlling bowler, the spinner, and therefore no great burden for any of your pacemen.

The Warne question surfaced again for the 1998-99 Ashes. A shoulder injury had wrecked his year, and indeed led to him missing the Test series in Pakistan, but his impending return had echoes of Dennis Lillee's will-he-won't-he scenario in 1974-75.

Getty Images

By 1981, I was beginning to lose some of my enthusiasm for county cricket, and starting to think about my future. You can just make out the glasses I was wearing underneath my helmet, which helped improve my form.

Mirrorpix

Soon after retiring, I became an umpire – here I'm standing at the Parks as Oxford take on Kent in April 1987.

As coach of Lancashire in 1995, with Mike Watkinson.

A photocall on the day my appointment as England coach was announced, in April 1996.

With England captain Mike Atherton ahead of my first game in charge, a one-day international at The Oval against India.

Pointing out the key to success – there's only one thing a coach needs to make happen.

With some of my coaching team, John Emburey and Ian Botham, during the controversial tour of Zimbabwe in 1996–97.

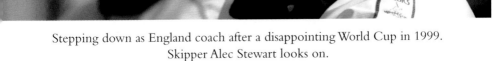

Stepping down as England coach after a disappointing World Cup in 1999. Skipper Alec Stewart looks on.

David Lloyd

It's always important to have a healthy breakfast before a Headingley Test.

Though it does mean I have to work it off in other ways – here I am training with my youngest son, Ben.

Graham Chadwick

The *Test Match Special* team for 1993. (Back row, L-R) Peter Baxter, Neville Oliver, Jonathan Agnew, Bill Frindall and me. (Front row, L-R): Fred Trueman, Brian Johnston and Trevor Bailey.

Since the beginning, I've been heavily involved in commentating on T20 cricket. (Above) At the launch of the 2004 competition with Ian Ward, Clare Connor and James Benning. (Below) In 2015, I had the chance to commentate at the IPL for the first time – there is plenty we in England could learn from this tournament.

Here I am fishing with Mark Taylor in Australia. It's much safer doing it that way than letting the fish come at you, as I did when I went underwater to get up close and personal with some sharks.

Life has always been about more than cricket. Playing with Tags in the garden, while proudly wearing my Accrington Stanley shirt; at the races in the Cheltenham festival; and with a pint of Leave the Car at Thwaites Brewery in Blackburn.

Presenting Sam Billings with his cap ahead of his England one-day debut against New Zealand in June 2015.

Back where it all started, at Accrington CC, with 'Jungle' Jimmy Hayhurst.

But even without Warne, the Australians had much the more potent spin attack, especially given Tufnell's selection omission. Stuart MacGill would have been a shoo-in selection in most other eras, and would undoubtedly have finished with double his Test-wicket haul of 208, but with Warne around he remained a peripheral figure.

We had prepared for high-quality Australia leg-spin in advance by engaging an expert in its art, Peter Philpott, a man I knew well from the Lancashire League, to work with the team. He had already lectured on the subject of leg-spin to emerging players in the ECB's development of excellence programme, and I wanted him to impart his knowledge to the seniors. In his sixties he might have been, but with age came experience and it included coaching both Warne and MacGill.

Peter was great on the theory – the idea was to get the players to understand the thought processes behind it, and what the bowler was trying to do – although for the practical side of things I drafted in Abdul Qadir, the former Pakistan leg-spinner. Abdul was no spring chicken and I wouldn't have fancied him in a race against anyone, but when it came to bowling he still bore the hall-marks of the magician. Being able to hire a quality leg-spinner was a real bonus.

What Abdul did was to deconstruct leg-spin by bowling within the parameters of his action at reduced speed. By slowing the whole process down, so that he went through it at only half or quarter pace, it was like facing a bowler in slow motion until he reached the point of delivery. That effectively let our batsmen see how the hand, the fingers and the wrist worked in unison. Once the batsmen got used to seeing the ball come out slowly, Abdul would build up his pace until it eventually came out properly. He was able to disguise his intricacies at full speed, and for him to strip everything back enabled our guys to train their brains and recog-nise what he was doing once he quickened back up.

Peter's work was more educational and revealed some intriguing information on Warne. We looked at his record in detail, and the research showed that those to have succeeded against him shared a certain trait – aggression. If it was an interesting revelation, there was also a caveat here as the number included Brian Lara and Sachin Tendulkar, the two best batsmen doing the rounds.

But Philpott simplified our strategy and made us see it from Warne's perspective. His primary objective, Peter argued, would be to be as economical as possible, going for as few as two runs an over, providing his captain with control and pressurising the opposition batsmen in terms of the scoreboard. If he succeeded in limiting runs, the opposition were in his trap before he struck. With McGrath at the other end you were not going anywhere in this scenario, and Peter insisted we needed to find ways of scoring at a more reasonable rate.

Unfortunately, we didn't manage that during my time as coach and there is arguably only Kevin Pietersen, of England batsmen, who has managed it since. Never during the time I was coaching, or watching Warne admiringly from the commentary box, have I seen anybody take him apart like Pietersen did at The Oval in 2005.

Our recruitment of Qadir, even on the most casual of terms, was not a commonplace move. English cricket rarely engaged foreign coaches at that stage, but I knew he was in Melbourne and wanted to make use of him. Of course, there were a clutch of overseas bowling advisors in the years that followed – Allan Donald, Ottis Gibson, Troy Cooley, Mushtaq Ahmed and David Saker to name a few.

We also had Chris Schofield, the emerging Lancashire leggie, as a temporary member of our travelling group. As a teenager at the end of the previous season, he had claimed eight wickets in a County Championship win over Gloucestershire. Over in Australia on a scholarship, he went with us whenever he was available to aid both his own development and our batsmen's preparation.

Warne did not actually appear until the final Test but his understudy was more than useful. In fact, he possessed a superior strike rate. We actually managed to get into the final match with the Ashes gone but the series still alive at 2-1 following victory at Melbourne. Predictably, perhaps, with Warne fit, the pitch at Sydney was a bit of a Bunsen. They picked Colin Miller, whose multi-skills saw him bowl seam-up with the new ball before reverting to off-spin, and he did so with incredible success, breaking Chuck Fleetwood-Smith's 63-year-old Sheffield Shield record of 60 wickets in a season with 67 in 1997-98.

I'm not sure of the last time Australia had gone into a match with three spinners in their line-up at home, but that is how they opted to go at the SCG and we could see why from the surface. With the conditions conducive to turn, we discussed playing more than one frontline spinner ourselves, and I proposed we pick Schofield. The selectors would not have been expecting a raging turner like this when the original tour selections were made months earlier, and we now found ourselves with all our eggs in one basket so to speak, with two off-spinners Robert Croft and Peter Such comprising our slow-bowling options. Michael Atherton had favoured the selection of Phil Tufnell despite his occasional off-field misdemeanours, but his successor Alec Stewart did not push for his inclusion.

Now, although not in the official party, I pushed for that of Schofield to give us some variation. But I just couldn't get the captain to sanction the idea, which was his prerogative. In the end, we included Ashley Giles, who had flown out ostensibly as a one-day squad player, in our twelve but the vote for the final place actually went to Alex Tudor, another pace bowler.

Australia had a decent battery of quality fast bowlers in Glenn McGrath, Damien Fleming, Jason Gillespie and Paul Reiffel, but our guys outbowled them at the MCG in the penultimate Test on what I would say was an English-type track. There were some really fine performances, none better than that of Dean Headley on the final day, and victory in Melbourne had kept alive our hopes of a drawn series.

But our chance of securing that went in the second innings, when Simon Taufel – the recently retired and very well-respected umpire, perhaps the best we had ever seen – made what in my opinion was a poor decision as a young third official.

At 60 for two in Australia's second innings, Michael Slater, going for a second run, was the subject of Headley's direct hit at the bowler's end. He appeared a couple of inches short, but when umpire Steve Dunne turned to television adjudication for the decision, instead of confirming that Slater was out, Taufel pressed the button to suggest he was in. Having conceded a 102-run deficit on first innings, we would have been right back in the game. Particularly when you consider that Slater went on to get 123 of Australia's 184 all out. His strokeplay simply took the game away from us. Small margins cost dear at the highest level and this England side, which possessed some very fine players in the late 1990s, had gone toe to toe with one of the great sides in Test history.

Steve Waugh, Australia's captain, was an utterly uncompromising character, who you felt would do anything within the spirit of the game to be victorious. He played it as tough as anyone that I ever saw, both as an individual competitor and a leader. Like Atherton, he thrived in the heat of the battle and relished verbal confrontation. In the knowledge that he wanted to engage in chat while at the crease, team orders were for our lads to keep quiet.

As with all Ashes series, it was customary to have a beer with your opposite number after play, and at the end of that 1998-99 series, the complimentary nature of Australia coach Geoff Marsh's comments as we shared ours were most welcome. 'You're getting closer,' he told me. Others had higher pre-series expectations of us than you might have considered too, with Dennis Lillee saying he thought this England team 'had the capacity to win the series'.

Arguably, however, we lacked Australia's depth. That much was evident when in mid-December, between the third and fourth Tests, in a match against an Australia A team in Hobart, we suffered a humiliating defeat that left me seething. In a high-scoring match, the Australian second string were dangled a carrot by Atherton – who was captaining, with Stewart and his vice-captain Nasser Hussain opting to sit out. He offered them a 376-run chase on the fourth and final day. Greg Blewett, in particular, took his toll on an attack fatigued from the exertions of the Test series with an unbeaten double hundred, leading the A side to a nine-wicket win with three-quarters of the final session unused. He and Corey Richards shared an unbeaten stand of 197 in 29 overs during the afternoon.

It didn't happen regularly but not for the first time I let rip in the dressing room. 'It's all right for you f***ing lot, I roared. 'But who has to front up and explain it? Joe C**t here.' Timing is everything, they say, and Darren Gough, another of those given the match off, just happened to be entering the room dressed as Santa Claus. 'And as for you, Father Christmas, you can f*** right off,' I added.

Once the postmortem was over, we moved on. Team spirit, something I viewed as essential, was still intact and the Ashes were still alive. At the Christmas dinner it was like that Hobart defeat had never happened, and that's the way it should be. Not to say that there were not frustrations at our repeating of the same old mistakes. Our habit of getting into good positions and either letting them slip completely, or allowing opponents off the hook in some way, was chief among them.

We were too inconsistent, and that reeked of fatigue to me. We had the talent but displaying it across an entire match, let alone a series, was often beyond us. The core players lurched into games knackered, and preparation could have been so much better.

By the end of that winter, it was becoming clear that my tenure had run its course. Whispers were getting back to me while we were in Australia that the board were interviewing Bob Woolmer. To hear that kind of thing when you are committed in a job is not nice. I don't know whether they did carry through with this interview or not, but it was deflating to consider they might be scouring the world markets for a replacement. I felt there had been some significant steps forward, yet we didn't necessarily win enough for either me or my employers to be fully satisfied – they had shown doubt in one sense by removing the rolling aspect of my twelve-month contract. In shaping the fortunes of the England team, I felt we were heading in the right direction after nine wins in thirty-four Tests, but I concede we could have done better. For the ECB's part, there could have been greater support, particularly when my passionate nature got the better of me.

Discussions were already underway on my future – Tim Lamb said he didn't feel able to give me any promise of longer-term commitment – when in mid-March, six weeks before the 1999 World Cup squad were due to meet up, I travelled to Ian MacLaurin's London offices to map out my own career from that point forward. Although it was the best job in the world as far as I was concerned, and my coaching instincts alerted me of potential reward to come, the pragmatist inside me offered a contradictory view. I needed clarity over my future. My contract was due to run out in August and now into my fifties I was looking for some security.

So it was that on the eve of a global tournament we agreed I would leave ahead of schedule, thus allowing my successor time to bed in against New Zealand ahead of that winter's tour to South Africa. From a self-preservation point of view, I didn't want to be in a position where I left that meeting in New College Street,

London, with the potential to be sacked weeks later with no other employment lined up. From the board's point of view, they saw the World Cup as a massive competition and didn't feel compelled to make a decision at that time.

Yet I didn't feel that the planning replicated their thoughts on the competition's importance. Lots of small things that would have made a big difference just weren't right. We were based in Canterbury when I had tried to make an advantage of being the host country by requesting we were based in Leicester, a more central location. We were under-prepared courtesy of a payment dispute by the players and we got what we deserved. Meanwhile, I got the career change that I was aware of becoming a possibility the previous winter when the BBC's *Test Match Special*, the new players in televised cricket Channel 4, which had started screening home internationals, and Sky Sports all made tentative approaches towards me. Neither was there time to lick my wounds as the inquests took hold in soggy Birmingham – because within hours of our exit John Gayleard from Sky Sports was on the phone, telling me I was starting my new job with immediate effect.

CHAPTER 11

The Engine's Running

It could have been 'Don't panic, Mr Mainwaring,' or 'Oooh, I could crush a grape.' Just as easily it might have been 'I don't believe it,' or 'You plonker, Rodney.' All these catchphrases have one thing in common. None of them is mine. Then again, to tell you the truth, neither is 'Start the car,' my signature on commentary. Sure, it has become synonymous with my stints behind the microphone for Sky Sports, a job I began immediately after the 1999 World Cup campaign, but it wasn't a line I can lay claim to because I pilfered it during my days on the northern after-dinner circuit.

During the 1980s, I would often be paired on evening bills with a comedian from Blackpool called Mick Miller, and we were each booked in half-hour slots. Being a meticulous time-keeper when it came to his stint, Mick would always be keeping an eye on his watch. If you ask me, that was natural enough because I always wanted my time to be over as quickly as possible at these dos. Speaking in front of a hundred blokes plied with booze was certainly more of a means to an end than a labour of love, as far as I was concerned. Glancing down at his wrist, when he realised he had ticked over past the 29-minute mark, Mick would tell the floor: 'I've almost done my time, the money's mine, start the car.'

I couldn't tell you the exact game in which I first used this magpied phrase, but I always liked the idea of the getaway when the job was done and so began using it to signify to the viewers that in my opinion a run chase had been broken or that a team's pursuit had been thwarted. Furthermore, I'm not sure how it stuck with me, as it wasn't a conscious decision to use it repeatedly, but cricket's audience must have latched onto it, because if there is one line that recurs with my time behind the microphone, that is the one.

There is a chance I muttered it in those first few weeks of work for Sky in the summer of 1999, immediately after defeat to India had us in the England camp reaching for the car keys ahead of schedule. That spring saw seismic change for me. I became a married man again, and with that came a new life in Cheadle Hulme with Diana. I also became a television commentator again.

During my discussions with Ian MacLaurin in London, I let it be known that other job offers had to be considered in the absence of anything concrete being promised from August onwards when my employment with the ECB was due to expire. I proposed a post-World Cup departure as the most suitable for all parties. Of course, professional pride triggered a desire in me for him to shout me down and turn talk to a future that involved me. It was not forthcoming and the Team England identity we had worked hard to create was going to be given to another to safeguard. To the last, I have to say MacLaurin was supportive, and he gave the distinct impression that he was sad rather than glad that we were parting, and that he didn't want to sack me. Conversely, he was in no position to give any promises.

But as I left the job with England I walked straight into another with Sky. News of my departure was released immediately, and within twenty-four hours I was being given a ten-minute deadline in a phone call with Gayleard. I asked for extra time to consider and was given a firm no. Within the hour, a faxed copy of a contract offer was in my hands, and my official departure press conference with England was immediately followed by another with Sky in which they presented me as their new man. 'David Lloyd, Sky Sports, Old Trafford,' sounded all right to me.

Suddenly Ian Botham, Paul Allott, Bob Willis, Michael Holding and David Gower, all guys I knew personally, were going to be colleagues. I would be made to feel very welcome, but it did rankle a touch at first that these guys had been critical of the work I'd been doing as coach. That didn't last long, though. You have to come to terms with a few things when you jump the fence. As soon as you're on the other side of it, you appreciate that little bit more that you are going to get praised and you're going to get criticised. There's an expectation on you to have opinions if you are commentating for a living. It's a public service, lest we forget.

My first ever commentary was for BBC radio in the 1986 NatWest final between Lancashire and Sussex when I was used as the Lancashire expert and John Barclay chosen as the equivalent for Sussex. My first mistake was to turn up in a suit. Of course, for radio you don't need that. But I believed that working for the BBC meant I had to look smart. Naively, I also expected there to be rehearsals in advance when I agreed to the gig, so it was something of a shock to the system when I was thrown live on air. It's a simplistic way of looking at things now, but all you really need to know in that position is your subject, and I was pretty well qualified there.

In the course of time, I was also to discover that when it came to another of the broadcaster's gifts, I had struck gold. You need to have a voice for radio, and I know I'm so lucky in this regard, because (and I don't know why) according to people whose expertise is TV or radio, lots have told me that my voice is perfect.

Not that my initial experience with the Beeb proved a smooth ride, despite that first engagement at Lord's being followed by further offers of work. For when Peter Baxter, the producer of *Test Match Special*, wrote to me during this period as an irregular summariser and offered me a more regular position, I declined. At that jack-of-all time in my life, I considered myself too busy to take on a regular position. I was trying to earn a living through my dinners, coaching and other things besides, and was fearful of throwing all my eggs in one basket.

After this, Peter wrote back to me instructing me to think again. I chatted to Christopher Martin-Jenkins about the situation and he advised me that although I might find that the remuneration was quite modest, radio and a flagship show like *TMS* provided a profile from which came many, many spin-offs. So that, in a nutshell, is how the broadcasting part of my career started.

Needless to say, Peter's forthright correspondence, and CMJ's supplementary advice, made me re-evaluate where my split work life was heading. It was one that was becoming more and more hectic and varied, and certain parts of it were more lucrative than others. If my ambition had briefly taken in a desire to be part of a new international umpiring panel when it was first floated in the late 1980s, it proved a fleeting one.

When I was learning the ropes behind the microphone with *Test Match Special*, I was grateful for the generosity of spirit shown to me by trained broadcasters, those who knew the tricks of the trade. As with most things, being part of a commentary team becomes easier with practice. Back then, the main commentator, the lead, described the action. The summariser, someone to have played the game to a high standard and more often than not a former international such as myself, then came in between overs to provide expert analysis. Your job was to reflect on what had just gone on and what might happen. Then it was time to shut up, allowing the lead man to call the full over before you interjected again. That process was sacrosanct, although the contemporary template is much less structured and at times resembles a free-for-all.

At the time I was dealing with broadcasters of the calibre of CMJ, Brian Johnston and Don Mosey, unbelievably accomplished lead commentators, so there was little chance of me straying off course, and from the back of the box I was able to listen for guidance from fellow summarisers such as Trevor Bailey and Fred Trueman. Yes, we had great fun but there was a real discipline to it all, and it was as much for their skill at the job as my understanding of it that I would never cut in out of sync. Johnston, Martin-Jenkins and Mosey were like conductors, guiding you in and out.

Another who made commentary look like a cakewalk was Richie Benaud, an outstanding cricketer for Australia, an ace as a captain, but lest we forget someone who went on to become the finest of broadcasters on retirement. He put in the hard yards to learn the skills, and he used the greatest trick of them all regularly. It is a misconception that commentating is solely about speaking. It's not. It's about knowing when to speak. Equally, it is about knowing when to stay silent. Richie was a master of this.

There's a lesson here for a few of the blokes who pick up a mic in this day and age. Not long after television channels made a move to three commentators, I had the honour of being asked to do a stint on Australia's Channel 9 during an Ashes Test over there. Richie's modus operandi was to keep his utterances to a minimum. In so doing, when he did have something to say, you listened.

On this occasion in question, the usual economy of words had been employed by him when he picked up on something in the middle and flicked what we call the lazy switch, so he could have a quiet word with the director without the viewers hearing him. He wanted some footage of an incident he'd spotted a couple of overs earlier – Shane Warne had done something in the slips and it had passed the rest of us by. After a short interlude, the footage he wanted was located. Warne, who hadn't bowled yet – but who would go on to skittle England for the umpteenth time – had picked up his bowling marker, a small white disc, and thrown it to where he thought he'd be starting his run-up. Between overs, they broadcast Warne's gesture, with a simple accompaniment: 'Shane Warne's just put a marker down.'

That was Richie's only contribution in the half-hour we were on together, but it beat anything else we had to offer. One line! It was classic Benaud: he had the eagle eye to see what Warne was doing in the first place, the confidence to stay quiet while we rabbited on, and the perfect choice of words. As he might have put it himself: marvellous.

The coverage at the 2015 World Cup emphasised just how good he was. Ill health meant he couldn't take his place as scheduled, and absence made the heart grow fonder for his laconic style. For some reason Star Sports, the tournament's global broadcasters, used a team of rookies to commentate and threw their least experienced together, it seemed, for the final. Some of them were among the game's greatest modern-day players, wonderful talents, but with bats and balls in hand, not mics.

Frustratingly, it was painfully evident that none of them had done much commentary. Neither was it apparent that they had observed how the job is done properly or been given any meaningful advice by those who had offered them a place in the commentary box either. It was terrible TV. They just couldn't pinpoint the moment – no emotion, no elation, no despair. At times, you had to remind yourself that a cricket match was being played as they regaled the viewers with tales of their own careers. They had plenty to say, it seemed, just not much on the most significant one-day match played anywhere for the last four years.

How we missed Richie that evening. He never went overboard, and the size of the occasion would not have changed him one little bit, but he could have captured all those qualities in that understated way of his.

Sometimes he could be very understated indeed. I remember talking to Michael Slater, who teamed up with him in the commentary box in his later years. He told me about one day when Richie did two half-hour stints as one of Channel 9's trio, and did not utter a single word. That was Richie – content to sit on nought and make hay later when the opportunity presented itself. If there was nothing to add to the picture the viewers could see, he wouldn't offer anything.

One thing that you have to remember on TV is that the viewer can see the cricket. Your voice is supplementary. It really pains me now, for example, when some commentators start reading out a graphic that has appeared on screen for all to see. It might be the top ten leading run-scorers at a particular ground, or the best batting averages of players when chasing in one-day internationals. Visual aids are part of television coverage. They are meant to complement the topic of discussion. So to read out the list from top to bottom is incredibly naïve, even patronising. Perhaps it's indicative of a spoon-fed generation. I would be having a quiet word, reminding them that the viewers in 99 per cent of cases will be able to read.

In contrast, Richie would consider the list, and then say something like: 'The way things are going number four could soon be moving up as high as number two.' He wouldn't even name names – he respected the intelligence of the viewer. And I know how much viewers respond to that.

One of his best qualities was that he never sought the limelight. He wasn't in it for the ego. He'd turn up in the commentary box and if he was off-air, he'd set up at the back of the box, take out his computer, have a gander at the latest horse racing cards or do his homework on the newest player on the scene, recent performances from a team or the characteristics of previous matches at the ground in question.

He was always fully equipped when he took the chair. The chemistry he had with the likes of Tony Greig and Bill Lawry was amazing. It was unmissable. And it was based on a deep mutual respect and love of the game.

Boy, he loved the game. One evening, Richie, the former Manchester United manager Ron Atkinson and I were treated to dinner in Birmingham by the *News of the World*, which we were all working for at the time. Ron was covered in his signature bling and telling us all how he could get into any nightclub in town. He was clearly ready for a lively evening. Richie wasn't a big drinker but he'd allowed himself a couple of glasses of red, and he started telling this story about the great Australian leg-spinner Bill O'Reilly. It's fair to say the story was on the longish side, and by the time Ron had disappeared into the night and Richie was being bundled into a waiting taxi, we were still learning all about the man they nicknamed Tiger. We had got as far as his third Test appearance, I think.

That enthusiasm was typical of Richie's devotion to the game. But he possessed this wit that made all other commentators want to be like him. He didn't really go in for after-dinner speaking, but he might occasionally be asked to say a few words at functions. Once he spotted me in the audience at one, and quickly remembered the time I had my virility challenged by that hoodlum Jeff Thomson (have I mentioned that before?).

'Ah, there's David Lloyd,' Richie said. 'I remember him telling us in 1974–75 how he could play Thommo with his c**k … and then he proceeded to do precisely that.' The joke was all in the pause and the timing.

He was a great leg-spinner, a superb tactician, and a lovely bloke who won respect with his demeanour. I can just imagine how warmly he'll be welcomed by some of the other great commentators up in the sky: Brian Johnston, Alan McGilvray, John Arlott, even Fred Trueman. Fred was often known to splutter: 'I just don't know what's going off out there.' Richie, it's safe to say, never suffered from the same affliction. He was the doyen of the commentary box because he was so astute.

If there has been anything that has linked me to Benaud it has been attitude, I hope. 'What I want most from being a television commentator is to be able to feel that, when I say something, I am talking to friends,' he once said. That's how I feel about my job. I share his mantra of engaging brain before speaking (although some might not believe that at times). What I mean is that it's much better to get whatever point across in as few words as possible. Whether you are trying to make a serious reflection on the match's progress or raise a smile or a chuckle, do it succinctly. Do not rabbit on.

Richie was the master of delivery. With famous lines like, 'Captaincy is ninety per cent luck and ten per cent skill ... but don't try it without that ten per cent,' he had people hanging on his every word.

When you are on lead commentary, on the first morning of a Test match, say, it feels like you're batting for the folks at home. They're not alongside you but they're with you nevertheless, and there is always a moment of excitement when it's your turn to set the scene. Sometimes, when David Gower hands over from the studio you have to give it a moment's pause to allow the rest of the world to come in. Then, once you have composed yourself, you're away. It's a little bit like the start of an innings. You want to get going; to get that single to get off the mark. And hopefully once you get going, you will have painted the picture for the viewer, helped them to qualify what they are seeing, and started the process of getting them on the edge of their seats. Then, it's time for the players to keep their part of the bargain.

Being a commentator is to be part of the entertainment industry, and I view my job as one to entertain. On occasion I am sat there imagining that Bryan Henderson, who as producer sits behind me, has Lloyd, the letter P and number 45 swirling around his head. But the skill is to know when it's time to dumb down and when to be deadly serious, and it's the cricket that generally dictates the mood. The fun is between overs and during lulls in the action – it's then that a flick of the lazy switch and a search of the Western Terrace leads to sweepstakes on the size of the beer snakes or the number of fancy dress Elvises. Sometimes a steward confiscating a beach ball can be compulsive viewing.

What the public don't like, I'm certain, is being shown a bank of dignitaries in the crowd, which is becoming an annoying trend in some parts of the world. Who are these people and what do they do? Well, they certainly didn't play cricket, even when they were twelve stone lighter. For some reason, though, the Indian broadcasters insist they have to be shown because they're important. But if I'm out on loan to another broadcaster as part of my contractual obligations with Sky, I refuse point-blank to say who they are, and never will. I just shut up. It's different if you happen to spot a Hugh Jackman, Michael Parkinson or Mick Jagger in the crowd, but gratuitous plugs for non-cricketing, non-celebrities? No thanks.

Brian Johnston was one of a kind in his search for gentle mischief, but I'm not sure in these days of the politically correct he would get away with his tactic of avoiding tricky names for overseas players by dubbing them something completely different. Peter Baxter was a stickler for getting names right, but the 1991 tourists from Sri Lanka had a couple of particularly tricky names to pronounce, and when the seamer Kapila Wijegunawardene made his Test debut at Lord's, Johnners said: 'I'm going to call him Wagner, after the great composer.'

But there was never any malice, just unadulterated fun in that *TMS* box, with Fred Trueman playing up to his billing as the clown prince. One of Fred's foibles was his time-keeping, always turning up at the last minute, worrying about where to park his car, and making sure his wife Veronica was comfortable for the day. On one particular occasion in 1992, on his home ground of Headingley no less, he had made his way up to the rickety old commentary box at the top of the rugby stand behind schedule. The Test match between England and Pakistan had already started and it was the famous occasion when Neil Mallender had been chosen as a horses-for-courses selection.

Fred came blustering into our chicken coop after the first over had gone down: 'What a job I've had getting in, parking up, and getting Veronica to her seat. I've sat her with Sir Lawrence Somebody-or-other.' This was Sir Lawrence Byford, president of Yorkshire County Cricket Club.

'Fred's arrived, everyone, wonderful to see you,' Johnners greeted him on behalf of the nation.

Fred had got his pipe with him and it was stoking up like Ferrybridge Power Station. Within a couple of minutes, the entire box was covered in fog and visibility became a challenge.

Johnners rejoined: 'See you've got the pipe going, Fred. You don't inhale, do you?'

Before Fred could get a word in, Bill Frindall raised his head from his scorebook to interject: 'No, but we do.'

Then Fred chips in by asking: 'Who's that running in from the Kirkstall Lane End?

'Neil Mallender, Fred.'

'And who does he play for?'

'Northamptonshire, Fred.'

'Well, I am here to tell you that there have been some great bowlers run in from the Kirkstall Lane End – and he's not one of them!'

He added: 'Neither does he look like a well man, to me.'

Of course, Mallender's nickname was Ghost because of his milky white complexion, and a target for Fred's curmudgeonly treatment of any rival seam or swing bowlers. It would not have mattered a jot to him that Mallender claimed eight wickets, and returned the best figures on debut by an England bowler in a decade, to help his side to victory. In my mind, from an English perspective, there has never been anyone to touch Fred. It was clearly the same in his mind too, although he didn't half play up to the caricature of himself that everyone was so fond of developing.

When Jonathan Agnew came on board as the BBC's cricket correspondent, he and I would playfully masquerade as listeners and send in questions via fax, then sit at the back of the box giggling as Johnners would ask things like: 'Who in your opinion, Fred, are the six fastest bowlers that England have produced?'

'Well, there were me ...'

'Oh, there must be seven,' Johnners would say, in that wonderfully understated tone.

Cricket lends itself to the most serious analysis and slapstick humour sitting side by side, and that is why *TMS* has been such a well-loved institution. But, like me, these men were true patriots and cared deeply about the fortunes of the England team, none more so than Fred.

Back in 1984, after David Gower's declaration set West Indies 342 in 78 overs to win a Test match at Lord's, Fred was being teed up by the lead commentators with lines such as: 'Well, it's going well for West Indies here, Fred,' and 'What a start, England would have thought there were only two results possible on this final day ...'

Other than a grunt, Fred didn't say a word, leading to him being asked: 'Would you like to expand on that?'

'No. They're that bad I am saying nowt!'

Of course, that was not what was expected of a radio summariser, and the quick-witted Christopher Martin-Jenkins replied: 'Well, the general idea on radio is that somebody does so, so I'll continue.'

On another occasion, the 'it-was-always-better-in-my-day' Trueman was in full flow when discussion turned to the best batsmen to have graced the game. 'Well, there was Leonard. He was a wonderful player, Leonard,' said Fred, referring to Len Hutton.

'Then, there was the great Wally.'

To which Johnners said: 'Which great Wally's that?'

Fred added that the great Wally in question was Wally Hammond, one of the most difficult batsmen he had ever bowled against. Cue guffaws when Frindall, whose brain was the equivalent of a Cricipedia, said: 'That's strange, Fred, because you never actually played against him.' It turned out that their careers had just missed each other's.

Two things you could be sure about in the *TMS* box: there was never a dull moment and there would always be a glass of red wine or two after lunch. Trevor Bailey, a *TMS* stalwart for a quarter of a century until 1999, would get asked a question and be in such a state of relaxation that his initial response – a 'mmmmm ... mmwww' – sounded as though he was heavily constipated. Nothing much would follow. The Boil – as he became known because of the way Bailey sounded when pronounced by Australians – had a language all of his own. Nothing impressed him as much as a meticulous seamer: 'He's accr't, very accr't,' he would enthuse. To be honest, I'm not sure what Trevor would make of the disparity between bat and ball these days, because rather than condemn the beamer he would be all for one being slid in every now and again to keep the batsman honest.

No one was more eccentric than CMJ, whose position as a most respected broadcaster, author and national newspaper cricket correspondent was offset by his absent-mindedness. Known as the Major, it might have passed for Major Mishap because he was renowned for such madcap errors as trying to ring *The Times* sports desk with a remote control rather than his mobile, mildly agitated at the lack of reception. On another occasion while at his hotel, he was listening to music on his MP3 player while cutting some newspaper articles out to paste in his scrapbook. When the music stopped he assumed he had run out of batteries. So he put a new set in, frustratingly and confusingly to no avail. In need of help, he tracked down Mike Selvey, of the *Guardian*, for some technical guidance. It turned out he had cut straight through the wire.

There was great joy in the *Test Match Special* box in the summer of 2014 because Henry Blofeld celebrated forty years on the team, and I doubt his level of enthusiasm has dropped. I cannot imagine how many pigeons and buses he's called over the years. Probably a similar number to wickets and maidens. He may not have been a professional cricketer himself, but Blowers is as calamitous as the rest, and with commitment to boot. For the opening Lord's Test of the summer, he turned up looking his usual resplendent self in his red trousers, which must have been touch and go after setting fire to himself during his own dinner party. Apparently, an errant candle found its way onto his attire. The old boy said he thought he was being cremated but he lived to tell the tale and was in sprightly form – if slightly scorched.

Talking of dinner, it's a presumption that the Sky Sports commentary team hangs out socially after hours. But that is absolutely not the case. There are lots of people with lots of opinions in that box, some iconic cricketers who played for England and many former captains, and as in a dressing room environment we all have different interests and different people we click with: Ian Botham and David Gower like fine dining, fine wines; Mikey Holding is devoted to his computer and horse racing; Michael Atherton, Nasser Hussain and myself generally tend to be beer-and-curry men with producer Bryan Henderson and Mark Lynch, the director. Ian Ward is great company and has a permanent thirst.

Some things we do religiously, such as the grand slam of naan in Nottingham. On a short stretch of Maid Marian Way, there are about half a dozen Indian restaurants and we are in a different one every night. Starting off with a couple of pints at the Old Bell, the Lincolnshire Poacher or Olde Trip to Jerusalem, we then slip off down to one of the curry houses. We tend to let off more gas at a Trent Bridge Test than anywhere else.

On other occasions, Atherton does go off piste to join the pompous dining club, attending restaurants that serve things called jus and foam, and provide tasting menus with twenty little bits of nothing on them. On one occasion, Gower and Derek Pringle were tasting some wines at £120 a bottle. One was slatey and the next one was gritty, apparently. I told them that they sounded ridiculous, like they had experience of sampling roof tiles and the remnants at the bottom of a budgie's cage, but they dismissed me as a heathen and told me to jog on.

It takes all sorts of different characters to gel to make a team, and Shane Warne and Hussain make quite a contrast. Warnie can be very dramatic early in a morning, regularly warning our producer Bryan Henderson that he has not had enough sleep, only to qualify it with: 'But I am here – I've turned up for ya.' Goodness knows what he has been up to. Unfortunately, the most trouble he has ever got me into was when a ball slipped from my hand during one of our lunchtime masterclasses and struck the lens of one of the £34,000 cameras. Our previous boss Paul King told us off like a couple of naughty schoolboys.

Sometimes Nasser will tell us he has seen enough of us during the day and will stay in his hotel room on his tod. Who do you think the winner is there? When he does come out, it can often lead to disaster. On one night out in Hampstead, first his car wouldn't start and had to be trailered back to Essex. Then the hotel lost his luggage, so he had to come out in his work gear. Finally, the boss promptly spilled Sauvignon Blanc over him. Not sure Nasser saw the funny side.

In contrast to the slapstick of *TMS*, Paul Allott and Bob Willis are very serious broadcasters, some would even argue dour and boring in Bob's case, but away from the camera they can be outrageous fun. Bob has found himself a great niche on Sky Sports with his Verdict – the part of the highlights show during which he tells it exactly how it is. For me this has become compulsive viewing; everyone is waiting for what he is going to come out with next, and social media is always abuzz in anticipation of Bob's appearance when England have done badly. After losing 5-0 in Australia during the winter of 2013-14, he was asked for his thoughts. 'They should all be sent home, economy class,' he said. 'Some of them strapped to the wings.'

When Duncan Fletcher oversaw the previous whitewash down under seven years previously, Bob got out of his seat, sending wires flying everywhere, to lean into the camera five metres away, prod it and say: 'I know you are watching, Duncan Fletcher. Go now!' At times he is unmissable.

There have been other great Bobisms over recent years. One day Charles Colvile expressed the opinion that it was a shame rain had stopped play, and that it had denied the Barmy Army their money's worth. 'What do you think of the Barmy Army?' Charlie asked him. 'They should all be gassed.' He also got hounded out of the St Lawrence Ground in Canterbury to a cacophony of boos in a domestic game after Colvile got him going again on the subject of the lime tree that once famously stood within the boundary before nature and high winds took their course. In contrast to Colin Cowdrey, who eulogised it to the extent he claimed if he had a wish for a final act on earth, it would be to speed a cover drive towards it for four, Bob simply snarled: 'Should have been chopped down years ago. Whoever heard of a tree in the middle of a cricket field?'

Comedians like Frankie Boyle can get away with that kind of thing and much worse, but Bob does tend to upset people. You have to remember he is playing a bit of a role here. What should not be underestimated, however, is his passion for English cricket, and in his assessment of it he pulls no punches. If you had a chance, you would be hard pressed not to enjoy his company over a couple of pints because he lives life.

You are certainly left in no doubt that this is the case with Bill Lawry, a master of immersing himself in the action. He completely feels it, becomes like a fan in the very best possible way. People say that players don't leave anything on the pitch when they have played well, and it's a bit like that in his commentary. When he calls a game, he's out of his seat as it reaches its climax, and standing up is something I have copied. At the end of a match when the run chase is counting down, you are just in the zone. It's no good being too cool for school. You have to transmit the emotion involved. There's a winner and a loser here. There are viewers at home wanting one team to win and the other to lose, and part of the excitement of a good game is being taken on an emotional journey. When you know you have done it right, it's an exhilarating feeling. Sky are not a company that blow the wind up your backside, but when it's all finished and the guys are de-rigging after an epic conclusion and your producer gives you a slap on the back and a thumbs up, that is satisfaction.

Taking pride in what you do is a prerequisite of any job for me, and I have to admit to not enjoying the contrast in style when I have worked for Star Sports – who own the rights for International Cricket Council events such as World Cups. Undoubtedly, there has been a massive shift during my time with them towards incessant chat, and the motormouth style they do nothing to discourage is a total turn off for me. They get iconic players through the door and plonk them behind the microphone, which is doing everyone a disservice.

Graeme Smith, Rahul Dravid and Brian Lara were examples of wonderful cricketers, but as I mentioned earlier subjecting these giants of the modern game to stints alongside each other for

World Cup knockout matches, without appearing to have given them any practice or experience, was totally wrong in my book. When I watch cricket on television, I find myself studying the production rather than the action itself, and I was so horrified during the semi-final match between South Africa and New Zealand, arguably the best contest of the whole 2015 tournament, that I had to switch the volume off.

Some people can make commentary look easy, and they tend to be the ones who do the job regularly. These guys were badly exposed for their lack of mileage in the field, but they were not wholly to blame. The majority of the fault lay with the producer, I'm sorry to say, who should have been telling them to get off peripheral subjects and focus on the monitor alongside them. When a game is going on, there is a huge vista in front of you and a tiny monitor that you work to. Primarily you work to that monitor, not the full field, as you need to know what pictures are being screened and what is coming up. You work off the monitor and glance at the game, not the other way around.

When commentating, you're not only communicating with the rest of the world, you're communicating with the rest of your colleagues. Instructions through the earpiece tell you what is coming up – you are listening to the director for what happens next while the assistant producer alerts you for advert breaks, taking you in and out on a one, two, three count. The producer is sat behind you, alongside you are your co-commentators and the assistant producer is downstairs. It's a skill that takes some mastering and I defy anyone to present evidence of it being completely mastered first time.

You simply cannot be coming in halfway through a sentence when the rest of the world is joining you, because the audience naturally thinks: 'What the hell are they on about?' This takes some getting used to and some are unable to do it, and don't even try, refusing to either listen to or wear the earpiece altogether. I know when we at Sky invite players or coaches in for short stints in domestic matches to give them an insight into what goes on, nearly all of them are reluctant to wear these essential accessories because they find it a distraction. The knack is to have the volume turned down so the voices are there, in the background, passive rather than active but audible, so you can navigate your way through.

The absolute no-no for us is to be talking when the play is live. The golden rule is 'run up, shut up'. Simply, when a bowler has started his run up and you are off on one, telling some story about 1992, you cut it short. If that delivery is a wicket ball or a six, it cannot be used for the edit for the highlights, because as good as your story might be, a ten-second clip of it sounds odd. Another thing that I hate with a passion is when, during action in a cricket match, the coverage leaves the middle to move to the boundary edge to talk to somebody. This is live sport. Why do I want to see two talking heads when there's a game going on? It's a total non-sense. Why would you want to sacrifice the chance of seeing a match-turning moment for an interview with a non-playing member of the squad or an assistant coach? Can you imagine Chris Kamara on the touchline talking to Jose Mourinho with Arsenal on the attack? Would Ray French be in conversation with Kevin Sinfield, sat on the Leeds Rhinos subs' bench, when Wigan's winger was sprinting down the touchline? No. Yet the Indian broadcasters are obsessed with doing it.

Whatever people say – and there is a lot of muck thrown at Sky – one thing that the company cannot be faulted on by any critic is the quality of the product. Sky Sports invests heavily in cricket, and the bottom line is that it is a company that finances the game in England, whether you like that or not. As far as I'm aware, and I am just a commentator, there were no other bidders for the product of live international cricket when it last went out to tender in 2012. All the talk about terrestrial versus subscription television is all well and good, but there are some fundamental questions to be asked before you even get to bidding and Sky's £65 million a year contract.

For a start, where would these terrestrial channels be putting it? Cricket matches finish sometimes at seven and eight o'clock at night, if there has been an interruption. How would that be factored into their scheduling, and where is a mainstream channel going to put a day-night match, when its timing would eat into your primetime schedule? That is a massive problem and the very reason why terrestrial stations are lukewarm in putting live cricket on. I'm not wishing to dismiss other people's opinions lightly, but I do believe that Sky get a raw deal. They are able to use their platform of multi-channels to put the product on and pay handsomely for the privilege. One thing that is forgotten is that Sky have been committed in the long term. Since 1991 every England match overseas has been screened, and even in those days there was not a rival to show anywhere near that level of commitment. Yet the discourse, whenever the subject of cricket on TV is raised, usually takes on a suggestion that Sky has somehow stolen live action from the majority of the population.

Equally, when panic spreads at a drop in numbers playing recreationally in England as was reported in late 2014, it's a very lazy assumption that the reason kids aren't playing the game is because cricket is no longer a terrestrial property. In this day and age, a lot of core sports are down on their participation figures and it's nothing to do with what's on in the living room. It's because there are so many other things to do: cycling, canoeing, abseiling, rock climbing just for starters. All these exciting activities, previously one-off leisure pursuits, have come into mainstream life. It's not where they existed two decades ago. Now there are so many avenues of sport to go down.

The one question I would pose is: where would English cricket be without Sky's money? Of course, the compromise is that there are not as many Sky households as terrestrial, and I cannot argue with that. But in defence of my employers, I have calculated that at the time of writing the cost of Sky Sports is the equivalent of four pints of lager a week. There are lots of housing estates dotted with satellite dishes, so it cannot be out of the reach of everyone. If you are a real lover of sport and want to watch it live you have to pay for it, and in turn that pays for the sport.

CHAPTER 12

The Kapes Crusader

Kevin Pietersen is the best England batsman that I have ever seen. You can go through a list of Tom Graveney, Peter May, Colin Cowdrey, Geoffrey Boycott, Graham Gooch and David Gower – but to me Kevin's the number one, because when he's at the crease you cannot take your eyes off him.

How sad then that he should have spent so much time on the outside of the team in a saga that seemingly ran longer than *The Mousetrap*. Let's be frank, it's not a situation in which anyone involved has come out smelling of roses. For a start, to have issued a 'sacking' and then reiterated that Pietersen would not be picked due to 'trust' issues shows that the entire affair was not handled brilliantly by the England and Wales Cricket Board. And yet to focus solely on the acute sense of loss of the paying public – a proportion of whom were involved in a social media clamour for him to return at the start of the 2015 international summer – would be to overlook his own faults.

These days I'm very much on the outside looking in when it comes to the England team, and my views on Pietersen as a dynamic cricketer are those formed as a privileged spectator. At his swashbuckling best I would happily part with cash to take my seat in the stands, but maverick players are high-maintenance. Pleasing the masses and annoying one's bosses appear to go hand in hand for his type.

I remember asking the Manchester United footballer Denis Law why he never went into management. 'Managing players?' he said. 'Players are complete arseholes. I know. I used to be one.' It was a fairly coarse assessment but I got his drift. It can be hard work handling players, particularly those who have a tendency to break away from the norm, and there are only so many times you can reinforce the guidelines before patience runs out.

There was plenty of history, of course, when it came to Kevin falling out with the England management. First, there was his relationship breakdown with Peter Moores back in 2008-09 that led to the demotion of the pair of them. Then came the exile following the breakdown with the rest of what had been a successful England team in the summer of 2012. Finally, there was the 'disconnection' that Paul Downton revealed the bosses felt he displayed during the Ashes whitewash of 2013-14.

Kevin pushed and pushed as far as I can see; he has tested his bosses to the limits over the years. Ian Botham and to a lesser extent David Gower, around the same time of his flying expedition in Australia with John Morris, did the same thing during their careers but they are Isthmian League compared to Kevin.

It's easy to say blithely that the best team should always be picked, and I for one wish it was possible for that to be the case, but you cannot carry on irrespective of someone's behaviour. With English cricket in a right old mess following the World Cup botch-up and a disappointing Test series draw in the Caribbean, clamour for another 'reintegration' was inevitable. But for Andrew Strauss it was not a viable option, particularly if rumours that he would have lost Alastair Cook, the man he invested in as captain, were true. Strauss hinted that others would have considered their futures, too, and that would have threatened a mass break-up.

I got to know Strauss during his post-playing stint as a Sky Sports commentator, and I'm convinced his decision would have had nothing personal to it. I don't think for one minute he dwelt on the textgate scandal with the South African team in the summer of 2012. Simply, he would have weighed everything up and decided to move on. Happy for all the flak to come his way, he just wanted the team to be freed from KP's shadow and be allowed to develop. For months it had been suffocating under a groundswell of criticism against the ECB – a bandwagon that developed on Kevin's behalf – on just about any subject going.

It's difficult for people to accept, and I rue the fact that he was consigned to history, but as Margaret Thatcher once said: 'The lady is not for turning.' On this occasion, neither was the lord of Lord's. Strauss made his decision. Investment would continue to be made in the players lampooned on Twitter in a grossly unfair manner every time they contributed a low score. Then his supporters made a point of publicising that in their opinion, X wasn't as good as KP, at every twist and turn. But his exile was nothing to do with Gary Ballance, Joe Root or Adam Lyth.

Unfortunately, the PR campaign came too soon after he appeared to consign himself to the international scrap heap. Remember that only six months before declaring himself prepared to give it another go with his annulling of his Indian Premier League deal with Sunrisers Hyderabad, he went into print and, among other things, accused the two bowling mainstays, Stuart Broad and James Anderson, of presiding over a bullying culture in the England team. That is quite a claim, and not one to be made lightly.

It seems a shame that Kevin didn't wait until the end of his playing days before publishing his character assassinations. These days should not be a thing of the past because he is a special talent, but they are because that is the way of the world. There are bosses and workers, and while you can certainly challenge a boss, there has to be a level of respect, and that means you can challenge them only so often. Unfortunately, through his writings – the book, newspaper columns, interviews and social media comments – it showed he had scant regard for some bosses and some colleagues.

From a pure cricket perspective, you could hardly blame him when at the age of thirty-four the penny dropped that the clock was ticking for him as a top-level sportsman. The best players in any field want to be competing against their elite peers, and for all the Twenty20 glitter that decorates the globe, that means Test cricket.

It was even commendable that he opted to throw his lot in with Surrey in a bid to score some first-class runs on his interpretation of what Colin Graves said about his need to play domestic cricket and perform to have any chance. Grasping at lifelines, it appeared reasonable to Kevin and to a number including myself to assume that, with Graves and Tom Harrison coming in as ECB chairman and chief executive respectively, this meant everyone started 2015 with a clean slate.

It all appeared set up for him. Pietersen had a great chance to excel in Division Two, and did with his wonderful unbeaten 355 against Leicestershire. In the winter of 2014-15, though it was only Australia's Big Bash League, he appeared to be in a good place with his batting, and to extend that into the English season would have pleased him. Because of his devotion to preparation and a decent lifestyle, he has tended to be ready to play as soon as he is fit, despite a recent history of niggling injuries.

He might also have been keen to give it a go because the main targets for his ire in those pages of his autobiography – Andy Flower and Matt Prior – were no longer in the England set-up. For the record, I thought the book was a sad read, dripping with bitterness and containing no joy whatsoever, which is a direct contrast to his batting which is full of it. To learn that he wasn't enjoying what should have been among the best moments of his life was a real shame.

Even after all this, however, he could not ignore the magnet of Test cricket. He wanted to make himself irresistible to the ECB once more, and it would have hurt to be told by Strauss that it was not a marriage about to be repaired any time soon before his triple hundred innings at The Oval was complete.

My preference in all this, and again I'm only speaking from a logistical point of view rather than one with any vested interest, would have been to place all the key players in this drama in one room and tell them not to reappear until they had bashed out a compromise. With his mojo back and commitment unerring, Pietersen is a batsman to strike fear into any opposition and, despite his extended absence and mega-money deals around the globe, it is clearly international competition that gets his juices flowing.

Call my proposal arbitration if you like. To me, it was necessary for a simple process to take place in the immediate aftermath of Graves's comments. It may have needed an independent mediator, someone who has dealt with high-profile figures at the top of their sports, such as Sir Clive Woodward or Sir Alex Ferguson. They would be chosen not because of their knight-of-the-realm status, but because they have dealt with similar situations over the years with characters who have excelled in the highest company and come with huge egos and pay packets in tow. Think of Cristiano Ronaldo, Wayne Rooney, Martin Johnson and Lawrence Dallaglio.

I would have said something like: 'Kevin, we want you playing because we recognise that you are a player of match-winning potential, but these are the rules. You have previous, and lots of it. How are we going to make this work? Because the minute you step out of line – and we will be watching – that will be it. Our patience has a limit, we have stretched it for you but one more transgression and it will be very thin.'

For the record, I would also have allowed Kevin to bring his mate Piers Morgan with him. No doubt it would have become quite lively, but it would have got everything out in the open and stopped all the innuendo on Twitter and the like. The default position, if I had been coach, would have been to make it clear that I wanted him in, but if he was to be in, it was all or nothing and no more dealing in the shadows. Everything onwards would become transparent.

It was all very well when Kevin turned up at Lord's for the Test match versus India in 2014 sporting a baseball cap with Pasadena emblazoned on the front. As the band of that name sang: 'I'm doing fine now – without you!' Yes, England were for a while, but they certainly were not over subsequent months.

I'm all for including characters that challenge the norm. One of the beauties of cricket to me is that the best teams contain players of all different shapes, sizes, colours, creeds and social status. And so one of my contemporary concerns has been an apparent one-size-fits-all attitude that now prevails.

One guy in particular who I swore by in my days as a coach would never have got on the park. In an age where 12 was always an acceptable score on the bleep test and 15 was achievable by the fittest, Ian Austin would not get anywhere near double figures. What's more, he wouldn't even try.

Using the bleep test would tell you if someone was strong. But when I was at Lancashire, there was no one like Austin when it came to strength. Yet one pre-season, Oscar, as we called him, set off and got to seven, which is a brisk walk, coughed and said: 'That will do for me.' 'No, Oscar, the challenge is to go until you can go no further.' 'Yep, that'll do,' he said.

Now no one could tell me that Ian Austin was not strong. He was like an ox, and he would bowl all day for you, and never go off injured. So, unlike the parameters they use these days so meticulously, I would only ever use them as loose guides. The evidence I would want to see is how players coped physically in the middle.

Tests like the bleep were devised not to discount players from being able to do six to seven hours a day on the field. This was a guideline to differentiate between them doing seven hours a day okay and five hours leaving them knackered.

I would be looking at what Austin did with ball or bat in hand, and when it came to this he was in my Lancashire team every time. In fact, moving up a level, when it came to the 1999 World Cup selection we surveyed domestic cricket's opening batsmen to ask who they found the most difficult new-ball opponent, and the name that kept coming back was that of Austin.

I would certainly not use it to preclude someone from playing, like they did with Samit Patel, for example. That's a nonsense. Jack Simmons used to tuck the local newspaper under his arm, with biro circles all around the properties he liked in the district, and stop off and have a nosy on our pre-season run. For him it was a glorified shuffle. But ask him to shuffle in and bowl his off-spin all afternoon and there would be no problem. Job done. I don't think Colin Cowdrey and Tom Graveney would get much over nine on that test, but could they bat? That was a given. Could they bat a long time? Yep. It should never be the criteria for whether someone should play or not. What I would be interested in is whether they could do the job.

For what he could do to the best bowlers on the planet, it was obvious that Pietersen was more than capable. When he whacked the great Shane Warne against the spin into the stands at The Oval back in 2005, trying to save a Test match to win the Ashes, it was the first time I had ever witnessed anyone render the Australian leg-spinner powerless.

Pietersen's outstanding effort of 158, his first Test hundred, was as good an innings as I have witnessed. What made him stand out for me over the next ten years was that, like Brian Lara and Ricky Ponting, he possessed that ability to get himself in, and to then shift gears once he was 'in'. Part of the art of batsmanship is to use your defence to work yourself into attack mode, and there are endless examples of Pietersen doing this.

In South Africa the previous winter, he built his hundreds slowly before bursting down the home straight like Usain Bolt. His management of an innings is truly masterful. At The Oval that famous September afternoon, he went into overdrive. Much later, during the winter of 2012-13, he showed that perfectly with his hundred in the Test match at Mumbai. Just a few days previously in Ahmedabad, he had not got a clue how to get started, and looked a completely different player. Yet the genius players are able to find answers mere mortals cannot. By getting into the nets and working tirelessly on tightening his technique, he realised how to prosper on those subcontinental surfaces.

Then in the match situation, you saw that once he got a measure of it all, he knew when to step on the gas. The reason that Mumbai innings was so special was because he gave the innings the impetus it lacked. That has been a problem for England for several periods when Pietersen has been missing over the past decade, and is the one thing I would have been fretting about as coach. What we witnessed with Nick Compton and Sam Robson making their way in international cricket, and Jonathan Trott and Gary Ballance also taking their places in the top three at any given time, was a tendency for the innings to get stuck before it had moved anywhere.

Alastair Cook tends to play at a fairly sedate pace whether in form or out, and Trott was never much of an upgrade on steady; Compton seemed so intent on crease occupation and Robson in the 2014 series against India kept looking at every pitch like it was about to explode. Goodness knows what he would have made of some of them in 1964.

But when Pietersen arrived at the wicket at the Wankhede Stadium, the team run rate sat exactly at two, at 68 for two. By the time they dismissed him for 186, it was 3.4, and England had scored in excess of four runs per over while he was at the crease. He had moved the game on, in the manner he did at The Oval when he neutered Warne and Co and then hit England out of range, and that in a nutshell is why he's so special.

He saved that Test by taking it away from Australia. Certainly, as a commentator I was making the point that survival was all well and good, but you need to score runs to get yourself out of dangerous territory. In that instance, it's necessary to be the team dictating the terms. The requirement in that situation is to change the equation – to get the runs up and the minutes remaining down, to a point where the opposition cannot win.

Of course, it was Andrew 'Freddie' Flintoff who set up that brilliant 2-1 win in 2005 in what I have to say is the best series I have ever witnessed. He was immense across those five epic matches, confirming beyond doubt that he had fulfilled the enormous potential I witnessed in him when he was a young lad at Lancashire. He copped some flak over the years for his off-field transgressions, but Pedalo Fred was worth every minute.

During my time as Lancashire coach, he was a diamond in the club's youth system who progressed through all the age-group sides. Later, it became obvious given his physicality that he was ready for men's cricket – although he was tall and slim with powerful shoulders rather than the powerful force he was to become.

His plus points were there for all to see – a capable fast bowler and hard-hitting batsman with buckets for hands. However, it meant that others around the county circuit knew about him too, and he had already been made another good offer from a rival suitor when Geoff Ogden, chairman of Lancashire's cricket committee, and I went to his family home in Preston to express our commitment to his future as a cricketer.

Northamptonshire were keen enough on him, in fact, to offer him support in his education by getting him placed in one of the region's best schools for A-levels. Shortly before that visit to his house in 1994, I went to see him play for St Anne's against Leyland when Malcolm Marshall opened the bowling and Andrew opened the batting. Uncharacteristically, he poked about and was cleaned up a few deliveries later. My presence had proved a distraction. Truth is, though, our decision had already been made at Old Trafford.

So to see this one-time teetotaller go through the England Under-19 system and then on to topple the big boys of Australia a few years later has given me immense pride. We always liked to see one of our own do well in Lancashire, and it has been an equal buzz to witness James Anderson, the shy boy from Burnley, transform into the world's most masterful swing bowler and reach 400 Test scalps.

Perhaps too much too soon was expected of Flintoff, because due to his physicality and ability to get the ball through at a decent pace, we relied too much on his fast bowling to the point where we began to jeopardise his fitness. So, for a period as a young player we drew back from pressurising his developing body and played him as a specialist batsman. Only later, when the medical specialists that had advised us to reduce his workload gave the all-clear, did we re-release him on his destiny to become a world-beater.

Some things never changed with him, though. Even in his teenage years, Flintoff had that problem with his front foot when he bowled – it landed at a funny angle and his entire body weight went across it. That's some force on impact. Ideally, a bowler's front foot points down the pitch but he never felt comfortable with it in that position. Duncan Fletcher's England regime, primarily through Troy Cooley, attempted to realign his landing at the crease but to no avail. No matter how perfect it looked when he walked through his delivery and released the ball in slow motion, whenever it came to game-time that foot angled awkwardly again.

Alec Stewart and I considered him ready for England in 1998, and although there were not necessarily excellent results from the off, this is nearly always the case with young players. Seven years later he was in his prime, and Michael Vaughan used him as his chief weapon in a wondrous bowling attack. It had helped deliver seven Tests the previous summer between historic away series wins in the Caribbean and South Africa, and even Australia, the number one team of the decade, were forced into submission at the hands of Flintoff, Steve Harmison, Matthew Hoggard, Simon Jones and Ashley Giles.

Despite their stellar cast, whenever Australia batted in that series you expected to see wickets tumble, and you were rarely disappointed, with Flintoff leading the procession. The 2005 Ashes was completely different to every other series I have been involved in as a commentator, because you couldn't take your eyes off five minutes of the cricket for fear of missing something memorable. This applied to when you were sitting at the back of the Sky Sports commentary box too. Usually, when you finish your half-hour stints on the microphone you nip off for a breather – a coffee, a chat, a flick through the newspapers. Not that summer.

From the moment Steve Harmison left his marker, in blood, on Ricky Ponting's cheek of all places, it was compelling theatre. The devil was in the delivery – one that reared up into the grille of the batsman's helmet – as well as just about every one that followed it from England's pace attack over the five matches. This was Australia's warning – Justin Langer is reported to have turned to his former Middlesex team-mate Andrew Strauss perplexed that no England fielders had rushed to Ponting's aid. He later required the aid of a decent plastic surgeon.

But Flintoff was the spearhead, the leading wicket-taker, offering scant respite and no easy runs for an Australian batting order under siege. Even Giles, in the holding role as left-arm spinner, was not to be underestimated in that quintet. As captain, Vaughan knew he could rely on Giles to keep it tight whenever a partnership developed, so that his pace bowlers could recharge their batteries.

With Australia's never-say-die attitude thrown into the mix, it made for some sensational finishes. Moments like Ponting's wound at Lord's; his run-out at Trent Bridge; Geraint Jones clasping that series-levelling, leg-side catch off Harmison to complete victory at Edgbaston; Flintoff's double-wicket over earlier in that same match; Kevin Pietersen slog-sweeping Shane Warne for six during what was supposed to be a final-day rearguard at The Oval; and a barrow-load of others besides – this was the series of the lot from an English perspective. If the 1934 Australians were the Invincibles, our lot of 2005 were the Unforgettables.

As with all great dramas, though, there were twists along the way. Primarily when that champion of fast bowlers Glenn McGrath, whose disciplined five for not-many on the first evening contributed to Australia taking a 1-0 lead, trod on that loose ball in Birmingham before play on the first morning. As one wag suggested, it was the first loose ball McGrath had ever been associated with. Disruption like that scrambles a captain's thoughts and perhaps that's why Ricky Ponting opted to insert England minutes later.

As was the general pattern, England preyed on the mistake. Cyril Washbrook all those years earlier had given me the benefit of his wisdom on the subject and ensured that, if as captain I ever considered bowling first, I should think again. It was always the way for me as a general rule, even in one-day cricket when the onus was to pile up a score and defend what was yours.

England's scoring rate of five runs per over in that first innings of 407 told another tale. They were uber confident despite the Lord's setback. Here, Flintoff and Pietersen, a combination I for one wish we could have seen more, went into overdrive in trying to out-hit each other.

But it was with the ball that our Fred the Ped put his name in

Ashes folklore. Virtually every spell he sent down was spellbinding. For years, every English all-rounder had been bullied into submission by the ominous shadow cast by Ian Botham. Yet here, as was the case when he returned to Edgbaston for his heroics in the 2014 Twenty20 finals day, Flintoff had the Brummie crowd playing to his tune. There was plenty of the showmanship of Botham in the way he gently loosened his limbs to show he was warming up for another spell. With that, a gentle crescendo of anticipation would wash around the stands.

Now let's get into them, he no doubt thought, every time Vaughan handed him the ball. For the Australian batsmen, it must have had a psychological effect. Flintoff would crash into the crease with the force of what must have felt like 20,000 people.

On commentary, I likened him to a steam engine during that second Test match. As it happens, I have been on the footplate of one of those and I wouldn't have liked to have tried to stop its progress. In my youth, I was a trainspotter and used to take my bicycle on the train and go for a week's spotting somewhere like Crewe. I've always been a big fan of the Princess Royal Class. Flintoff was as pristine in 2005.

A great source of satisfaction for Vaughan would have come from the fact that his team were relentless in going for the kill, no matter what time of day. Fatigue never became a factor, which is something I wasn't able to say about my England team just half a dozen years earlier unfortunately. As a captain or coach, if your team is still harassing opponents at six o'clock in the evening, you are almost touching perfect.

England got under Australia's skin in every way possible: the biggest example coming at Trent Bridge when Gary Pratt ran out Ricky Ponting during a short stint as twelfth man. Ponting was furious as he left the field, sharing his feelings publicly with the raucous crowd, and Duncan Fletcher, perched on the home balcony, added to his chagrin by refusing to engage in a verbal spat as he departed. England were focused on one thing by that point – getting over the finish line.

Not since the 1980s had an England team done so against Australia, and there were obvious similarities to the first of those three triumphs two decades earlier. In fact, the portents for England were good once you recognised that in 2005, just as in 1981, we had a dead Pope, a royal wedding and a victorious Liverpool team in the European Cup final.

The other was a good team with some gold-dust players. Flintoff certainly got a similar amount of credit to his replica Botham, and Vaughan's leadership was favourably compared to that of Mike Brearley. Two of the men not to get as much credit as was due, perhaps, were the two fast bowlers Bob Willis and Simon Jones. Truly top-class fast bowling takes place in partnerships – you need pressure from the other end at the top level – yet Willis's contribution is often overlooked, while Jones showed the value of a bowler able to reverse swing the ball at ninety miles per hour.

The key for England was continuity. Until the final Test, their first-choice XI stayed fit; there was no discernible weak link. The best teams prey on any sign of it in an opponent. The best teams also possess great depths of resolve, and it was a sign of Australia's quality that they were in the shake-up for victory at Trent Bridge despite defending a modest target of 129. Australia and Ponting in particular did not give an inch. His rearguard hundred to save the third Test at Old Trafford was the ultimate captain's knock and, typical of the ebb and flow, ensured that Australia saved that match with one wicket intact.

For those few short weeks the country was gripped by cricket, and it was similar to the 2012 Olympics in that regard. The gridlock on Manchester's roads on that final morning of the fourth Test proved it. With people streaming into queues desperate to be part of history in the making, it gave me flashbacks of when the 'sold out' signs went up for Lancashire's home Gillette Cup semi-finals. I remember Angus Fraser, who always liked a chunter in his playing days, grumbling away that morning after abandoning his car some distance from the ground and walking, because his first commentary stint of the day with *Test Match Special* was in jeopardy.

There were almost as many there in Trafalgar Square when the victorious team was paraded the following month, just hours after Pietersen's innings well and truly drew him to a nation's attention. In years to come, there will be people proudly saying: 'I was there.' Apart from one particular chap who was so nervous he couldn't bear to watch.

He had made it into the ground through the turnstiles next to the Alec Stewart Gate, and was clutching a ticket as sought-after as one of Willy Wonka's golden ones when he approached me as I made my way from one of our Sky Sports TV trucks into the OCS stand, the building where the commentary box was housed. There was a little bit of rain around and he was inquisitive as to whether play would start on time. When I informed him that in my estimation it would, his heart sank. Naturally enough, I asked him if everything was okay. Had he heard me properly? I said that I thought they *would* be starting at 11 a.m.

'Oh, I'm not bothered about seeing them play,' he told me. 'I just want it all to be over.'

What shouldn't be forgotten is that things could have been oh so different for Pietersen, English cricket and the history of the Ashes had Shane Warne not dropped him at slip on 15 in that momentous second innings. But then the very best players make the most of the slightest opening, and that is why I consider Pietersen to have been the best among England players. I was lucky enough to have played alongside one of the two other men to remind me of him, Caribbean kings both. To me, Clive Lloyd was the Kevin Pietersen of his day, a box-office player who made you feel like something special could happen at any moment.

There were other similarities too: Clive was also one who could switch modes with a click of his fingers, they shared a similar gait at the crease, both standing over 6 ft 4 ins tall and with a work ethic. Practice was the secret to each player's success. All spectators see is the flamboyance of KP's trademark peacock flick through midwicket or Clive's languid pick-up off the legs – Warwickshire, with four West Indian players in the opposition, saw it far too many times for their liking in the 1972 Gillette Cup final as the ball kept disappearing into the Tavern Stand during Clive Lloyd's wonderful, match-winning innings of 126. But they don't see the hours of tinkering with technique that precedes it.

For his personality at the crease, the other is Viv Richards. It sounds masochistic to admit it, but I used to love playing against Viv, because he was so exhilarating to watch. He had this menacing presence on the field, so that even when you were pitched against him, you couldn't take your eyes off him. When I was umpiring, I used to be fascinated by him, standing there banging the butt of his bat, snorting. His mannerisms were so distinctive, and the walk to the crease was undeniably as intimidating as some of the deliveries from his fast bowling colleagues. I used to say that if I could have walked like that, I would be looking back at a career with thousands more runs; equally so, if I had possessed any of the other-worldly shots from the Kevin Pietersen repertoire.

CHAPTER 13

Climbing the Ladder

From my first day on duty back in July 1999, all I ever wanted was exactly what every other cricket supporter in the country desired, and what I had previously been trying to achieve. That quite simply was for England to be top of the pile when it came to international cricket.

Changing jobs had not changed my outlook one bit, and to witness the England team under first Duncan Fletcher and later Andy Flower climb those Test rankings, and reach the summit, has been a real joy. Our limited-overs cricket even promised greater returns for a while, certainly when the team under Alastair Cook briefly took over as number one in the standings, and when Paul Collingwood fronted the most dynamic short-format team we have ever thrown together to win the World Twenty20 in 2010. But these lofty perches have not been inhabited with any regularity, proving exceptions rather than the rule.

The England team I left, and immediately witnessed losing to New Zealand in its first series under the temporary tutelage of Graham Gooch, improved immeasurably over subsequent years as the effect of central contracts and a change of emphasis, a modernisation if you like, from county control to a more natural order took hold. I have always loved county cricket but the tail was wagging the dog for too long, and only when it was addressed did we begin to see countries that had passed us by tracked down. It was with great satisfaction that I saw others reap the benefits of having rest and recovery periods for players, greater resources and true world's-best ambition.

Not that the ascent was plain sailing. Far from it, in fact, and the pendulum of fortune has swung much in the same way as that of the Ashes. Its modern chapters have been fascinating, not least because after such a long period of dominance by the Australians, nothing can now be discounted when these two great rival countries meet. Just when England appeared to have an iron grip on the urn with four wins out of five, back came Australia in 2013-14. Never is there more intrigue, more drama, in terms of cricket than in an Ashes series. Bill Shankly once said football was not a matter of life and death, it was more important than that; and the way England and Australia have acted over the years has been like espionage. Think only of the England bowling plans that found their way into Australian hands in 2006-07, or the leaked Justin Langer dossier on the home team in 2009. Then there has been the hiring of double agents – men like Troy Cooley, Dene Hills, Graeme Hick and John Buchanan, whose own 'consultancy work' on Australia did not, like Langer's, make the public domain.

Using his vantage point in the Somerset dressing room, Langer dubbed England 'shallow' and claimed they had a 'sing when you're winning' attitude. In my opinion, it was pretty run-of-the-mill stuff, with a couple of glaring inaccuracies. I have always viewed James Anderson as a wholehearted performer, a real trier – certainly not a 'pussy' – and the way to bowl at Matt Prior was certainly not wide, as recommended.

If there was a moment to show that despite its prestige the Ashes really is not comparable to life and death, it came in the winter of 2014-15 when the precarious nature of our mortality was so painfully emphasised through the loss of Phillip Hughes, a competitor in both the 2009 and 2013 series, to a freak accident in the course of combat. As we found through our own loss of Ben Hollioake in 2002, nothing brings a sport together like a tragedy. When that ball from Sean Abbott struck the back of Hughes's neck at the Sydney Cricket Ground in November 2014, it was a horrific reminder of the dangers involved. Sport is not supposed to end like this.

The loss of Hughes, so desperately sad for his family, friends and the whole of Australian cricket, showed how empathetic a sport ours is. Its spirit is founded on respect for one's opponent in the heat of the battle, and one of the most touching moments for me was when the grieving parents publicly absolved Abbott of blame. Coming back from something like that must be treacherously difficult, and it reminded me of the incident between Peter Lever and Ewen Chatfield during a Test in Auckland in 1975.

The New Zealand leg of the tour came at the end of that 1974–75 Ashes series after I had returned home nursing an injury. Peter, a team-mate of mine at Lancashire, hit Chatfield on the head in the days before helmets, causing the Kiwi batsman to collapse and swallow his tongue. He had to be resuscitated by the England physio Bernie Thomas, who said his heart had briefly stopped beating. Technically, I suppose you could say he was dead for a few moments.

Mercifully for everyone, Ewen pulled through, but I couldn't help feeling that Peter was never the same bowler after that. He was a thoughtful chap, and the fact that Chatfield came so close to dying was tough for him to deal with. The following summer during a county match, we were playing on an uncovered pitch – and Peter just didn't want to bowl. No one blamed him. How as a bowler do you get over it? I guess you never can, but my heart went out to Abbott when he made his return to action the following month.

Batsmen have better protection these days, and I don't see this as being an issue about the safety of helmets – attempts have been made to update and improve them ever since their introduction into the mainstream during the 1970s. From all accounts, Phillip's fatal blow was dealt not because he was too late on a delivery that beat him for pace but that he was early on it, and in spinning around he exposed this vulnerable area. Now batsmen like Ian Bell and Joe Root, among others, have begun wearing extra protection around the back of the head.

Helmets came in after Roger Davis got hit at short leg. He died for a short period after being struck by a ball turned off his pads by Neal Abberley, of Warwickshire, in a match in Cardiff in 1971, before being resuscitated. After suffering convulsions he was treated by Dr Colin Lewis, who, as luck had it, was among the crowd and gave him CPR. Thankfully, Roger came round in hospital after further treatment.

That was the first time that helmets were thought of. Then, with the barrage of West Indies fast bowlers, they became an issue. Evidence of my general concern, however, is that I went to Tyldesley and Holbrook, the sports retailer in Manchester, because I knew the owner Bob Cooke played lacrosse and hockey. I bought a lacrosse helmet and wore it for some time, following Roger's misfortune, when stood at short-leg. As players we were wary of wearing protective gear – batsmen had always relied on evasion to stay safe, the dangers you accepted as part and parcel of the game, and it was frowned upon by peers, with some even suggesting it was a sign of cowardice. I spoke out about the need for facial protection during the 1976 summer, yet it was still taboo for a batsman to walk out to the middle in a helmet. The erudite Mike Brearley and India's Sunil Gavaskar came the closest, by sporting protective temple pieces under their caps.

Not wearing one had its consequences, of course, as I found out when I came up against Bob Cottam, the Northamptonshire fast bowler regarded as one of the quickest on the domestic circuit, when he left me hospitalised. Wearing just a cap, I went for a hook and the next thing I knew I was waking up on my way to the infirmary. Seldom did I shun the chance to hook, but on this occasion the ball beat the stroke and hit me flush in the face, causing me to collapse onto my stumps.

Wearing helmets certainly took some getting used to, and the first few had a Perspex protector covering your face with breath holes to get rid of the perspiration. This served only to tickle people, and due to a combination of the design and the size of my hooter I had to have one specially made. Others, like tail-ender Peter Lee, were totally unaccustomed to them. In 1981, on a quick pitch at Old Trafford, the contest against Somerset featured some seriously impressive fast bowlers: we had Michael Holding and Paul Allott and they had Joel Garner and Ian Botham. The game was going fine, until out of the blue, it kicked off.

It all got a bit spiky, and having dismissed the visitors for 89, we set off in pursuit of a score of 155 to win. Lancashire were still in need of more than 30 when Lee — who batted for us only because the roller could not get into the middle in time without being timed out — strolled out. In the first innings, Leapy had an almighty slog and got to nine, which was a gargantuan total when you considered his ability. Joel had pitched the ball up looking to castle him but the mood in the middle was more sinister this time, and the rest of us warned him to put a helmet on as a feature of the innings had been the high number of bouncers sent down.

'Nah, I've never worn a helmet,' he said. 'Joel will pitch 'em up, like he did the other day. He's my mate. We go back a long way.'

We persuaded him that this would not be the case and ensured he walked down the steps with this helmet under his arm. He had never worn one before, so not until he got to the middle did he start putting it on. Unfortunately, Leapy mistook the breath holes for peep holes, and so stood waiting for Joel to spear the leather sphere at him with his head looking up at the sky.

Sure as eggs are eggs, Joel struck him a blow on the side of his head, cutting his earlobe, before cleaning all three stumps up soon afterwards.

'Good job you put that helmet on,' we said to him, passing him a packet of Elastoplasts. 'Your mate Joel's sent you these.'

Hughes took his place in the Australian team at the start of the 2013 Ashes, as hostilities took in back-to-back series – a move designed to aid both countries' preparation for the 2015 World Cup by leaving the build-up free.

As sporting turnarounds go, England were on the wrong end of arguably the biggest witnessed over those six months. For the first time in living memory, England had spent a decade in the ascendancy when it came to the greatest series of them all, and a 3-0 home victory was no less than expected.

But where I come from, you're brought up with a rather rough-and-ready set of principles, a primary one among them being to get your retaliation in at the first opportunity. Not to put too fine a point on it, that's what Australia did to England that following winter. Talk about a kick in the biffs. And if you've come with me this far, you'll know I'm one of the northern hemisphere's leading authorities on such blows.

Yes, I fully anticipated spending the entire year of 2013 in some of my favourite watering holes, at home and down under, chatting about England's series successes over a pint, hearing folk tell their stories and a good few from yesteryear to boot. I even prepared my own ale for the 2013 Australians, one suitably named for drowning the sorrows. A nutty number going by the name of Leave the Car (more appropriate than Start the Car if you are supping) brewed by Thwaites in Blackburn.

Thwaites invited me along to open their new micro-brewery in 2012, and it was all very interesting to a pub enthusiast like myself.

These days you can go on their website and brew your own virtual pint. But I was pleased to be able to go for the practical rather than the theory. I wanted a flavoursome beer, which means the percentage has to be quite high, and Leave the Car came in at 4.5 per cent. We produced twenty-nine barrels of the stuff, and I have to say it was superb. A few of those would have helped the Australians escape the pain of reality for a while. Equally so, for Englishmen a few short weeks later.

What a shift in fortunes. When you considered where the respective England and Australia teams were three months into 2013 and then at the same juncture the following year, the change in the balance of power between our sport's two great foes was mind-boggling. England ended up whitewashed for a second time in three visits to Australia, against a team that could not previously buy a win.

On the eve of arriving in England in mid-summer 2013, Australia were undoubtedly at sixes and sevens. Their tour of India had been disastrous. Some had forgotten to hand their homework in on time, several were suspended and one was even dispatched from the tour of India back to Australia (I told a couple of my antipodean pals how good it was to see some Victorian punishments becoming trendy again). It was the birch for us at Peel Park Primary: three strokes and a flea in the ear to boot.

They were never going to do much against that kind of backdrop. Disciplinary issues were plaguing them. They arrived in England with questions on whether Michael Clarke was part of the team or not, and he was their captain. His relationship with Shane Watson, or indeed lack of one, was a hot topic which cooled only once they started winning again. While back in Sydney for the birth of his son Will, Watson said he was weighing up his international future. Pat Howard, the rugby man in charge of Australian cricket, had suggested that Watson was only a team player 'sometimes'. The in-fighting, I would argue, was at a similarly disruptive level to what England experienced across that summer of 2012, when Andy Flower used his power as coach to remove Pietersen on a temporary basis.

Events were chaotic to say the least. A few days later, with Clarke ruled out through injury, Watson was back on the tour and named as captain. This kind of domestic plot is exactly what I would expect in *Emmerdale*, which is one of my life's guilty pleasures, but not in international sport. It was completely chaotic.

'Homeworkgate' smacked of a team losing heavily, lacking direction, and with no idea how to get back on track. They were on their way to a 4-0 defeat in India, but they weren't going to find answers jotted on A4 sheets of paper, next to half-finished games of Hangman and scribbled Half Man Half Biscuit lyrics. The fact of the matter was that they were just not good enough and they had picked the wrong players. It wasn't what they could or couldn't produce with the aid of protractors, calculators and a thesaurus that was the problem. They needed direction from their management. Mickey Arthur, their coach, should not have been asking Australia's players for suggestions on how to improve as individuals and as a team. Ultimately, that was his job as the coach – to facilitate practice, and create an atmosphere that allows individuals to relax and operate to their maximum potential.

It wasn't as if he was new to the job; this was a team he had been moulding for two years, which suggested the changes in squad personnel and rotation policy were wrong. In short, Arthur was on borrowed time from the moment he 'drew a line in the sand' at 2-0 down with two Tests to play against the Indians.

This whole episode showed that change can possess recuperative properties, as long as the right appointment is made as a replacement. In contrast to Arthur, Darren Lehmann was an old-school cricketer with a rather impressive-looking coaching CV. In fact, the moment he was placed in charge of Australia A that summer, it was curtains for Arthur because Lehmann is a born winner. Within the previous twelve months he had won the Big Bash League with Brisbane Heat and led Queensland to one-day cup success. In his first ever coaching post in 2009, he turned Deccan Chargers from Indian Premier League chumps to IPL champs.

What we have witnessed of Australia over the next two years bore his stamp – he forced the team to reclaim some of their country's culture. If a moment of self-doubt enters an Australian cricketer's head, he gives it a hard shake, reminds himself of his heritage and goes bloody hard at whatever task has been set him on the field. The first alteration Lehmann made was to attitude: Australia had become un-Australian.

During the summer of 2013, he couldn't change the personnel he had been given, so he had to focus on how to play, rather than who was playing, the game. They came into that first Ashes Test match without David Warner, Ryan Harris, George Bailey, Mitchell Johnson and Nathan Lyon. It was the wrong call. By the end of the tour they were all in the equation, and two months later they were at the forefront of Australia's assault in Brisbane. It revealed how much planning Lehmann had been doing while on the tour of England.

By the end of the 2013 series, they were getting lots of things right. Lyon, an incredible non-selection throughout the first few Tests, had reclaimed his rightful place as the team's first-choice spin bowler. He had got nine wickets in his previous Test match in India, for goodness sake, only to be discarded. Warner was back at the top of the order where he is most dangerous, rather than sat waiting for the ball to go soft at No. 6, and Harris's new-ball skill was making life difficult regardless of the surface. They had identified the right players to go with their tough-as-old-boots coach.

Among the computers, analysis and theorising in the modern game, there is room for an old-school coaching ethos, and Lehmann doesn't stray far from it. He expects his players to know their game plans, creates an environment for them to express their ability and he has a beer at the end of the day's play. Players will always respond to that kind of attitude. They respond in a different way entirely when, after being at a cricket ground for nine and a half hours, they clamber onto the team bus to watch a DVD of their faults in defeat. International cricketers tend to be good at self-analysis.

My own view is that there are certain teams that need one of their own when it comes to the appointment of a coach, and Australia is the country I think that applies to most of all. When I left the England job, my preference was for an Englishman to inherit it, but reflection from afar, no doubt influenced by the great success of our Zimbabwean imports Duncan Fletcher and Andy Flower, has made me realise that was more idealistic than a necessity.

But Mickey Arthur didn't necessarily get the Australian way and it contrasted massively to Lehmann. When David Warner needed straightening out in 2013 following his Birmingham nightclub altercation with Joe Root, he got the arm around the shoulder, a 'fair dinkum, mate, you've cocked up but I'm going to do the right thing and give you a chance'. There is just something about giving a fellow Aussie another go, no matter their transgression. They love the idea of mateship. Sticking together is part of their national identity, and it needs an Australian to implement it. Naturally, with a South African in charge, that is lost in translation.

Under Lehmann's stewardship, Warner was disciplined for his punch of Root, jettisoned for a short period, told to get his head down and switched on to his game. Lehmann had been a bit of a larrikin at times too, and he seems to get on his players' wavelengths The difference in Australia's fortunes since then tells you as much.

Ultimately, results dictate whether a coach is going to be persevered with or not. That's the same all sports over. But the timing of the change, so soon after Australia had arrived on tour, was still a seismic shock. It was a bizarre press conference when Arthur sat down to talk about his departure, then vacated the chair for Lehmann to come in and discuss how he intended to go about the role. Quite simply, Arthur had done his best, it had not been good enough, and Lehmann was the correct fit. Credit Cricket Australia for recognising it and grasping the nettle.

They had gone from high intensity, 'do this, do that' instruction from high command to a bloke who knew exactly what it was like to be one of those sat around him. 'I've played for Australia, I know what it's all about, we're going to play hard, tough cricket and enjoy ourselves.' That's exactly what they did, and although it didn't work immediately, it didn't take long to come good.

Although not universally popular, Michael Clarke became a very good leader that summer. Up in the Sky commentary box, we can hear on-field chatter through the stump microphones and there was no question who was captain out there. He barks his orders, rather like a general, and his field placements were precise and revealed a great attention to detail. Team decisions became less odd as the summer unfolded – batting Ashton Agar at No. 11 on debut was clearly ridiculous. In fact, he looked a more likely pick as a batsman than as a left-arm spin bowler.

Australia started to improve over time. After Lord's, where England dished out a right good hiding – if your memory's a little hazy the margin was a whopping 347 runs – they were in with a chance of victory at Old Trafford but for the rain, they were competitive before losing up at Chester-le-Street and they made the running at The Oval. All in all, Australia might have felt hard done by, but I also thought that while England had won 3-0 they hadn't played very well either.

In terms of quality, cricket fans had been utterly spoilt both by the awesome Australia under Mark Taylor and Steve Waugh, and by England's history-makers of 2005 under Michael Vaughan and the change of power under Andrew Strauss that followed. There was nothing to match the epic moments of 2009 – the James Anderson–Monty Panesar axis to preserve parity in Cardiff, Andrew Flintoff's five-wicket haul at Lord's, Stuart Broad's spell, Jonathan Trott's debut hundred and Flintoff's slingshot run out of Ricky Ponting at The Oval. In contrast, the 2013 Ashes was low-key, safety-first cricket. It didn't capture the imagination of the general public like it had in 2005 – nevertheless England won by three clear Tests.

Commentating on that England team's rise and rise was something to be cherished. I'm as patriotic as the next bloke, and there were times when I sat back at the end of a day's play and thought: 'Crikey, this is fantastic to watch.' The brand of cricket that was being played eight years earlier against a world-class team was irresistible. In comparison, this was ruthlessly dull. If you want to put it into football terms, it was like abandoning Brazil's 1970 team for George Graham's Arsenal of the 1990s. It was as if the mantra was to be tight at the back, masters of the offside trap, content to take 1-0 thanks very much. There was nothing sexy about it; nothing to catch the eye of your average English cricket fan. Folk wouldn't have been going down the pub to talk about fantastic performances. It was effective, no more.

Cricket tends to go in cycles and perhaps this was reflective of a trend. Earlier that summer, and indeed in the away series against the same opposition in the spring of 2013, New Zealand showed how tricky they could make it for England when they tightened up. Life became very difficult. In emulating this, Alastair Cook's team were always well positioned when the tricky moments arose. Throughout the five matches they invariably came out on top in them. Part of that reason was because Australia had suffered nine Test defeats in the previous twelve-month period, whereas England were used to winning.

Previously, not enough has been made of home advantage when

it has come to our international series. Recall the pitch presented to Sri Lanka, for the one-off Test in 1998, as evidence of an overly hospitable welcome to touring teams. I, for one, have never viewed preparing surfaces to suit one's owns strengths as being unethical. The sluggish ones of that summer proved a test for Australians who learnt their trade in conditions where pace and bounce prevail. This request by England – their away victory twelve months earlier in India, where slow pitches are king, contrasting to the Aussie whitewashing there – was coupled with Australia playing into home hands. When confronted with the best off-spinner in the world, what on earth were they doing playing so many left-handed batsmen? It was no surprise that Graeme Swann finished as his side's leading wicket-taker with 26. The Australians had no answer to him, really.

That was one of the major differences between the home and away series. Once Lehmann had his feet under the table, he made explicit instructions to his players not to allow Swann to settle. Where once they were apprehensive, suddenly they were getting after him, hitting him to all parts. He certainly wasn't going to get pitches to his liking over there. Australia were confident England weren't going to get the runs on the board, and that would further pressurise him. They weren't shy of letting him know prior to a ball being bowled that they were coming after him, either.

In fact, in a reprise of pre-2010-11, lots of Australians had lots to say. They were right behind their team and guys were selling yellow T-shirts emblazoned with 'Stuart Broad Is A Shit Bloke'. There were plenty of people in the queue to part with their dollars when I walked past on the opening day at the Gabba. It's a well-known fact that Australia is home to some of the most poisonous and deadly creatures on the planet, and someone appeared to have rounded them up and shoved them through the turnstiles at the Vulture Street End of the ground.

These predators tore into England like sharks, and having had a face-to-face altercation with a Great White that December, I can tell you it's not pleasant. For some reason, our bosses at Sky Sports thought it was a good idea for Nasser Hussain and me to warm up for commentating on the second Test in Adelaide in unorthodox fashion. Blackpool Sea World with Dolly the Dolphin this was not. And for this excursion to Port Lincoln, I was thankful for choosing a slinky aluminium number. Never could I have imagined being so pleased at being caged up as they dropped us into the water near the Neptune Islands. Twice I went for a dip in the area in which these big fellas hunt seals and was shocked that the experts pipe heavy rock music into the water to attract them. Would you believe it? Like most Australians, these brutes could not get enough of AC/DC and Cold Chisel.

At the Gabba, Broad's treatment all stemmed from his refusal to walk in the first Test of ten back in July. He was hammered for standing his ground when, with England 232 runs ahead and the game finely balanced, his thick edge off Agar's bowling flew to Michael Clarke at first slip via a deflection off wicketkeeper Brad Haddin. The furore was ridiculous. Let's face it, all batters try their luck. There might be the odd exception, but I can't think of one. People offered up Adam Gilchrist as a paragon of virtue, but he had long gone. If you want to talk in those terms, then you might as well talk about the 1960s and 1970s when 97 per cent of English cricketers walked.

The game has changed. The modern player stands and waits for the umpire to make a decision. Broad was no different in allowing Aleem Dar the chance to judge the situation. Some people might want to twist that around and say that the batsman is cheating when he knows he's hit it, but that's how it is. I admit I was absolutely gobsmacked at the time. On commentary, the words just flowed out of my mouth. 'What's he doing?' But casting Broad as some sort of Antichrist? I was mystified by the reaction. Clarke and Haddin didn't walk in the match, either, a fact that was conveniently forgotten by the Aussie brethren. Recall the image of England celebrating, then calling for a review to confirm that Haddin had become James Anderson's tenth victim of the match for a 14-run victory.

Players don't walk, even if they know that they've hit it, and in this instance in question, the umpire didn't see it and it was a genuine mistake. The suggestion coming from some quarters that Broad should be disciplined was ludicrous. If he deserved a punishment, then there would have been a long queue in front of judge and jury.

His office as Public Enemy Number One was strengthened when Lehmann went on an Australian radio station and joshed that crowds down under should ensure he went home crying. I've done umpteen of these knockabout interviews, and when heard in a broadcast situation when words can be put into context through tone, it is obviously a bit of banter. However, the same words appearing in print can look pretty ordinary and not befitting an international coach. Not that Broad is the kind of character to let things bother him. Typically, he claimed a five-wicket haul in the first innings of the series to a cacophony of boos. It was real pantomime stuff. The local Brisbane newspaper even refused to name him in their reports, such was his treachery.

Things were going pretty well on that opening day, and there was certainly no sign of things to come when half a dozen Australian batsmen were dismissed for 132. What happened next was to set the tone for the five-match series. Whereas England were often five out, all out – usually in the face of a Mitchell Johnson onslaught – when Australia were five down, Brad Haddin came in. In this series, he was the immovable object.

For some reason, the England lads felt the best way to unsettle Haddin was verbally. But he had something of the Steve Waugh syndrome about him because the more they chatted, the greater his desire to stick around and extend the conversation. His series reaped 493 runs – a phenomenal statistic for a No. 7, and one even more impressive when you consider that not one England player breached 300.

It was perhaps when the tails of the two respective teams were batting that the differences in quality were most evident. Their bowlers' speeds and disciplines were far superior to ours, and somehow they got the ball to swing. Perhaps you just needed that extra yard of pace to acquire that movement. They certainly made that argument plausible by consistently showing up their new-ball adversaries.

From the mid-point on that opening day, we were absolutely spannered by Australia. Battered, bruised and bashed, the batsmen were unable to cope with that pace. There was no answer to it at all. Until that lad Ben Stokes came in and hit that wonderful hundred at Perth. There were no misgivings from him, and at twenty-two he appeared to be a wonderful find.

I had very few problems with England being beaten by a better team. I had very few problems with the assessment that this Australian pace attack was the best doing the rounds on the international scene. England were being beaten fair and square, but when they were dismissed in 31.4 overs in Sydney, that was quite different. Commentating is such an instant process, you're never searching for words, they just come out and you can't take them back. 'This is like watching a pub team,' I said.

The cricket was downright dire for the loyal folk who had travelled halfway around the world to see it. Believe me, my job is nowhere near as enjoyable when there is a gulf between the two teams either. On a personal slant, things did get better as the series concluded. Not least because Channel 9 – to whom I was seconded when not on air with Sky Sports – allowed me a stint on air with Bill Lawry, one of my commentating heroes, during the Melbourne match.

I love the real Bill almost as much as the great mimic Billy

Birmingham's caricature. If you're not familiar, Birmingham is the voice behind the Twelfth Man tapes – a take-off of Australian commentators that cannot help but raise chortles. Unfortunately, when I met the legendary Billy, as great an occasion as it was, he could not perfect an impersonation of me. And as for his Mark Nicholas, think Austin Powers. 'Yeah, baby!'

There was nothing groovy about England's performance, though. The towel had gone in early and the performance would have rocked Andy Flower sideways. His team had been pummelled and now they'd had enough. He would have expected more resistance, more bloody-mindedness about performances. He would have been reeling that a team of his had played in that manner.

Flower spoke of necessary change when addressing the English shortcomings in the series aftermath. One assumed he was referring to the make-up of the backroom staff, the preparation of the players, and the need for those players to play more county cricket. Not about his own position.

As a team during the Flower era, England coped with just about everything thrown at them. A prime example is when we went to India to play on spinning pitches, lost the first Test but still came back and won 2-1.

The one thing that hit us hard was pace, and Mitchell Johnson was terrifyingly good in his home conditions. To take 39 wickets was a phenomenal effort. Johnson is what you would call a confidence cricketer. Following his mid-year work with his mentor Dennis Lillee, it was evident that he was in a decent place with his bowling during the one-day series in England, when he rushed Jonathan Trott in particular. For Trott, that was the beginning of the end of what had been an accomplished career.

One of the challenges that series presented – if not the major challenge – was replacing Graeme Swann. His excellent control allied to his wicket threat allowed England to play a four-man attack for the majority of the five years that followed Andrew

Flintoff's retirement in 2009. When Swann himself called it a day, I didn't see anyone other than Monty Panesar who was going to bowl effective spin at Test level. Time will tell if Moeen Ali can follow a promising start with something sustainable over the long term.

At the age of thirty-five, Swann's top-level career did not have long to run when he quit mid-tour with the urn in Australian hands. Speaking with my coach's hat on, I had absolutely no problem with him calling it a day when he did. I have never been one who has taken to players announcing in advance that they're retiring at the end of a series or an impending season, because I believe once you make that announcement your ambition wanes. Once a player states that, I wouldn't want him around the team. Had Swann stayed, I think it would have been an extra distraction.

People posed questions on Twitter such as: 'Why desert a sinking ship?' Pardon me, but the ship had already sunk. This was a chance to get him out of the way and move on with what they'd got. I just couldn't see any point of keeping on a lad whose body was telling him his race had been run. All of us players have been there: you wake up one morning and your mind is clear that you don't want to do it anymore.

Others suggested he should have shown unity in the light of Jonathan Trott's early-tour departure. Codswallop! Everyone wished Trott the best in his recovery, but their decisions to depart were entirely unrelated and both undoubtedly for the best for individuals and team alike.

England came away from that Ashes tour in need of rebuilding. Not only did coach Flower leave his position, but Pietersen was sacked as England began a new era. That is why, for the record, I would never have gone back to Trott as England did in 2014-15, as it served only to delay Adam Lyth's opportunity when a series in the Caribbean would have been the perfect environment to break him in.

CHAPTER 14

Cleaning up our Act

Apologies here for indulging my own theme but I really think life has come full circle. For I recognise that England have undergone a proper scrub up this year. They needed one too, because they had been pushed way back in the queue when it came to lots of current issues. My fear had been that English cricket would be completely left behind, and lots of areas need cleaning up.

Sport is cyclical and there is no doubt that things were great for a while – Test top dogs for a full year between August 2011 and August 2012 lest we forget, a period in which we were also 20-over world champions – but equally, if you stand still others will delight in passing you by. For decades, England was the centre of the cricket world, a magnet for the very best players, but not any longer following a failure to grasp the Twenty20 nettle. We are no longer the primary hive of activity but a satellite stop-off among many.

As other rival countries' limited-overs cricket has strengthened and expanded through their 20-over Premier Leagues, ours has withered, and the evidence presented at the 2015 World Cup was that we had become a second division outfit as a consequence, as far back in the pack as we have ever been. Seldom few of our players have regular exposure to the best in the field, and the way to improve any cricketer is to challenge them against as high-class opponents as possible.

With Andrew Strauss now at the helm, it is time to be brave and empower him to take England in a direction we have never headed before. This is not a journey that will be completed over-night, but the regime change and appointment of Trevor Bayliss as coach suggest we know where we want to head after the wreck-age of the winter, and the 3–2 Royal London series win over New Zealand in June 2015 provided an enthralling start. Bayliss is a coach with a wonderful limited-overs record – taking Kolkata Knight Riders to two Indian Premier League titles, Sydney Sixers to Big Bash League and Champions League glory and New South Wales to 50-over successes. His credentials are excellent, and it's about time we employed more out-of-the-box thinking. It's early days yet, but I wouldn't be surprised to see another specialist coach or two recruited for each format to work under the Australian. We certainly need to release the manacles that tell us 'this is the way because it has always been the way'. To get level with the best in the world, you have to aim higher than they do – because they are moving forward at a rate of knots.

There are already some excellent coaches in support, of course, and the presence of Paul Farbrace within the England set-up should not be underestimated. For a start, without him I'm not sure Strauss would have got his man. After all, Bayliss was only a month into a new two-year contract with New South Wales and had turned England down twice previously, before he finally agreed at the third time of asking. The bond the pair have after being involved in the terrorist attack in Lahore in March 2009 while working as coach and assistant coach for Sri Lanka is some-thing you simply cannot measure. Their trust in and respect for each other is deep.

Back on England's tour of Sri Lanka in late 2007, Bayliss invited me over for a cup of coffee and a chat at the team hotel in Colombo. We just chewed the fat, but I did register what an impressive bloke he was. He possesses a natural ease about him, and everyone speaks highly of both his ability and attitude as a coach. No wonder he was shortlisted when the job ended up going to Peter Moores for a second time in 2014. Speak to the great Sri Lankan players like Kumar Sangakkara and Mahela Jayawardene and they have nothing but praise for him.

Equally, Farbrace will be vital to this pairing, just as he had been at Yorkshire with Jason Gillespie. The bottom line is that players play and these men all seem to share the same ethos of allowing individuals to express themselves. It's clear that Bayliss's values are to work hard but enjoy it, and he encourages players to be themselves with no inhibitions. Indeed, those were his instructions to the new-look one-day team when he left Farbrace in charge of that series against New Zealand between accepting the job and arriving on these shores, and boy was it enjoyable to observe. Here were a group of players expressing themselves – and how. Here was an England team on the front rather than the back foot. The initial signs were that he will pave the way for the players and they will perform for him. Farbrace will be crucial in the whole bedding down process, and I'm talking about the first year or so, not just the first few months. He knows results need to be good in the here and now, but there will be a longer vision too.

Strauss has shown he's not shy of making strong decisions by removing Peter Moores upon taking office. Unfortunately, results define how long a coach stays in position and Peter's were not considered to be up to scratch.

Of course, I know about the disappointment of losing an international coaching job before you feel your role has been fulfilled, but I would dismiss any notion that Moores and I suffered similar fates. He took over a Test team that was ranked second in the world and slipped to fifth in his first time in charge, and was moving in a similar direction again, for all the talk of his popularity within the dressing room. The team I inherited was nowhere near that level and the resources incomparable. Everything provided for an England coach in this day and age is set up for success. There are seemingly limitless amounts of cash to be invested, a player system that is run with counties as an afterthought, not the other way around, and a structure underneath the full team that is light years ahead of where we were in 1999.

This is not to say I don't have sympathy for Moores, a man who worked hard to demonstrate he deserved a second chance at international level by heading back to domestic cricket and delivering the County Championship title to Lancashire. He spoke about developing a young England team, although I'm not sure his remit was to win in three years' time. You have to be successful in the present.

His biggest mistake, I would argue, was not his long-term focus but his extreme loyalty in the short term. In international cricket, a captain and a coach come as a pair and he stood by Alastair Cook too long. Perhaps he had been influenced by the breakdown of his relationship with Kevin Pietersen in 2008-09 and was fearful of rocking the boat. But showing faith in Cook into the winter of the World Cup created a monster. The decision for change was made too late. At that level, there is no time for pussy-footing around. If the captain is not good enough, you get rid, no dramas. It was the same when the vice-captaincy switched from Ian Bell to Joe Root. Strong management is about choosing the best men for any given job.

For the record, following the drawn Test series in the Caribbean – a thoroughly underwhelming result – I would have been in favour of retaining Moores as coach but removing Cook as captain. Moores spent several months defending Cook in the aftermath of the 2013-14 Ashes whitewash. Yet when the tables were turned and Moores was dispensed with, I was shocked at Cook's silence as the last man standing.

Of the management team that went to Australia that winter, only he was left. This unseemly period had seen England hit rock bottom and yet the England captain apparently had nothing to say about it. Previously, whenever his own leadership was challenged, he vowed to carry on, which was his prerogative, but his determination to lead, admirable on face value, detracted from his primary role in the side – to score runs.

With a coach's hat on, if you watched Cook bat during a hundred-less two years between 2013 and 2015, you would have recognised a hesitancy and indecision to his game. Previously, he always appeared to be crystal clear in what he was trying to do. So many players will talk about batting with a dominant top hand, but I think his bottom hand became too dominant, so his bat was skewed when it came down. His strokes, never what you would consider things of beauty, had nevertheless regressed and any fluency had given way to clunkiness. He did score a run or two in the 2014 series win over India, but he was forced to dig very deep into his levels of resolve to produce them and did not look natural.

When asked on air for my World Cup squad at the end of that international season, I did not have him in my starting XI. My feeling was that if he continued to play in this static way, he would hold us up. Ironically, of course, immediately after breaking his three-figure drought in the Caribbean, his dismissal triggered a domino effect. England lost that Test in Barbados, against opponents the outspoken incoming ECB chairman Colin Graves branded 'mediocre'; then Strauss came in, immediately poured scorn on a Kevin Pietersen comeback and left Cook to dwell in the background as the public looked for answers as to why.

To me, it was this issue that the new England director needed to address more than any other. Strauss is a strong appointment – I would have been equally happy with Michael Vaughan or Nasser Hussain being persuaded to take it on – but repairing the image of the national team is paramount and not a job to be carried out overnight.

Quite simply, the England regime needs to open up. It has been looking like a real closed shop for far too long. Arguably, the downside of central contracts is that the players have become too powerful, and have forgotten what it means to walk onto a field to represent your country. Because when you pull on an England shirt, you're not just playing for yourself, you're playing for the paying public sat in the stands and the ones who are sat on the sofa with a cup of tea at home.

We have entered into a period in which there has been a recurring disconnect between the players and the people they represent. The public seemed to have been turned off by the grubby in-fighting, a perceived treatment of Team England as a cosy club, of which only a privileged few are members. It is not. If it's a club, it has no exclusivity. It's *our* team. If it belongs to anyone, it belongs to us all, the thousands of people who want it to perform to the best of its ability. The privileged few get to do *our* bidding.

Some of the behaviour we have seen over recent times suggests that there have been those who make up its number who do not think like that, or at least they have not been encouraged to think like that. It's almost as if they have lost their soul. At times, they appear downtrodden, think the world is against them and believe they are down on their luck. When they went behind to a focused India in the Test series of 2014, they developed a real siege mentality. It was a real 'us and them'. You were 'us' if you had a peg, in the dressing room – actually no dressing room on earth can have enough pegs, given the bloated nature of the backroom staff, but you know what I mean – and 'them' if you didn't. They became a rather faceless, loveless, uniform entity.

I firmly believe every team needs its characters, not least to sell the sport to the next generation. At a time when England were deciding against reintegrating the flamboyance of Kevin Pietersen, they should have been promoting cricketers with a similar on-field modus operandi more fervently than ever. I would argue that Team England can become too insular, too English. Post-Pietersen, those in the PR department, of which there are many, should have been getting the message across that we have some exciting new kids on the block. This was the time to turn Jos Buttler and Ben Stokes into A-list stars, not after we had been humiliated at the World Cup.

Instead, conservatism prevailed to the extent that when in a one-day international in May 2014, Buttler hit a thrilling 74-ball 121 off a Sri Lanka attack fresh from World Twenty20 glory, Cook, as captain, claimed he was not yet ready for Test cricket. Buttler himself, when asked about filling in for the injured Matt Prior, claimed he was not certain he was ready. There were question marks over Rod Marsh and Adam Gilchrist when Australia first picked them, but they were not concerned about their rough edges, only that they had the potential to be very special performers.

Similarly, Alex Hales blasted a hundred at that World Twenty20, against the damned winners no less, and was not considered ready for a crack at the ODI team. What an absolute nonsense. Decisions like this, and the choice to bring in Jonathan Trott for the Tests in the Caribbean, heart-warming comeback story as it was, led me to conclude that the selectors have been dreadful. Trott, not as accustomed as Adam Lyth to opening, also lacks the dynamism of the Yorkshireman's batting. All our decisions were backward rather than forward-thinking.

My advice would be to give these players their head and let their personalities out. They need to be able to express themselves without those above watching their every move or to be discouraged by fears of their limitations. Folk love a tainted hero, and I would not want them to inhibit the career of someone like Stokes. He will trip up, do something daft – as he did when he punched that locker in the Caribbean – but they should not stifle that. Ask those who witnessed his truly outstanding all-round display at Lord's against New Zealand in 2015 how they felt about him. If you had stifled Ian Botham, you would have denied cricket one of its great protagonists and some of its richest history. Somehow, you have to allow free spirits the room to breathe.

The Yorkshire pair of Gary Ballance and Joe Root certainly seized the moment when it came to international cricket, and sports fanatics don't want their heroes to be square. Neither, however, do they want to see them topless on a night out, a treat the Nottingham public got after a draw with India at Trent Bridge in 2014. Thankfully, it was for innings like his hundreds either side of that strip that Ballance was named the ICC's emerging player of the year. Despite the mid-2015 loss of form that followed, the way he coped in his first few months at the top level suggested he possesses the attributes to have a successful career. Get your shirt on him being an England regular for years.

One thing I would tell any of the up-and-coming players in this squad is to relax and remember their job is supposed to make them happy. They are being paid to have fun, and when they are being interviewed it is 100 per cent good news. Every single time a player is asked to be interviewed by either TV, radio or by the written media, it's because he has done well. He has a positive story to tell. At worst, it's because he is the best performer within the team at that particular time. As I discovered first hand, if you're interviewed as a coach it falls upon you to explain away a defeat more often than not, and that's the way it should be. When I was a coach I saw protecting my players from criticism, particularly when they were already disappointed at failure, as a prerequisite of the job.

At times, I have heard contemporary players dictate that they are not talking to X, Y or Z in an interview because they do not happen to like the X, Y or Z in question. Forget personality clashes, though, because in thinking like that you're missing the point. When you're being interviewed, you're really not talking to the interviewer at all but the public who are watching, listening or reading. This is a chance for players to project themselves; the bloke in front of them is only asking the question.

Find me a professional sportsman who would rather be centre of attention in an empty stadium than in front of a full house. By that token, let the people you want to entertain know something about yourself. Let's not be hearing about the nation getting the wrong impression. Come and front up. In TV situations, I would be telling these young men to learn the technique of talking to the interviewer while giving a glance at the camera.

There is an art to creating your own image. Not for one minute do I think that Michael Clarke is well liked within the Australian cricket fraternity, but he's very good whenever you get him on screen. He might struggle to win a popularity contest, but when he does an interview he sells himself by being *himself*. The skill he has is to talk as normally as possible. Unfortunately, that is one of the areas where Peter Moores fell down. Pete had the chance to talk in normal terms, to get his messages across on what the team was trying to do on multiple occasions, but all too often failed to deliver in clear and simple terms and ended up tripping himself up with reflections on data. Personally, I never saw a problem in admitting that the opposition was superior.

Worryingly, England seemed to be woefully out of touch with the rest of the top nations at the 2015 World Cup. Their cricket was just so outdated. They were out-hit, out-fielded, out-paced, out-thought. When it came down to group qualification, it meant they were plain old out.

England stumbled out of the traps against Australia and New Zealand, and to be honest they were pitiful to watch in those opening two matches. Yes, they were up against the best two sides, but there were no redeeming features to be found in their style or tactical approach whatsoever. Poor old Moores appeared to be ageing by the day. His team looked powerless and shell-shocked. No one could deny that England worked their proverbials off at practice, and that appears to have been their mantra for success, but it all seemed to be in hope rather than expectation. How different it all was just three months later when a team liberated and focusing on skills struck a record 408 runs off the New Zealanders at Edgbaston, and then chased down a target of 350 with four overs to spare. It was simply scintillating, and a far cry from the spring.

It was pretty clear from a long way out that reaching the World Cup semi-final would be a good effort. But the frustration was that they were trying to win games with old-school tactics against opponents playing a very different style. The warning signs were there for all to see when they were playing to make scores of 250. You need a lot to go your way, and a lot to go wrong for your opponents, to be successful in modern-day tournaments with that kind of approach.

It was no coincidence that the best two teams, Australia and New Zealand, the ones that embraced breaking down the ceiling when it came to constructing scores, reached the final. Those two teams completely got what was required in a one-day international era that uses two new balls. That change, between the 2011 event and the one in 2015, was perhaps more significant than any previous tinkerings with the regulations, because it made hard hitting and wicket taking more important than ever. Only when they were playing against each other did either of the two co-hosts fail to post a score of 330-plus batting first.

New Zealand were all over England like a cheap suit in that record-equalling loss in Auckland that highlighted Brendon McCullum as the undisputed best captain in world cricket. He doesn't do funky fields. He just knows where to put the fielders for every batsman, and allows his bowlers to reap the rewards. And when Tim Southee started taking wickets, he just got more and more aggressive. Ten years ago, you simply could not have imagined seeing so many slips in a World Cup match between two major nations. There was not a single thought of holding back once they were on top; New Zealand were simply spurred on to greater acts by their success-driven captain. After he orchestrated that demolition, he then went after England's bowling as if he had a train to catch. To lose after facing just 12.2 overs must have been devastating for a team already low on confidence.

One-day international cricket has moved on massively and it just left England producing echoes of a different era. A decade and a half earlier, a score of 250 was steady. But changes to the regulations through extra powerplays before the 2011 World Cup in India – there were three lots during that period, if you recall – raised the bar of an average score to 300. By 2015, you needed 340-350 to be firm favourites, such was the quality of the pitches. It demands picking a team devoid of fear – undaunted at scoring above a run a ball at any stage of a game and not easily distracted in their bid to dismiss batsmen who are trying to monster them out of the park. Holding bowlers, so effective in my coaching days, now get panned, and you have to have the potential to dismiss batsmen and disrupt the innings.

Of course, the super-sized scores attracted some negativity from critics who suggested the balance of power had shifted too far towards bat over ball. But I have no quibble with the amount of wood being used by the manufacturers, who became targets for the anti-big-bats brigade. To me, the six-hitting only adds to the 'we'll get one more than you' attitude of the elite nations. Great bowlers of their time will still claim wickets, as we witnessed with the standout left-armers Mitchell Starc and Trent Boult.

In contrast, England didn't get out of third gear. You have to promote power players at the top of the order and yet not only did we ignore that until it was too late, we committed one big no-no:

the number of times we left the ball was galling. If there was a bit of width, we were letting it pass unchallenged on its way through to the wicketkeeper. See what happens when you give a bit of width to David Warner – he would rupture himself trying to hit it as hard as he could. Glenn Maxwell gets the billing of the Big Show. He's a quiet lad and isn't fond of his nickname because of the attention it draws, but you can see where it has come from. Boy, does he go big when he puts on a show.

But the modern way is for competitors in all sports to be bigger, fitter, faster, stronger. You only have to walk across Regent's Park to Primrose Hill, as I do to get to the pub during a Test match at Lord's, to recognise that. You will see mixed soft-ball, and touch rugby teams powering over the grass, and there are some big'uns turning out … and the lads aren't small either. Big Jilly, the hooker, made my old mum look tame. What a unit she was. If it was time to scrum down and she said it was Tuesday, it would be Tuesday.

The one common denominator for those that were clearing the ropes for fun and those that were not was bat speed. That displayed by the likes of Warner, Maxwell, McCullum and AB de Villiers was in a different league to anything our players were able to produce. From what we were witnessing there, it didn't appear that we had it in our thinking to get the levers through the ball at such veloc-ity. By mid-2015, when England appeared to have ten McCullums of their own, this theory was already ripe for the unpicking.

These blokes clearly worked out that to generate the kind of phenomenal power they do, it is primarily the speed and not the weight of the bat that is essential. The old English way is to barely pick the bat up and defend, defend, defend as default. In contrast, blokes from overseas have a real flow of the arms, possessing golf-like swings. The first thought when they have the bats up at shoulder level behind them is to hit the ball for six. If they can't get it all the way over the rope, then they downgrade and look for a four, a three or a two and so on. This is clearly the mentality of players like Buttler and Stokes, and I hope we now have ten years of unbridled fun watching them win international matches. To hit 43 sixes in a five-match series represented a phenomenal start to a new era.

Things might not have been going well on the field from an England perspective, but you cannot be miserable on tour in New Zealand and Australia. Although there was some sobriety offered on a walk around Christchurch, now an eerie experience four years on from the earthquake. I attended the memorial service for the victims of that particular natural disaster and it was very moving to see people, arms round each other, who had obviously lost loved ones. A sign of how long it would take to get this beautiful city back on its feet was provided by the fact that portakabins still act as some banks and shops.

Socialising took its toll on me, though, as some of my co-commentators can get very thirsty. Ian Smith and Simon Doull, the former New Zealand internationals, took me to what they said was a quiet spot in Wellington called the Bangalore Polo Club. But it was not horses that proved to be the trouble. Drinks are served alongside bowls full of monkey nuts and the club's party piece is to encourage everyone to eat them, throw the shells on the floor and allow the pigeons to come in to eat them all up. It reminded me of the way my dear old dad felt about his budgies. Here in Wellington, in fear of having my head given a Jackson Pollock-style design by these feathered friends, I made my excuses and left pretty sharpish.

On a more cultural note and a break of routine for me, I accepted an offer from Mark 'Tubby' Taylor, the former Australia captain, to join him and his Channel 9 colleagues Brad McNamara and James Brayshaw on a tour of the Barossa Valley wine region. It was over three days and I'm sure I lost one of them. It was one of the best experiences of my life, fun from start to finish. I would tell you more about it, if only I could remember. Suffice to say there were lots of vineyards involved.

There was something to celebrate in Ireland's performances again, though, and it was a delight to share a few drinks with their squad in Adelaide after they were eliminated – I was allowed to do so only after Ed Joyce demanded I wear an Irish shirt, mind. It will be criminal if Ireland, a side that has beaten Pakistan, Bangladesh, England and West Indies in its past three World Cup finals, are not involved at the next tournament in 2019 as per the ICC's current plan. There is no reason why Ireland cannot be a Test nation by then, particularly considering that Bangladesh have been in for some time. Just imagine how good they would be if they were able to retain their best players, instead of losing people like Eoin Morgan and Boyd Rankin to England.

They played some really good stuff again and will realise they are only a couple of penetrating bowlers shy of moving up another level still. We so need these Associate nations involved if it is to be truly recognised as a world tournament. Yes, I am with the majority who urge a reduction in its length, and two matches could be played on the same day to condense it. As someone who works on television, I'm aware of the problem in carrying this out but do not believe it's an insurmountable problem that can't be resolved with some persuasion. Overlapping matches reduce the number of advert opportunities for broadcasters, and having worked for Star Sports I get the impression that getting the adverts on is more important to them than having all their equipment fully functional. Cricket has to be spread to new territories, not trapped in a colonial past, and everyone with a vested interest in its wellbeing should be finding solutions right now.

One other thing I would like to ensure stays in the game is traditional forms of spin. The guile of Daniel Vettori and Ravichandran Ashwin, who I thought was terrific throughout the World Cup, showed that if you are any good, there is still a place for you in the very highest company. Unfortunately, with Graeme Swann and Vettori now in retirement, the number of quality traditional spinners is dwindling.

Some of the modern variety would look more comfortable chucking darts at Alexandra Palace than bowling at Lord's, but I still feel the likes of Sachithra Senanayake and Kane Williamson were victims of a haphazard and slightly unfair system when they were sent off to be laboratory-tested. Personally, I would rather see anyone with a suspect action being put on notice and then monitored in match situations instead. Get them to bowl in short-sleeved shirts so the umpires can see exactly what they need to, and then act if they keep transgressing. If they do, the authorities have a case. Under the current system it feels like those pulled are guilty until proven innocent, whereas I have preferred the benefit of the doubt to work the other way as it attaches less of a stigma.

These mystery spinners dominated Twenty20 cricket for some time. Just think how influential Saeed Ajmal and Sunil Narine were in helping Pakistan and West Indies win respective World Twenty20 tournaments. But their influence has reduced in competitions like the Indian Premier League – in part due to suspicion and their own independent testing procedures – which I was lucky enough to take in first hand in 2015.

These games leave our domestic Twenty20 matches looking like another sport. We have missed a trick in 20-over cricket, something I feel able to say with authority as I have been Sky Sports' commentary figurehead on the format since its inception in 2003. IPL games are absolutely full on – the players come off the field exhausted – but the focus is on the entertainment side of things. Huge sums of money have been invested in the product and that's reflected in its popularity. In contrast, we remained a bit village green, threw our lot in with Allen Stanford's crooked empire in 2008 and have been left isolated ever since.

From a personal point of view I loved the IPL, and it was only when stood doing my own ironing one night that I realised how much I missed Vipers (that's my pet name for my wife Diana, as in My Little Nest of Vipers, in case I hadn't mentioned it). Those shirts and waistcoats they kitted me out in – getting the creases out of those would have made a suitable round on *The Krypton Factor*.

One of the intrigues of the IPL is how the world's most deco-rated players mix with India's up-and-coming talent. You can see the effect this has when a young lad like Sarfaraz Khan, the seventeen-year-old Royal Challengers Bangalore batsman, comes to the crease and from a technical point of view is trying to get as low when striking the ball as his team-mate AB de Villiers, the best player in the world, who is stood at the non-striker's end. For aspiring cricketers to be able to work with the cream of the game's global talent is a pretty special and extremely valuable educational experience. It's a similar process to that which young English play-ers went through in a bygone time. We used to attract the crème de la crème for seasons on end. Players of the calibre of Zaheer Abbas, Mike Procter, Imran Khan, Wayne Daniel, Andy Roberts, Viv Richards, Barry Richards and Joel Garner used to be part of county cricket's fabric.

Yet the only one on the county scene to match the kind of dedicated commitment of those traditional imported signings is Warwickshire's Jeetan Patel, whose affection for the club is matched by his team-mates' affection for him. One of the things I don't get, and I am old so perhaps I'm on a different wavelength, is some players coming in from overseas for three weeks. They have no sense of the history of the club, and I don't know how they fit into the dressing room. It's all a bit too mercenary for my taste.

I guess it's to do with market forces, and you cannot change the fact that on the world cricket scene the number one draw is the

IPL. We have to accept that is the way it is, but I hate to think county cricket has become a resting ground for players who have come out of international cricket. These iconic figures of the 1970s and 1980s were current international players, the best of their era. Using my own county Lancashire as an example, in 2015 they had three southern Africans no longer involved at international level in Ashwell Prince, Kyle Jarvis and Alviro Petersen. Can they match the ambition of their great predecessors, who still had much to prove, or are they on a last pay cheque? They certainly came up with some impressive numbers when it came to wickets and runs, but I cannot shake the fear that the County Championship is becoming Easy Street. They are playing alongside Tom Smith, Simon Kerrigan and Jordan Clark, cricketers aspiring to be top competitors on the international scene. I hear the argument that they can pass on their knowledge of that environment, but there has to be a willingness for that knowledge to be shared or exchanged.

For me, from the outside looking in, Kumar Sangakkara is a fantastic signing by Surrey, because he's of such great career pedigree and a thoroughly good bloke. He spoke of his love of the smell of a county dressing room and how he wanted to finish his career here, as it was one of his remaining ambitions on his cricket bucket list. Conversely, I sat next to Tillakaratne Dilshan in Colombo in November 2014, and he told me in no uncertain terms that county cricket was laughable. Not the standard, he insisted, but the scheduling it keeps. Although he signed up for Derbyshire, it was a concern to him that there was so much switching between formats. We need to react and start blocking off tournaments like the NatWest T20 Blast in three and four-week passages.

Cricket is all that matters in India so we'll never match the IPL in the UK, just as they will never be able to get near us in terms of a Premier League in football. You need an inherent love for the game – something traditional, deep and established – to exist before you can develop something of such high quality. In India, it helps that cricket doesn't have to compete with football, rugby, golf, tennis and flat-racing events that overlap our domestic seasons. They also have the advantage of the weather, the odd Armageddon-style deluge aside.

But if we want to advance our own game and offer the British public a product that will engage and excite, then we certainly have the capacity to stage something very similar to the Big Bash League. My proposed template – eight teams, who play each other twice – would replicate that used in Australia and India. Where we have an advantage in scheduling, however, is that we are not like the other two countries as there is no need for plane travel to get around the venues, enabling us to get through the same number of games in fewer days.

You'd have to play it alongside Test match cricket, as they do in Australia, to shoehorn it into the domestic itinerary and make it attractive to the best players in the world, because it needs that to give it credence as a proper event. When you consider that players such as Glenn Maxwell, Darren Sammy, Eoin Morgan, Dale Steyn, Chris Gayle, Morne Morkel and Virender Sehwag are not guaranteed to play, you know you are talking about a top competition. Every one of those players has featured in county cricket at some stage, and some in the past couple of years, but hosting something on a grander scale would attract more of the top global names for longer periods.

You need big money for big ideas, and the IPL model gets its money back from their TV coverage – and that means commercial sacrifices like strategic time-outs, breaks in play just so they can get more adverts into the live coverage. From an advertisers' perspective it is perfect, because there are so many people watching and having fun that it looks like a great event to be associated with. Grounds are rammed with up to 75,000 people.

In contrast, some of our counties can get 4,000 tops and for them that's a good return. But it's not enough to justify top-level investment. No wonder then that there has been such resistance to an English Premier League from around the shires. Only those with traditional, international venues – that house 20,000 plus – could be accommodated in the kind of franchise system I propose.

I have a great affinity with Twenty20, but I'm still to revise my opinion that this is not serious cricket and has to be treated in a different way to the proper stuff. It may make people lots of money, and good luck to them. Kieron Pollard is a very good Twenty20 player, but there will be no one talking about him in the pub when the subject of great players comes up. Talk turns to people like Sachin Tendulkar and Ricky Ponting. They marvel at our own James Anderson. A player is judged by what he does in Test match cricket. It has always been thus. Rewind twenty years and we were not judging Sachin, Brian Lara, Muttiah Muralitharan and Shane Warne on what they were producing in one-day cricket. We judged their credentials on Test match cricket ability.

So, what of Test cricket? For some time, there has been concern that although it is still embraced by us in England and over in Australia, it has been losing its appeal in other parts of the world. There was a feeling developing that like their former captain Sourav Ganguly's bell-ringing – he made such a bodge of the job before the start of play one morning at Lord's that it failed to register on Snicko – India were becoming out of sync with it.

There has been talk of modernising it, although when I heard Colin Graves mooting his idea of four-day Tests after succeeding Giles Clarke as chairman of the ECB, it struck me that we would be looking at one hell of a long day in the office. Graves proposed each day to contain 105 overs rather than the current set-up of five days of ninety overs, but the sad truth about Test cricket is that it just seems to be getting slower when it comes to over-rates.

If players are struggling to bowl ninety overs, how on earth are they going to get through an extra fifteen? A day's play would be finishing just before *News at Ten*. It drives me mad watching the numerous stoppages that take place, from drinks breaks, and the twelfth man running on for a natter, to groundsmen arriving with all manner of implements. Then there are the stoppages for technology reviews.

I played at a time when eighteen overs an hour in county cricket was mandatory. They didn't even need a minimum number in Test cricket, because bowlers simply got through their six balls without being given a hurry-up. I'd keep Test cricket at five days of ninety overs each, but empower match officials to clamp down even more than they do now on slow over-rates. If a captain can't get his bowlers moving along at fifteen overs an hour, he's banned for a Test – no questions asked.

One of Graves's concerns was about fifth-day crowds, but I would have a solution to that. As a Yorkshireman he should know – and I'm a temporary resident of the county, so have some experience of their thinking – that folk like something for nothing. I would propose throwing the doors open for free against opponents other than Australia. It certainly worked at Headingley in 1998 when 13,000 turned up for the half an hour it took to wrap up South Africa's tail. And those that shelled out to be cut price fifth-day Ashes spectators in Manchester and The Oval in 2005, and Cardiff and The Oval in 2009, will testify what great value for money it was.

One thing for certain is that there are challenges ahead but after more than half a century in the game, after starting out as cricket's great unwashed on Water Street, I have come to accept that times move on and attitudes will alter. But the more it changes, the more it stays the same.

There have been several periods when county cricket has been dismissed as obsolete, but it's still here. We have shifted from three-day to four-day cricket and even had seasons of both; we have seen players on strike, others banned; the world's brightest talents have been shipped in, and the world's brightest talents evacuating for other destinations. On the international stage, the revolutionary World Series Cricket threatened to split the game in two, and did so temporarily at least. Others have tried to form breakaways and failed; some have had fleeting success, some will keep on trying.

But none of this has diminished my enthusiasm for traditional cricket – for the purest contest between bat and ball. English cricket has provided me with a wonderful life in various guises, and continues to do so. As a player I was knocked off my feet; as a coach I was kicked when I was down; and in the commentary box I have been in and out of my seat as its number one fan. I will continue to champion its cause and make no apologies for doing so.

Index

INDEX

DL's road journeys with, 62–3
Boyle, Frankie, 231
Boys from the Blackstuff, 60
Bradman, Don, 142
Brayshaw, James, 283
Brearley, Mike, 145, 146, 250, 256
Broad, Stuart, 88, 239, 264, 265, 266–7
Brown, Ali, 184
brown cow (sports drink), 134
Brown, Dougie, 180
Buchanan, John, 254
Bumblies, 40
Burnley CC, 28
Burnley FC, DL's time with, 16–17
Buttler, Jos, 277, 283
Byford, Sir Lawrence, 226

Caddick, Andrew, 205, 207
Cambridge Street Methodists FC, 18, 19
Cambridge University CC, 50, 167
Campbell, Alistair, 190
Carr, Donald, 132, 144
Carroll, Paul, 162
Cedar Swifts FC, 15
Cellino, Massimo, 165
Champions League, 272
Champions Trophy, 181
Chance to Shine, 162
Chandrasekhar, Bhagwath, 116
Channel 4, DL approached by, 215
Channel 9 (Australia), 220–1, 222, 268
Chappell, Greg, 124, 142, 143
Chappell, Ian, 28, 124, 137, 139, 141–2, 143
Chatfield, Ewen, 255
Church CC, 27
Clark, Jordan, 287
Clarke, Giles, 289
Clarke, Michael, 259, 260, 263, 266, 279
Clay, John, 78
Clayton, Geoff, 55, 56–7, 92
Close, Brian, 57, 79
Coleman, John, 164
Colley, David, 136
Collier, Jack, 25, 27–8
Collingwood, Paul 'Colly', 253
  DL's similarities to, 22
Colne CC, 28
Colvile, Charles, 191, 231
Compton, Nick, 244
Constant, David, 168

Cook, Alastair, 238, 244, 253, 274–5, 277
Cooke, Bob, 69, 157, 256
Cooke, Martyn 'Buzzer', 163–4
Cooley, Troy, 210, 246, 254
Cork, Dominic, 189
Cottam, Bob, 256–7
County Championship, 43, 88, 106, 107, 131, 150, 173, 206, 210, 274
  weather hits, 151
Cowdrey, Colin, 129, 130–1, 141, 231, 237, 243
Crawley, John, 173
Croft, Colin, 195
Croft, Robert, 196, 211
Croft Roplasto, 155
Crompton, Jack, 67, 68, 69
Crowe, Russell, 165
Cuddihy, Russ, 158
Cumberland CC, 166
Cumbes, Jim, 102
Cunliffe, Bob, 30–1, 32

Daily Express, 37
Daily Mail, 149
Daily Mirror, 117
Dallaglio, Lawrence, 241
Dane, Alec, 4
Daniel, Wayne, 195, 286
Daniels, Craig 'Donkey', ix
Danvers-Walker, Bob, 4
Dar, Aleem, 266
Darden, Steve 'Dasher', 161
Davey, Jack, 194–5
David Lloyd Sports, 157
Davis, Roger, 256
Dawson, Richard, 73–4
de Silva, Aravinda, 173–4
de Villiers, AB, 282, 286
Deakin, Alan, 13–14
Deakin, Elsie, 13
Deccan Chargers, 261
Decision Review System, 52, 179
Denness, Mike, 115, 121, 131, 135, 142
Derbyshire CCC, 104, 105, 111, 146, 159, 170, 187, 287
Dewhurst, Lindon, 25
Dharmasena, Kumar, 197
Dhoni, Mahendra Singh, xiii
Dick, Frank, 202
Dilshan, Tillakaratne, 287
Donald, Allan, 193, 195, 210

INDEX

INDEX

INDEX

Ogden, Geoff, 245
Old, Chris, 79, 93, 141
Old Trafford:
Pit of Hate at, 54, 101–2
pitch characteristics of, 79 (*see also* pitches)
Omar Kureishi, 124
O'Reilly, Bill, 223
Ormerod, Dave 'Dibber', 161, 162
Ormrod, Alan, 173

Pack, Simon, 198, 199
Packer, Kerry, 109
Padgett, Doug, 57
Pakistan national side, 123–4, 146, 175, 226, 285
complaint against MCC by, 124
exceptional bowlers in, xiii
Panesar, Monty, 264, 270
Park Inn FC, 20
Pasadena (band), 242
Patel, Jeetan, 286
Patel, Samit, 243
Paynter, Eddie, 37
Pelé, 67
Petersen, Alviro, 287
Philpott, Peter, 209, 210
Pietersen, Kevin, 87–8, 89, 132, 210, 237–45, 248, 251–2, 260, 270, 274, 275–6
autobiography of, 240
career-best triple-hundred of, 89
ECB sacks, 88
first Test century of, 243
Lloyd, C., compared to, 251–2
'Pasadena' baseball cap of, 242
and Textgate, 239
Pilling, Harry, 53, 60, 112
pitches:
varying characteristics of, 79–81
Headingley, 79
and loams, 80
Old Trafford, 79
Pitt, Dave, 20
Pollard, Kieron, 289
Ponting, Ricky, 243, 247, 248, 249, 250, 264, 289
Potts, Harry, 16, 17
Prasanna, Erapalli, 121
Pratt, Gary, 249
Prince, Ashwell, 287
Pringle, Derek, 230

Prior, Matt, 240, 254, 277
ProBatter, 179
Procter, Mike, 93, 193–4, 195, 286
Professional Cricketers' Association (PCA), 109–10, 176
DL as Lancashire representative on, 109–10
DL as president of, xi, 109, 156
help and support given by, 156
Prudential Trophy, 146
Pullar, Geoff, 43–4, 68, 75
DL encouraged by, 43

Rajasthan Royals, 181
Ramadhin, Sonny, 28
Ramprakash, Mark, 178
Ramsbottom CC, 28
Ranatunga, Arjuna, 201
Ranji Trophy, 26
Rankin, Boyd, 284
Ratcliffe, Bob, 112, 158
Ratnayeke, Ravi, 159
Rawstron, Billy, 159–60
Rawtenstall CC, 28
Redpath, Ian, 142
Reidy, Bernard, 158
Reiffel, Paul, 211
Rhoades, Cedric, 46–8, 57, 58–9
as players' champion, 46
Richards, Barry, 32, 286
Richards, Corey, 213
Richards, David, 188
Richards, Viv, 76, 252, 286
Ridding, Bill, x, 65–7
Rishton CC, 24–5, 166
Roberts, Andy, 106, 127, 195, 286
Robins, Derrick, 149
Robinson, Amos, 61
Robinson, Eddie, 27–8, 158
Robson, Sam, 244
Roebuck, Peter, 167
Ronaldo, Cristiano, 241
Rooney, Wayne, 241
Root, Joe, xiv, 239, 256, 262, 274, 278
Roses matches, *see* Yorkshire CCC
Royal Challengers Bangalore, 286
Royal London series, 272
Rubber Duck, 101
Russell, Jack, 175

Saeed Ajmal, 285
Saker, David, 210

301

INDEX